Colin Shindler is an author, broadcaster and lecturer in history at Cambridge University.

For twenty years he was a Bafta award-winning television writer and producer being responsible for the series *Lovejoy* and the motion picture *Buster* starring Phil Collins and Julie Walters, for which he wrote the screenplay.

In recent years he has written a series of books on British and American social history and written and presented documentaries for BBC Television and BBC Radio Four. He lectures in British and American cultural history with an emphasis on the impact of both sport and film on twentieth-century society.

NATIONAL SERVICE

From Aldershot to Aden:
Tales from the Conscripts, 1946–62

COLIN SHINDLER

SPHERE

First published in Great Britain in 2012 by Sphere
Reprinted 2012 (three times)
This paperback edition published in 2013 by Sphere

7 9 10 8

A CIP catalogue record for this book
is available from the British Library.

ISBN 978-0-7515-4620-0

Typeset in Bembo by M Rules
Printed and bound in Great Britain by
Clays Ltd, St Ives plc

Papers used by Sphere are from well-managed forests
and other responsible sources.

MIX
Paper from
responsible sources
FSC® C104740

Sphere
An imprint of
Little, Brown Book Group
Carmelite House
50 Victoria Embankment
London EC4Y 0DZ

An Hachette UK Company
www.hachette.co.uk

www.littlebrown.co.uk

To Katherine
Without whom Life, to say nothing of Art,
would be infinitely the poorer

ACKNOWLEDGEMENTS

My first and greatest debt of course is to the men who shared with me their experiences of their time as National Servicemen. Although a few belonged to organisations like the Royal British Legion, some of them had not spoken of it to anyone outside their own social circle for many years. Invariably, whether they had a good time or a bad time they seemed to enjoy re-living that pivotal time in their youth and I felt privileged to be there with them as they did so.

In order to find these men from all over the country I required a great deal of help from many people and the list that herewith follows is related entirely to the order of the appearance in the book of the men they helped me to find.

In particular I would like to thank Brian Viner and John Beaman down in the glorious Herefordshire countryside and Mike and Ann Johnson for their hospitality in Ilkley, along with Mike's diligent correspondence around Yorkshire on my behalf. Jo Krasner and Iris Hyland and their outstanding A-Team of researchers at BBC Radio Merseyside rescued what looked like was going to be a fruitless journey to the Wirral, Liverpool and North Wales. My very good friends Ruth and Tony Badger, to whom I owe a lot more than this rudimentary acknowledgement, provided me with a link to their happy days in Newcastle and the North East. In London, the British Legion branches at Muswell Hill, Teddington and Friern Barnet provided me with valuable leads and my old friend Barry Garman located contacts from the heart of Old Islington. Stephen Chalke, the greatly respected cricket author and publisher, generously led me through the county cricketers of the 1950s, most of whom experienced National Service, and my thanks are also due to Shaun Pomeroy, my source for National Servicemen in Somerset.

My apologies go to all those whose stories didn't make the final line up; to all who helped, to Adam Strange at Little Brown who first approached me with the idea, especially to my friend and literary agent Luigi Bonomi and above all to my dedicatee and partner Katherine go my grateful thanks.

'We must not send the youth of Britain from the barrack square to the street corner. Some substitute must be found which will have the same beneficial effects of character-training as National Service.' Mentally I phrased a reply. 'I think it will be difficult to find a substitute which will inculcate bad habits, bad language, idleness, slothfulness and the amiable philosophy of "I'm All Right, Jack" half so successfully as National Service . . .' For the vast majority, National Service was an irksome suspension of freedom, rather like being forcibly compelled, as an adult, to go back to school — a particularly bad type of boarding school, staffed by brutal, snobbish, cynical and incompetent masters.

David Lodge, *Ginger, You're Barmy*

PREFACE

'This is an odd sort of book for you to write, isn't it?'

In September 1960, on my first day at Bury Grammar School at the age of eleven, the class stood to attention as Mr Ferley, our form master, entered. 'Right!' he said, 'Who's going to join the CCF?'

Thirty-one hands shot up, including those of the class weaklings, the 'sensitive and artistic' boys, and even 'Happy' Appleby, who had contracted polio as a small child and wore a leg brace. Only two (or possibly four) hands remained down. One (or two) of them belonged to a boy called Shepherd, but for some reason Shepherd's common-sense approach to life and its preservation attracted no response from our outraged form master.

'Shindler!' he expostulated, clearly aghast and fixing me with the sort of stare he had presumably learned on being singled out at inspection. 'Are you a coward?'

The truthful answer was, of course, 'Yes, sir.' However, even

I knew that admission wasn't the best way to start Big School, so I mumbled something about religious and political doubts. 'Besides,' I said, perking up a bit, 'I thought there was a choice.'

'There is now,' agreed the normally jovial Mr Ferley bitterly, 'but there wasn't when they sent me to Korea. It's a scandal the way this government has stopped National Service.'

I've never forgotten that exchange, and that's why an old school friend who remembered me as an eleven-year-old pacifist/coward said to me on hearing of my new project, 'This is an odd sort of book for you to write, isn't it?'

Though I am still relieved that I went home after school on Tuesday afternoons instead of marching up and down the playground in a uniform so appallingly itchy that many boys wore their pyjamas under it, I remember only too clearly the sight of squaddies on the streets of Manchester where I grew up. Those squaddies are now in their seventies and early eighties and their stories deserve to be told before they are lost for ever. After all, National Service was, as the cartoonist Mel Calman defined it, 'half adult boarding school and half lunatic asylum'. That seemed to me to be confirmation of both my own instinctive suspicion of the armed forces ('Cossacks!' I could hear my immigrant grandparents crying) and David Lodge's acerbic analysis in *Ginger, You're Barmy*, informed by his own practical experience.

I soon found out that this is a somewhat partial and prejudiced point of view. Many of the men whose recollections of their days in uniform during National Service form the main part of this book did not share that possibly too cynical attitude. For many of them National Service represented an escape from the inevitable drudgery of manual labour and the opening of new horizons. For these people National Service was their gap year and what they experienced in the army or the RAF changed their lives, usually for the better.

Norman McCord, formerly Professor of History at Newcastle University, and still living in Cullercoats on the north-east coast near Tynemouth, looked at me sharply when the audio cassette clicked off after the first forty-five minutes of our conversation. 'You can throw that thing away,' he said caustically.

'Why?' I asked with evident surprise.

'You're leading the witness,' he replied critically. 'You are asking me questions designed to produce evidence of conflict. It is both unethical and unhistorical.'

I suddenly felt like I too was eighteen again, not as a National Serviceman being screamed at by a sadistic corporal for being too slow getting down from the three-ton lorry that brought me from the railway station to the camp but as an undergraduate, back in a tutorial, having submitted a palpably under-prepared essay after too many play rehearsals and football matches. I defended myself stoutly. 'I am asking the same questions of everyone. I am not looking to change your answers or transcribe the tapes in such a way as to make your positive experience of National Service any less positive. If I ask you "Were there any problems?" you are perfectly entitled to reply "No, I loved everything about it" and I will record that in a faithful Boswellian manner.'

He seemed only partially appeased, but I realised on the drive home that actually Norman was hugely enjoying my temporary discomfiture because it must surely have reminded him of his old tutorial self, and I hope it made him feel twenty years younger. I also hope he – and indeed all its readers – will feel that Norman's entertaining account paints a picture of National Service entirely consistent with his evident enjoyment of his time in the RAF. I hope too that all my respondents will feel I have given a scrupulously fair representation of what they said.

All the tapes have obviously been edited to a greater or lesser degree which, by Norman's exacting standard, renders them therefore useless as objective oral history. However, I have spent most of my life writing dialogue for film and television drama and I am always conscious that what people actually say in ordinary conversations is frequently dull, banal and rambling. If dramatists really wrote dialogue the way people speak, it would be unbearably tedious. 'Drama,' said Alfred Hitchcock quite rightly, 'is life with the dull bits cut out.' You only have to sit next to someone on public transport using a mobile phone to realise that many sentences in a conversation ramble pointlessly up hill and down dale, frequently ending in a ditch full of brown water, chocolate bar wrappers and discarded cans of lager. This book is full of different kinds of conversation but in editing them, creating sentences where none existed, incorporating my questions into what appears to be their stream of consciousness, I have at all times felt acutely aware of my responsibility to present all the men honestly and accurately.

That is of course based on the assumption that the recollections themselves are accurate. How many of us can remember where we were, what we were doing and precisely what we felt six months ago, let alone fifty years ago? Although as the ageing process gathers pace many people find the times of their youth shining ever more brightly, in the memory these men are recalling events from more than half a century ago and we should approach their accounts as memories that are honestly recalled rather than as sworn legal testimony. They have considerable historical value even if some events might have been recalled with colourful elaboration. 'Old men forget; yet all shall be forgot/ But he'll remember, with advantages, what feats he did that day,' declaims Henry V just before the Battle of Agincourt. The key phrase is of course 'with advantages'. It would only be human to exaggerate emotions for good or ill. Some interviewees might, for example, have struggled with the shock of basic training rather more than they are now disposed to admit but that is itself, of course, just a guess.

In setting out to find thirty or so men whose experiences would give readers a fair understanding of National Service and its many ramifications I had three guiding principles. The list of men should span the entire fifteen years or so that this unique peacetime conscription lasted; men from as many different parts of the country as possible should be included; and a reasonable balance between officers and 'other ranks' should be sought. It is something of a coincidence that men were gathered in roughly the proportion they went into the different branches of the forces. The figures I have seen demonstrate that only 2 per cent of National Servicemen went into the Navy, while 25 per cent joined the RAF and 73 per cent were swallowed up by the Army. The fact that Julian Mitchell is the only naval National Serviceman therefore seems to be entirely representative of the whole.

There is also a balance in many other ways. Some really enjoyed National Service and some quite clearly did not. Some felt they had a moral obligation to serve their country (though those numbers declined dramatically as the Second World War

receded into history) but most had no patriotic feelings whatsoever and just wanted to get it over with and go home as soon
as possible. Although I was vaguely looking to attract men with
experience of the different trouble spots to which Britain traditionally sent its young men in uniform, I was surprised how,
within the thirty interviews, it was possible to encompass Korea,
Egypt, Cyprus, Kenya, Malaya and Aden – and of course
Germany – as well as men who never passed Dover. Older readers may remember the posh male voice on the wireless
announcing, 'This is the BBC Light Programme and the British
Forces Network in Germany'; *Two Way Family Favourites* with
Cliff Michelmore and Jean Metcalfe maintained the link with
British servicemen in Germany for many years.

All the men were asked the same questions regarding their
early years and their experiences during basic training – which
was the first, frequently terrifying, introduction to forces life,
particularly in the army. Interestingly, nearly all of them knew
of fellow conscripts who had broken down under the sort of
harsh discipline they had never previously experienced,
although only one interviewee admitted that he too had been
of their number – well done, George Penny! What soon
became apparent was that public schoolboys who had long
been separated from their mothers found National Service
easier to bear initially than those who had lived all their lives in
protective and supportive homes. Julian Mitchell is particularly
entertaining on this score.

Their stories pretty much finish after demobilisation but in
most cases the lives they went back to after this unique two-
year experience have been briefly summarised. These are not
intended as mini-biographies but rather to give the reader a

personal and historical context within which it is easier to understand the National Service experience.

Slowly, in the course of the interviews, two significant factors emerged which still exist to a smaller degree in Britain today but which in the 1940s and 1950s were much more apparent. These are of course the issues of class and what we would now call racism. Britain has always been a country in which the class into which people were born frequently dictated the course of their lives. Because the Navy was looking primarily for officers in its National Service intake and the other services demanded five O levels before a man could be considered as a potential officer, the 'officer class' was distinctive. Geoff Bennett is one of the few men in this selection who rose from humble beginnings to be commissioned as a second lieutenant, and it is clear that he planned his rise meticulously.

The subject of racism is always a minefield and I asked the questions and transcribed the answers on this matter with great care and attention. All the men answered honestly about their attitudes to the local population. Ben Perry's comment that he was told by an officer that the local Malays were to be treated fairly but they were not his equal seemed to be very representative of wider British attitudes at the time. Some, though by no means all, of those sent to outposts in the Middle East would remember that they always referred to the native population as 'wogs', but if we can lay our 2012 anxieties to one side this has to be typical of the way in which British soldiers in the 1950s saw the local population they had been sent to keep 'in order'. Rewriting the past to avoid current sensitivities does not make good history.

At the end of Part Two, we meet Nicolas Hawkes, who is

the first to see the locals, in his case Ghanaians, as people he felt privileged to help as they achieved their independence. Here is an indication that immersion in the schoolboy adventure stories about empire did not automatically lead to an imperialist posture and it could foster a point of view of African natives that could be reconsidered in the light of experience. To the British, African leaders like Kwame Nkrumah, Hastings Banda, Jomo Kenyatta and Kenneth Kaunda were, bewilderingly, terrorists who were quite rightly in jail one moment and Commonwealth heads of state the next. The wind of change that Harold Macmillan was to speak about in 1960 was already blowing through Africa. The Gold Coast, which had been reassuringly pink for the lifetime of most British people, was now in the hands of 'natives' and we weren't sure that this new country called Ghana was a particularly Good Thing, which makes Nicolas Hawkes's liberal, unprejudiced attitude so remarkable.

However, we begin back in the late 1940s, in the days of the Attlee government, with Britain trying hard to recover from the shattering effects of six years of total war. So welcome now to that grey world of postwar Austerity Britain in which these children and teenagers were going to have to make their way. It was the Britain of *Passport to Pimlico* and Denis Compton, of snoek and spivs, of rationing and optimism about a better tomorrow. In short, it was a long time ago, but these men all lived through it.

PART 1

THE BEGINNING
1946–1951

There was something very endearingly British about the start of the Attlee government that was to revolutionise society in the late 1940s. On 5 July 1945, less than two months after Germany had surrendered unconditionally and more than a month before Japan was to do so, the country went to the polls. The ballot boxes remained sealed for three weeks to permit the collection of those votes which had been cast by men and women in the armed forces who were still overseas. Although Labour won a landslide victory with an overall majority of 146, the result, in an era blessedly free of today's ubiquitous opinion polls, came as a surprise, particularly to the Conservative Party leader Winston Churchill. Mrs Churchill, worried about the strain of continued high office on the health of her husband, called the result 'a blessing in disguise'. Churchill growled that as far as he was concerned it was very well disguised indeed.

On the evening of 26 July, having tendered to the king his resignation as Prime Minister, Churchill left Buckingham Palace in a chauffeur-driven Rolls Royce. Fifteen minutes later Mrs Attlee drove her husband in the family Standard Ten into Palace Yard. As revolutions go, it lacked the iconic symbolism of the storming of the Bastille in July 1789. During the election campaign, Mrs Attlee had sat patiently in the Standard Ten knitting the time away as her husband made his speeches from the hustings. Now she was driving Clem in his best formal clothes to kiss hands with the mystified monarch who had admitted that the result 'had come as a great surprise to one and all'. The crowd of Labour supporters who lined The Mall cheered and shouted, 'We want Attlee,' as the Standard Ten clanked its way towards the Palace. The new prime minister waved politely from the passenger seat. This was not an image to inspire future film-makers as the attack on the Winter Palace in 1917 had inspired Sergei Eisenstein. Mr and Mrs Attlee and their Standard Ten were more likely to inspire an Ealing comedy than another *Ten Days That Shook the World*. It was, however, the start of a particularly British revolution.

There were two things that almost everyone who voted for Labour was agreed upon, male or female, middle class or working class. There must be no more war, and there must be no return to the economic and social conditions that had existed in Britain in 1939. For all their genuine admiration of Churchill as the man who had won the war, there was an ingrained belief that he was more interested in foreign affairs than domestic concerns and that his party was still the party of appeasement, privilege and the dole. There had been much grumbling about the controls imposed by the coalition government during wartime but it was grudgingly admitted that they had succeeded in creating a fairer society. The Conservatives would, judging by their past record, be only too keen to return to the *laissez faire* economics that had in part created the Great Depression. The new Britain that everyone wanted to see rise from the ashes caused by the German bombs had therefore to include significant government intervention and legislation. Attlee was just the man for this kind of job.

The problem was that the nation was virtually bankrupt and what Attlee believed the Labour Party had been elected to do was drastically to reform society at all levels. The railways and the mines were to be nationalised into new organisations called respectively British Railways and the National Coal Board; a national health service was to be formed; the secondary school system was to be transformed by the provisions of the Butler Act of 1944; and the recommendations of the Beveridge Report, published in 1942, had to be executed to create a more just system of welfare in a society that would now care for its citizens from the cradle to the grave. Perhaps most significant from the standpoint of the men whose stories comprise the main part of this book, legislation also included the National Service Act of 1947, which enlarged the armed forces following the demobilisation of 1945, and raising the school leaving age to fifteen, although something like 80 per cent of schoolchildren still left school as soon as they could.

Traditionally there had always been a suspicion in Britain of a standing conscript army, but in the aftermath of the Second World War there remained military obligations as part of the need to administer the war-torn countries liberated from Nazi rule as well as the normal duties associated with maintaining an empire. Even though India and Palestine were to be abandoned in 1947 in the face of overwhelming local hostility, there was still the matter of Britain's prestige on the world stage as one of the Big Three. All this had to be paid for with money the country didn't have, particularly now that Lend-Lease had ended along with the victory of the Allies. John Maynard

Keynes was sent off to Washington to negotiate a loan from the only developed country with any money, but he found the USA unexpectedly unwilling to reward with cash the gallant sacrifices Britain had made in 1940 and 1941 and he returned home without the grant or gift that had been hoped for. Instead Britain had to make do with a loan of $4.33 billion at 2 per cent that at least permitted Attlee to begin his revolutionary legislative programme, although many critics regarded the interest to be paid as punitive. Only Marshall Aid, which arrived to save Europe from Communism a few years later, kept the British economy afloat in these desperate years.

People might have felt at the end of six long years of war, with all the sacrifices that hard-earned victory had entailed, that they were entitled to some of the fruits of victory. Instead the welcome arrival of peace did not diminish the queues, fill the shops with goods or end the rationing. It might be salutary to examine briefly what these men as hungry youths were allowed to eat *a week* in 1946:

1s 2d (6p) worth of meat
3 oz bacon and ham
8 oz sugar
2.5 oz tea
2.5 pints of milk
2 oz butter
2 oz cheese
4 oz margarine
1 oz cooking fat
1 egg (per fortnight)
12 oz sweets (per month)

This food of course could only be bought after lengthy queuing. In newsreels of the time it is rare to find obese young people, which is perhaps the only positive note to strike as the full implications of rationing sink into our overfed, over-privileged minds.

Houses that had been destroyed by the Luftwaffe were not replaced, although the prefabs and the planned new towns offered hope to a small number of fortunate families. Couples who wished to marry frequently had to continue to live with their parents. Britain was, and continued to be for the first six years after Victory in Europe, a country of exhaustion and drabness, its towns pock-marked by ubiquitous bomb sites. Its population was grateful for the gift of life and the cessation of hostilities but it was still an unremittingly hard time for most of them.

Although people could now enjoy themselves without the constant admonition, 'Don't you know there's a war on?', the morals of the time returned to those of pre-war days after the relaxation caused by the experience of total war and the relentless knowledge that death was all around. In the summer of 1946, two young women who were permitted to go on holiday without adult supervision for the first time, arrived in Blackpool and paid their landlady in advance two pounds and fifteen shillings for full board for the week. That first night they went to a dance at the Tower Ballroom where they met two nice young men. Suddenly aware that their landlady had told them to be back by 9.30 p.m., they left the dance and their partners at 9 p.m. and ran all the way back to the boarding house. The following night they sat outside the boarding house talking to the boys. At 9.29 p.m. the landlady emerged and told them it was their bedtime. Their independent holiday notwithstanding, the young people knew better than to make a fuss. There was a deference to authority then that is unknown in the twenty-first century.

To make sense of National Service it is important to see it in its social and historical context. This was the Britain that Keith Bolderson, the first of the men to tell their stories in this book, was living in when he was called up in September 1946. He was perhaps particularly unfortunate in that within a few weeks of his induction into the RAF, Britain was experiencing its harshest winter for nearly seventy years. From the middle of December, a Britain already desperately short of coal faced paralysis. Heavy snow continued to fall day after freezing day and soon the entire country was deeply covered and frozen solid. It was the worst kind of freak winter and it could not have chosen a more unfortunate time.

Ships could not get in and out of the docks and the import/export trade was immobilised. London's commuters could not reach the city because the roads were impassable and train services disrupted. Schools were closed, and power cuts deprived people of warmth just when they needed it most. Even electric fires in the sitting room were banned at certain times of day, and it wasn't only homes that were deprived of gas and electricity. Soon there was no electricity for industry over huge areas of the country and two million men were out of work. Farmers suffered just as badly. Crops were ruined and livestock died, all of which had a knock-on effect on the production of food for the heavily rationed populace. The fledgling television service, tentatively restarted after the war, was suspended again.

These climatic scourges hit Britain with the force of biblical retribution and from flooded tube tracks to heavy snow in the

Channel Islands there was no relief for anyone. As late as March 1947 the blizzards and frosts continued, with hundreds of main roads still blocked by ice and drifts of snow which were alleged to reach thirty feet in some places. Then, in the middle of that month, came a sudden thaw. Ben Perry, working for the fire brigade in the Royal Army Service Corps (RASC), recalls not only the chicanery that went on as men tried everything to keep warm but also the chaos that came with the resultant floods. It was like a tempest loosing a swirling deluge, inundating nearly a million acres of farm land. It drowned sheep and cattle in their thousands and his job was to pump the water out. As the ice melted and the waters rose, rivers burst their banks and flooded houses.

The restrictions which had to be imposed as a result of this, the worst winter in living memory, were as stringent as any in wartime. Instead of the hoped-for gradual rise towards some form of prosperity the population of Britain shivered and groaned as imports were drastically curtailed. Even if you had a car there was no petrol to go anywhere in it. If you wanted to sit in your overcoat and read the paper it would be of brief duration because of the timber shortage which meant that newspapers reverted to four pages. Just keeping warm with the limits on clothing, footwear and fuel was a full-time occupation. The icy grip of the cold weather was numbing and created an indelible memory on the young people who experienced it.

The months of Arctic conditions were followed by the Brylcreem summer of 1947, as it was affectionately called in recognition of the record eighteen centuries and more than three thousand runs scored by the nation's favourite pin-up cricketer, the glamorous Denis Compton. Robin Wright, in the Royal Army Service Corps, was based in Aldershot and, maximising his leave and as a keen sportsman, he recalls with evident pleasure his days in the sun watching Compton and his regular batting partner Bill Edrich, who also scored over three thousand runs that summer, scampering up and down the sun-drenched pitches as county cricket enjoyed the best attended season in its history. It is perhaps salutary to add that as Robin was watching Compton and Edrich and Hutton and Washbrook putting South Africa's bowlers to the sword, the British economy was being similarly attacked. The convert-ibility of sterling, an integral demand of Keynes's American loan the previous year, caused an immediate and catastrophic drain of Britain's dollar reserves. The result was yet more cuts in government expenditure at a time when it seemed that there was no flesh left on the bone to be cut.

Robin, who was born in 1928, looks and sounds twenty years younger than his age. John Dixon, whose interview follows and who was born in the same year, has not been treated so fairly by the passing years, leading to the inevitable conclu-sion that for all of us the ageing process is both unpredictable and capricious. John has fewer positive memories than Robin of his National Service, yet in a way it seemed to shape his life more significantly. There is a lovely description of his discov-ery of jazz and the evocation of a shared learning experience at his RAF station offers a sharp contrast to the conventional view of life in the army.

It seems to reinforce the belief that for a few years after the end of the war, there was a moral seriousness about life in Britain that was not to endure. I refer to the establishment of the BBC's Third Programme on the wireless, 'the envy of the world' and the forerunner of Radio 3; there was also ABCA, the Army Bureau of Current Affairs, and the Arts Council, which grew out of the wartime Committee for the Encouragement of Music and the Arts. Did this seriousness perhaps relate to the lack of alternative forms of entertainment? Certainly cinema attendances and football and cricket crowds were never as large as they were in the immediate postwar years. In the mid-1950s, with the end of rationing, the beginnings of commercial television and the 'affluent society', this high moral seriousness faded, but what one gathers from Keith Bolderson, John Dixon and Norman McCord is a delight in learning and a feeling that whatever their backgrounds, a place at university was possible because they were bright enough. Such an attitude of mind probably wouldn't have been possible before 1945.

The interview with Dennis Warwick confirms this sense of a Britain that was (very) slowly loosening its class ties. When he talks about his father wanting him to work as a draughtsman in the office of the factory where he himself was employed, one hears the authentic voice of working-class folk who wanted the best for their children but didn't dare hope for too much or encourage them to aspire to a station in life they could not achieve. When he speaks of his growing affection for his girl-friend Pam who lived in Tolworth near Surbiton in Surrey and his parents' suspicion of the relationship, we are confronted by the very common anxieties of the times. For parents in Wakefield who had never left Yorkshire, this southern girl was clearly not to be trusted, simply because she lived off the A3. We hear lots of stories of men who were confronted in the barrack room by accents they had never heard before, but this particular anecdote I find very revealing of northerners and southerners. I have to say, as a Mancunian who has lived most of his life in the benighted south of England, that I entirely understand that suspicion even though I have an American daughter-in-law and two half-American grandchildren whom I love dearly. Some traditional suspicions still linger in the breast of good solid prejudiced northerners.

This first period of postwar National Service coincided with Britain's early and awkward attempts both to re-establish her old position in the world and to readjust to what was clearly going to be a new one. Geoff Rock's description of his time in Libya brings this to life very vividly. Although he came from a quiet backwater of the country in Herefordshire, being conscripted into the British Army automatically conferred on him some of the privileges of Britain's overseas role. It wasn't just the automatic assumption that the Arabs would nick everything that wasn't nailed down but the casual mention that the British played them at football and hammered them – the Arabs playing without shoes, possibly because, in their artless native way, they were used to doing so. In May 1947 a select Great Britain football team beat the Rest of Europe 6–1, confirming the triumphant delusion that we were top dog again, at least in that area of activity. Six years later, Hungary, the Magical Magyars, came to Wembley and hammered England 6–3, though they could have scored ten. The myth was destroyed for ever – or at least until 1966. Geoff Rock might have come from rural Herefordshire but he was still surprised to discover that there was no lavatory to sit on in Libya, just a hole in the ground, and that the women wore the veil and walked behind their men.

Whatever problems the British had in the postwar years, we were still British and that jolly well stood for something.

Stanley Price's interview is probably the most amusing, because Stanley is a masterful writer of comedy and his view of life in the army as an outsider – National Serviceman, Irish and Jewish – is predictably both biting and thoughtful. I've known Stanley for many years but we had never discussed his time in the army until I started to write this book. Apart from sharing a profession, Stanley and I both married outside the Jewish faith. It was hard enough for me in 1972, but Stanley is nearly twenty years older than I am and it needed considerable courage to defy your parents in the 1950s and invite an almost inevitable family rift. Stanley's brilliant demarcation of the subtle gradations of the class system as evidenced by schools and regiment is particularly revealing.

Joseph Strode is your classic Scouser. The very idea of the young Strode, an Evertonian by genetic inheritance and nature, suddenly removed from Stanley Park and Dock Road, Liverpool, and deposited in Korea during the war would be amusing if it weren't so frightening. Amazingly, he has lovingly preserved the propaganda that the Communists fired at him. His recollection of the Chinese and North Korean shells bursting and depositing their Christmas and New York greetings all over the exploited working-class lads from the British proletariat is utterly priceless.

So here they are, the cast of the first act of our drama. All of them are delightful men and all of them enjoyed wandering back in time to the days of their youth. I hope you enjoy it too and, like me, are grateful that you are reading about basic training rather than about to go through it.

ROLL CALL

KEITH BOLDERSON	1946–1949	RAF CLERK
BEN PERRY	1946–1948	ROYAL ARMY SERVICE CORPS
ROBIN WRIGHT	1947–1950	ROYAL ARMY SERVICE CORPS
JOHN DIXON	1948–1950	RAF RADAR OPERATIONS
GEOFF ROCK	1948–1950	1st INFANTRY DIVISION, ROYAL ARMY ORDNANCE CORPS
DENNIS WARWICK	1948–1950	RAF CLERK, PERSONNEL SELECTION
STANLEY PRICE	1949–1951	GREEN JACKETS, ROYAL ARMY EDUCATION CORPS
JOSEPH STRODE	1951–1953	1ST BATTALION, THE KING'S REGIMENT
NORMAN MCCORD	1951–1953	RAF FLIGHT CONTROLLER

KEITH BOLDERSON

1946–1949

RAF Clerk

I wasn't much of a clerk because I couldn't type but ... my acting abilities stood me in good stead because he [the wing commander] once said to me in front of some visiting group captain, 'Bolderson, your bearing is superb so you're only fit for one thing – you'll have to become a bishop.'

I'd like to begin by quoting my serial number but I'm afraid I've forgotten it. I know it starts 2323. I was born on 17 March 1928 and I was eighteen therefore in 1946 when I went into the RAF. I had been brought up for half my life to that date in the East Riding of Yorkshire and then my parents moved to near Lincoln, which meant that I went to a small grammar school called the De Aston School in Market Rasen. I have nothing but fond memories of the place. I got involved in a lot of plays and drama when I was there, which had a bearing on my time in National Service. I finished my Higher School

Certificate in June 1946 and was called up on 19 September. At that time you didn't know quite how long you'd be in for – it was a flexible thing. In the event it was two and a half years because the Berlin Airlift happened when I was there and they thought they needed to keep hold of the manpower when Soviet Russia shut off access to West Berlin by land and the RAF and USAF had to supply the city by air for nearly a year.

I wanted to go into the RAF and my parents happened to know one of the chaps who worked in the recruiting office, because in Lincolnshire where we lived we were completely surrounded by RAF stations. We were only three miles from Scampton, from which Guy Gibson and the Lancasters took off on the Dam Busters raid.

My intention when I went in was to do my time and then go up to Emmanuel College, Cambridge to read History. When the letter arrived after the medical I was told to report for duty at an RAF base near Wilmslow outside Manchester. That was the input place, where they sort you out and decide where they're going to send you. I was quite looking forward to it because it was a release from the narrow background I'd experienced to date.

At Wilmslow we were kitted out – you got your paybook and your eating irons. There was a special place to hang them in your bag. After you'd used them there was a place to wash them at the end of the cookhouse. My tunic fitted all right but the trousers were made for a man with a 46-inch waist, but of course in those days you wore braces – in fact we were issued with canvas braces – so it didn't matter too much. I can't remember precisely, but I think we did some paper tests and it was on the basis of those tests that I was considered to be sufficiently intelligent to be allocated to Yatesbury to become a radar fitter. The atmosphere at Wilmslow was fine. The shock of basic training was yet to come. There was a special train that took us from Wilmslow to Yatesbury, and it took us hours and hours to get there so we were issued with a packed lunch.

I went from that small school in a remote part of Lincolnshire to RAF Yatesbury near Calne in Wiltshire, which had nearly six thousand airmen on it, and a whole new world opened up for me. Yatesbury was only for radio and radar fitters and operators. I had no aptitude whatsoever for becoming a radar fitter, but they had a radar and radio training school. Now that required a fifty-week training course, so I was likely to be at RAF Yatesbury for some time after I finished basic training there. The lesser fry were operators and they were only there for twenty weeks.

I was a village boy so I was used to mixing with all sorts of social types. I wasn't a town boy from a narrow suburb. I never had any difficulty in meeting people and getting on with them. I started out as a day boy at De Aston and then became a boarder so I wasn't surprised by sleeping in a hut with thirty other young men.

What I do remember is that you didn't have one mattress, you had three. The mattress divided into three, they were called biscuits, and the drill was that in the morning you had to pile these up and then fold your blankets (in the RAF we also had sheets – which they didn't, I was told, in the army), and you did rather a smart sort of package on top of these biscuits with one blanket outside and then the sheet and then the next blanket and so on, all very neatly folded on top of each other.

The huts we lived in had been very hastily erected on stilts because the ground was so marshy. This was the extremely bad winter of 1946–7, so when I looked out of my bed I could see the snow that had drifted underneath the bed.

Although the war had only been over for just over a year when I was called up, I had absolutely no sense of patriotism. I'd been in Piccadilly Circus when I heard the announcement that the Japanese had surrendered and I remember feeling that that was it, there would be no more wars in my lifetime – the Cold War hadn't really solidified then and the Russians were still our brave allies. They were awkward of course, but their suffering entitled them to be awkward. We knew nothing of Soviet atrocities. We weren't taken into the armed forces to fight the Russians. We were there so they could demob the older men as fast as possible and get them back into employment. The country didn't need useless creatures like me.

I think we were lucky at Yatesbury because we had a lovely flight sergeant, Chiefy Hale, and he was terribly nice – I think he was very tolerant of young lads. However, there was one really unpleasant chap, a corporal whose name I can't remember, and he was really fond of old-fashioned discipline. I think he was bitter because he was still only a corporal.

In some ways basic training was like being on the stage because I thought I was performing a part. We were all pretending to be military and providing you did the things that made them happy you were all right. There were some unfortunate lads who never looked military and they got into the most enormous trouble – constantly being shouted at – but I was reasonably tall, reasonably fit and I could perform. We'd had an Air Training Corps at school but I never belonged to it. It was totally new to me.

First thing every morning, whatever stage of service you were at, there was a parade at about eight o'clock. You were then marched off in groups to wherever your occupational training was happening. The basic training was largely square bashing and learning how to salute – longest way up and shortest way down. I can still do that – it only took me eight weeks. Then you had school sessions and one of them was the different ranks and how to distinguish them by the number of stripes and so on. Going up it was pilot officer, followed by flying officer, then squadron leader, then wing commander, group captain and so forth. We had proper classroom sessions to teach you and then there was the physical stuff.

As part of your kitting out you were given a set of gym clothes. If the weather was nice it was outside on the parade ground but if it was inclement you'd be doing it inside a hangar. You just followed an instructor like you did at school. I suspect the basic training in the RAF was much easier than it was in the army because they weren't training you for hard physical action in warfare. We didn't have to know anything about planes, that's for sure. At the passing-out parade the base commander was a group captain and he came down to take the salute. We practised that salute on the march past from week two. The NCOs were aware there were weak ones in the flight, so they made sure they were in the middle so they would be hidden by everyone else.

The grumbling was less about the discipline than about the food. Don't forget in 1946 rationing was very severe for the civilian population. Calne was the home of Harris's Sausages so we had sausages in all sorts of form – even the wretched shepherd's pie was made with sausage meat at the bottom. There was always plenty of bread so we weren't that hungry, and we'd come from homes that had been rationed for years, so we were used to it. School grub certainly was much worse than what we got in the RAF.

We were shocked by the start of the Berlin Airlift in 1948, mostly because it was going to delay our release and also because such a thing was happening, the danger of a real war. I don't think any of us were really conscious of what was going on in the outside world. The only newspaper we ever saw was probably the *Daily Mirror*, which was not known for its news content. There was no wireless so no *Dick Barton* or *ITMA* – there was no such thing as a portable radio. There may have been a big wireless in the NAAFI but I didn't go to the NAAFI much. I was running the theatre in the evenings. I never did any of the work associated with being a radar fitter.

Not very long after I'd finished the eight weeks of square bashing I got involved with the station theatre, and to cut a long story short within three or four months I was running it. As an aircraftman you were on the bottom rung of the ladder. No AC2 could do this but though there was an officer in charge, Pilot Officer Neal, he didn't want to be doing anything as stupid as this and he was perfectly happy for me to be doing it. He said to me that he wanted to keep me so he was going to arrange for me to become the senior training officer's clerk. So I was reclassified as Clerk GD and I became Wing Commander Wilkins's personal assistant, which was great fun. I wasn't much of a clerk because I couldn't type but nevertheless he and I got on extremely well, and my acting abilities stood me in good stead because he once said to me in front of some visiting group captain, 'Bolderson, your bearing is superb so you're only fit for one thing – you'll have to become a bishop.'

The first thing I had to do was to programme a wide range of plays to appeal to all the men, otherwise Pilot Officer Neal was going to get into trouble. There were WAAFs on the station to play the female parts. I remember Maureen, who had to appear in a bathing costume in our production of *French Without Tears* – that brought a few whistles. I can't say we treated them very respectfully. The WAAFs were regulars, they were usually a few years older than us and they tended to be referred to as 'that bag So-and-So'. There was a lot of lewd talk about women, certainly. I mean, these were eighteen-year-old lads and the general attitude of men to women at this time was that women were rather ethereal beings and very dependent upon men.

We got paid more than the pocket money I had at school and I wasn't a drinker, so I felt rich. There was one man I can remember, a very rough, tough Glaswegian. I had never met anybody like him but I learned more from him than from anybody else. He had the ability to sink a pint quicker than anybody else. He loved going to the pub and challenging someone else to a contest to see who could down the pint first and the loser paid for the winner's pint. He always won. He'd left school at fourteen and gone to work in a Glasgow shipyard. He was older than eighteen – I think he'd been deferred. He would say something like 'I was fucking this bint on a Friday and this bint says to me "Dona yae look so serious," so I says to her, "Course I look serious. I'm paying good money for this!"' I've remembered that story for sixty years but I haven't been able to tell it that often. I liked him. The only people I didn't like were the boring ones who were mooning over the girlfriend they'd left behind, and there were quite a few of them.

There was a training routine for how to behave on pay day. You were lined up in your hut and a corporal would come in with the cash, and he would call out your name and you had to be lined up in the order you were paid. We went up and saluted and said 'Sir' and gave our serial number and we got the cash, which was enough to take me to the theatre in London. We had lockers by the bed where you kept stuff, but I don't remember anything being stolen. If you were paid as a radar fitter you'd be paid that bit extra, but I was paid as a clerk. It wasn't easy to get that status – I had to go to Debden in Essex and take a test which included typing, which I could do well enough to pass the test – I learned the keyboard with two fingers but I didn't have to look down. Making mistakes was a nightmare, so you desperately wanted to avoid making a mistake – particularly as you always had to make at least three copies, and they had to be altered too if you made a mistake.

While I was doing National Service I met a whole new range of people and I decided that I no longer wanted to go to Cambridge and become a schoolmaster. I was much more interested in modern things, so I applied to the London School of Economics and I was accepted whilst I was in the RAF, so I knew I was going up to the LSE in October 1949. There was some talk about politics and it influenced me greatly. It was a genuine discussion – there were old-fashioned Tories and people who liked the nationalisation policies of the Attlee government. I wouldn't want to over-emphasise the intellectual nature of these discussions but I certainly became aware of the world we lived in while I was in the RAF, which I hadn't been before. I remember a lad from Leeds, the Alan Bennett of his day, who talked very vividly about what life was like in the back streets of Leeds. It was a huge eye-opener and mind-changer.

After meeting all these people in National Service I was making, I suppose, a social statement by changing to the LSE. All the dreary people I knew in my life had been to Cambridge so that rather put me off and I met my wife at the LSE. Mind you, at that time I think it was only 5 per cent of the population that went to university. I got a grant of £240 a year from the Further Education Training Scheme, and your fees were paid, of course. It wasn't the RAF that changed me. It was the chance that the RAF gave me to meet such a wide range of people that changed me.

National Service was certainly beneficial to me and I have always been grateful for the experience, but I can't argue generally today from my experience then. It is my belief that one of the biggest mistakes this country has made has been to send too many people to university instead of putting them through some kind of technical training that would enable them to do jobs that are needed in a modern society. I don't think you can do that through National Service, you have to do it through reform of the education system plus other incentives. At the moment universities are serving the purpose that National Service was partly invented for.

BEN PERRY

1946–1948

Royal Army Service Corps

We had a crew of eight locally enlisted Malays on the fire crew. We were told that they weren't our equal. Officers told us that we must be firm but fair with them but they were not our equal. I thought some officers, if they hadn't been to public school, wouldn't have made lance corporal in charge of the toilets.

I was born in 1928 and brought up in Leominster. I had five brothers and sisters. I was the eldest. Our dad was a carpenter and he'd been in the horse-drawn artillery in the First World War. He never spoke about it much, though we all knew he'd been wounded because he had a big scar on his back. All he told me was never to volunteer for anything. He wouldn't even let me join the Boy Scouts.

I left school in 1942 at fourteen but I'd been working as an errand boy since I was ten. I also had a paper round and I worked in a grocer's shop, so I'd done three jobs before I left school. Then I went over to Tenbury to work at a firm that was making landmines and parts for incendiary bombs and hand grenades. I looked for an apprenticeship as a carpenter but there was nothing going. The women went on strike and they cut the pay for that job in Tenbury, so I left there and went to work for Cadbury's at the milk factory at Marlbrook, and I stayed there till I was called up.

At sixteen you had to register and they tried to get you to join the youth services – the Air Training Corps, the Sea Cadets or the Army Training Corps. I was excused because at Cadbury's we had to do shift work at weekends and that was when the youth services met. My father was pleased because he didn't want me to join any of them.

I was looking forward to National Service because I thought that meant no one would treat you like a boy any more. I'd be in the forces and see the world. My father said I shouldn't join the infantry, and I really wanted to go into the navy so I put down the Royal Navy. I was sent to Worcester for the medical and I was temporarily accepted, but eventually along comes a letter which says my original classification had been cancelled and I was now to be available for a call-up to the army. I was really disappointed. I thought I'd see the world. Join the navy and see the world. Join the army and march round the bugger.

I was sent to the Norton Barracks at Worcester. It was called 72 Primary Training Wing because everyone did six weeks infantry-style basic training – squad drills, map reading and rifles – basic soldiering. I was in the General Service Corps and when you were in there you weren't told which regiment you were going into. They assessed you but it depended on what they were looking for at the time. They'd give you tests to see how thick you were. They'd give you maths to do and maybe some geography and then they'd give you simple things to assemble like a bicycle pump, a door lock, things like that.

I was called up on 1 August 1946, which was of course a bank holiday. When I first got there they cut my hair and gave me the inoculations and then told me to go home and come back after the bank holiday. That was unusual because usually the first ten days of basic training you weren't allowed out of the camp.

There were thirty men in our barrack room. Norton had some brick-built barracks and when it expanded during the war they built some makeshift huts. It was home to the Worcestershire Regiment, so there were a lot of full-time regulars there. It was six weeks of basic training, then some stayed for a further twenty weeks, I think it was, of infantry training. They never stopped chasing you. Parade would finish and you'd be shouted into the barracks to change into gym clothes or maybe full service battle order, different types of dress, best boots, belt and gaiters for marching on the square. It was very rapid and you were on the go all the time because they were trying to toughen you up and make you fit. I played football so I didn't find it a problem. Some people couldn't cope. They were homesick and they would spend the nights crying. There was one chap who was very homesick and we thought he was a bit of a baby. Last person out of the barracks got belted with a towel and I joined in, but after I'd done it once I realised it was just making things worse for him.

To begin with several wouldn't eat what was put in front of them, they spent all their money down the NAAFI trying to buy other food, but the next chap always ate theirs. It was basic and rough – it certainly wasn't your mother's home cooking.

The worst part of that basic training was the assault course at night. There was a big wide ditch full of water. It was dark, so you ran ten paces, jumped and hoped – I didn't like that. One person would have to lie on the barbed wire, then his mates would run over his back. You had to be able to run a hundred yards in twelve seconds, a mile in five minutes, five miles in fifty minutes; you had to do ten pull-ups to the bar, a high jump of four foot six inches and a long jump of fourteen feet. I couldn't do the hundred yards, I couldn't clear the bar at four foot six and I couldn't reach fourteen feet at the long jump, but the rest of it was easy – I could lap people when I was running the mile. They told me I hit 76 per cent of the target.

Some NCOs had the impression that because I came from a small town I was a swede basher, but there were more thick ones among the townies than there were amongst us. I knew people from Birmingham at Cadbury's and there was a grammar school from Walthamstow in East London called the Monoux School that was evacuated to round here during the war, so I had heard other accents. I played cricket with them – one of them was the Test player and selector Doug Insole. Bugger broke my bat.

The worst accents to understand were the Geordies and the Scots. Not all the Scots, because their accents vary so much – I'm talking about the hard Glaswegian accent and people from Lancashire and Yorkshire, because they say words in a different way, don't they?

At the end of basic training they said they wanted me to

become a clerk but I didn't, and I saw they wrote 'This man is averse to any clerical work.' I was good at maths, you see, and I was in the A stream at school. I'd have liked to have gone into the Engineers or been a driver. My final choice was an artilleryman but that didn't mean you'd get any of your choices. You might end up in the King's Shropshire Light Infantry if they wanted a lot of infantrymen. I ended up in Colchester in the Royal Army Service Corps at the firefighting centre. I did the RASC drivers' course and was classed as Grade B because you had to be an NCO to be a Grade A. They called me a driver but I didn't actually do any driving – it was all fire-fighting.

All my records were kept in Army Book AB 64 Part 1. Part 2 was your paybook. They also kept a list of your inoculations. Initially I was paid four shillings a day, twenty-eight shillings a week, out of which they stopped half a crown for barrack room damages. I didn't do any damage to the barrack room but every week they'd take out two bob or half a crown. After six months when you'd completed your trade training it went up to maybe five bob a day, but I think the basic had only just gone up to four shillings from three bob a day when I started in 1946. We thought we might be in for two and a half years, something like that, when we started but in 1947 they passed the National Service Act and we knew then it would be less.

After Colchester I went to Aldershot, then my first winter was spent at Bicester at the fire brigade. It was the worst winter of my life and we spent a lot of time pumping out water when the big thaw came. We had virtually no fuel that winter but there were a lot of old packing cases which burned up too quick. I remember once a train nearly got derailed and we ransacked their coal bunker before they came in the morning to get the train back on the line. We dug a hole at the back of the hut and buried the coal there, then we put snow back on top of it. We had some German POWs on the base at Bicester doing some driving, and they told us they'd been over to an RAF station at Brill in Buckinghamshire and they had plenty of coke, so we went over there and pinched it. I was amazed we got away with it.

In the summer of 1947, after I told them I didn't want to do any clerking, they sent me to be a clerk at Aldershot for A50 Army Company. No promotion, no pay rise. There were more officers than men down there. When I got there I found this large pile of papers that nobody had filed. It was typical army bumf that comes out every morning. Once I'd read the daily orders and put anything that applied to us on the major's desk, that was it. I had nothing to do and I was bored to tears. And if you went to a dance in Aldershot there'd be forty soldiers and two girls.

Anyway, eventually I got the chance to go to Singapore. They did me again for smallpox – I'd already had it as a child, so I thought you only needed one for your whole life, but smallpox was endemic out there. After embarkation leave I went to the RASC Battalion depot in Thetford in Norfolk. That was a horror camp. All they tried to do there was to think of things to humiliate you. It was worse than basic training. If you walked on the wrong path to get to the cookhouse they put you on extra duties. They did me for the way I was carrying my knife, fork and spoon. I had to peel potatoes or scrub buckets. Every day there was something like that. That was 10 Platoon and we were there for a fortnight. You could be waiting in the queue for dinner and they'd come in and grab thirty of us and double us up down the bloody road. No sodding reason. Just being nasty, and the sergeant major was a right swine.

They did everything to break your spirit. An officer kicked my boots across the parade ground. Another one told me to go and get my hair cut at three successive parades. I deliberately damaged the boots and got a chit from the cobbler so he wouldn't be able to do that again. They kept finding fault with the way the buttons on my greatcoat were polished so I cut them off and replaced them with plastic buttons. Fortunately when a new lot arrived they started on them.

Eventually we got a special train up to the pierhead at Liverpool where the troopship was supposed to be waiting. Trouble was there was no boat there and we were like snails with our houses on our backs – blankets and everything. Eventually we were sent down to Gladstone Dock. Nobody told us what was going on but one of the lads had an uncle who was a docker there and he said that the crew of the *Empress of Scotland*, the ship we were supposed to be going to Singapore on, were out on strike and they were intimidating others who wouldn't cross the picket line. It was a civilian crew, otherwise it would have been mutiny. Eventually they got tugs to take us into the middle of the Mersey, where they dropped anchor, and they brought another crew down from Newcastle.

It took twenty days to get to Singapore. We stopped at Penang, an island to the north of Malaya, and there they let us go ashore for the day because they'd refused to let us get off the ship at Port Said – that was our first stop, then it was Aden and Colombo in Ceylon. Penang was our first taste of the Orient and I was amazed by the bananas. Everything in England was so rationed. It was like being on holiday because we could have what we wanted. We reached Singapore on 20 November 1947 – the day the Queen got married. The temperature was in the nineties and the humidity was about 90 per cent. It was really hot. You were sweating all the time. We were part of 92 Brigade out there, but pretty much as soon as I got there they sent me up to Malaya, so I was only in Singapore for three weeks.

We were never fearful for our lives, though we had to be on our guard when we went out. We used to bathe in a stream which had a pool in it and then we found out that some men from the Yorkshire Light Infantry had been gunned down there just bathing like we were. I think about six of them were killed.

We had eight locally enlisted Malays on the fire crew. We were told that they weren't our equal. Officers told us that we must be firm but fair with them but they were not our equal. I thought some officers, if they hadn't been to public school, wouldn't have made lance corporal in charge of the toilets. The Malay people didn't seem opposed to us at all. They are a very gentle race. Most of them were cleaners. We had some Eurasians on the base and they were chosen because they were supposed to be a bit brighter. One of the locals on the crew started making fun of my accent so I turned the hose on him. Afterwards he said he wanted to box me. That was the biggest mistake he ever made. He didn't last the first three minutes and he threw the gloves away. We did get into Kuala Lumpur but we never touched the local Thai food, never went for Indian or Chinese food. We went looking for a steak.

The Malayan Emergency started on 16 June 1948. At the

end of the street with our fire station there was a big building, the HQ of the Communist Party of Malaya, and that was quickly closed down. Certain people weren't allowed to come onto the base – the ice cream seller and people like that. It was the Chinese that were the problem, not the Malays. They wouldn't have the Chinese in the local police force – they were all Malays. I had to be armed after June 1948. I was issued with a gun and live ammunition, which I hadn't seen since I'd left England. The Malays on the fire crew weren't given it but the regular Malay soldiers were, although after the Emergency started the Gurkhas were brought in. I never fired another shot, though I'd been on the rifle range at Aldershot, which I'd done to keep up my pay.

I replaced Sergeant Evans, who had originally been selected as a Bevin Boy miner, and the only way he could get out of going down the mines was to sign on as a regular soldier. It meant he had to do three years out there. I became a lance corporal and then a corporal but they wouldn't make me up to sergeant because they said I didn't have enough time left to serve. They tried to get me to sign up for another year and they said they'd make me a sergeant then, but I wouldn't do it.

I came back on the troopship *Devonshire*. I was delighted to be coming home, even if there was still rationing. I went back to work at Cadbury's for a while but I was put on shift work and I didn't like that.

National Service showed me parts of the world I'd never seen. It taught me to be smartly dressed – I see some kids today with their hair down the back of their necks and I wonder what the sergeant major would have made of them!

ROBIN WRIGHT

1947–1950

Royal Army Service Corps

The Germans were slowly starving. They were pale and undernourished and if the nutrition hadn't improved they would have died. There was an overwhelming majority of women to men because so many hadn't come back, especially from the Eastern Front. They were cowed, probably bitter, certainly resentful.

I was born in Leicester in 1928 and lived there until I left university. My father was a bank cashier and remained one until he retired. We were middle class, I suppose, though with a lower-middle income because my father was never promoted. I had a very happy childhood. I was an only child but I was never lonely. I played a lot of sport and I went away to school at the age of thirteen. After that I did three and a half years' National Service having taken a short service commission and went to Cambridge in October 1950. I worked in sales and marketing for most of my career.

Leicester wasn't in the direct line of the bombing like Coventry was but I remember sleeping in the cupboard under the stairs because that was supposed to be safe. Although my family remained in Leicester throughout the war, my school was evacuated from Canterbury to just outside St Austell in Cornwall. In 1943 thousands and thousands of Americans arrived and they used to give us Hershey bars and chewing gum, until one day we woke up and they'd all gone – it was 6 June 1944. I remember the election of 1945 and that I was totally unable to understand the Labour landslide. Winston Churchill had been my hero so it was quite mystifying to me that he had been defeated.

As the date of call-up got closer I was looking forward to it because it offered new excitement. It was a troublesome world and we'd grown up with war as part of life. I was a bad sailor, so it was the army or the RAF and I was perfectly happy to go into the army.

There was no regiment attached at the start and by sheer coincidence I was first sent off to the Glen Parva Barracks in Wigston on the edge of Leicester. I was very lucky, I suppose, because during those harsh early weeks I could get home very easily. It was January 1947, the coldest winter in living memory. The snow didn't melt until the beginning of May, although the upside was that we had a wonderful summer in 1947 and I was based in Aldershot so I saw a lot of Compton and Edrich. The army was not noted for making sure we were warm or comfortable. We spent a lot of time scraping and clearing snow and ice off the parade ground so we could parade. You huddled round the stove in the barracks or you went down to the NAAFI. I was used to wartime rations, so I didn't notice that the food was particularly bad.

Basic training wasn't too much of a shock to the system because I'd done a lot of it at school in the CCF. I was used to arms drill and I was used to living away from home, but it was a big shock to others. I was small, bespectacled, inconspicuous, while some of the chaps coming into the barracks were six foot two and I was in awe of them but when it got down to it I was the one who knew how to press trousers and clean boots so I had a great advantage. Many of the others had left school at fourteen and had been working for four years, so they were used to earning more than the twenty-eight shillings a week the army paid us, but I wasn't. The majority of the National Servicemen that I met came into the army never having experienced discipline and they found that very, very hard. Again I was used to it all but others really struggled. I was a boy and they seemed like men, so much more mature, but they couldn't make the beds and they were really unhappy. One or two of them, of course, went AWOL. It was the verbal bullying that did it. There wasn't physical abuse but there was a lot of unhappiness.

There was a little *esprit de corps*, but not as much as there might have been because you had to do your own stuff first. There was a big social and financial gap between the men in the barracks and I suppose the mixing we did was good for all of us. At school we lived in a rarefied atmosphere where we just met our own kind, but then working-class lads presumably mixed with pretty much their own kind too. In the army you met all kinds. I wasn't the poshest by any means – I met soldiers far posher than I was – but I do think that mixing was very good for everyone. There was the son of a lord, which was outside my experience, and labourers that I'd never come across either. National Service was excellent for that. It made all of us realise what a wide variety of people lived in this country. It opened everyone's eyes no matter where you came from.

Some of the people found the physical stuff quite difficult and in the army there was very little sympathy wasted on people like that when they got NCOs barking at them. Those who hadn't had the benefits of physical training and sport the way I had just suffered. One way or another, the majority got through – not necessarily comfortably or happily, but they got through. For those who couldn't get through it must have been pretty hellish. There were some who certainly didn't want to be there – they were earning so much less or they wanted to go to university and this was a pointless two years out of their lives (as they saw it). These were the chaps who probably had a bad time in National Service.

After passing out at Glen Parva I was told I was going into the Royal Artillery, so I was posted to Aldershot to train to be a gunner. That's where I applied to be considered for officer training. There was more money, obviously, but I think I was more interested in having a bit more status and comfort. However, if I'm being honest I think back to my school days in the CCF and although it sounds arrogant to say so now, I think we all thought that we were being trained to become officers eventually. It was certainly my intention to become a National Service officer and still do just the two years. I was genuinely thrilled when I passed my Wosbe, the War Office Selection Board, and was selected for officer training. There was some back chat when I went back to my unit but none of it was nasty. Everyone accepted there were differences in education, which was the result of chance, but by and large people accepted my promotion with humour and friendliness.

So I went off to Mons, which was for general officer training, and then after that you went off to a specific corps. The RASC was responsible for supplies and transport, and I went there as an officer in the autumn of 1947. My commanding officer in the Royal Artillery wasn't too pleased about it. The Royal Artillery training was six months and the RASC was six weeks, so that's why I opted for the latter. I wasn't a great lover of the Artillery particularly, I hadn't chosen to be in it, and if I could become an officer in six weeks rather than twenty-six weeks that suited me.

When I was at Mons I came across the infamous RSM Ronald Brittain, who had the loudest voice in the British Army. I've never forgotten him bellowing, 'That cadet in the Artillery with the glasses, pull on your butt.' I wore glasses and I was in the Artillery. He saw that my rifle wasn't at the right angle from fifty yards away. He was almost a caricature of a regimental sergeant major but I've never forgotten him. There was the story of a young officer I didn't know, a second lieutenant who decided to flex his muscles. He stopped him and said, 'Sergeant Major Brittain, I didn't notice you saluting me properly. I want you to salute me again. And stand to attention properly when you're talking to me!' The next day he had his commission taken away from him. Frankly he deserved it. It was a stupid thing to do. Brittain was a powerful man.

After Mons I shipped off to the British Army in Hamburg. The German population greatly preferred the British to the Russians. They were terrified of the Russians. I don't remember any physical abuse of the Germans. That would have been strictly against army rules. What was so remarkable were the effects of the bombing. It was two and a half years after the war had finished but as far as the eye could see it was just rubble and people lived in and under that rubble. That, to a naïve middle-class nineteen-year-old from a sheltered background, was a real eye-opener. The Germans were slowly starving. They were pale and undernourished and if the nutrition hadn't improved they would have died. There was an overwhelming majority of women to men because so many hadn't come back, especially from the Eastern Front. They were cowed, probably bitter, certainly resentful. They went about their business without any feelings of friendliness and we were not allowed to fraternise. We were an occupying power, and they knew it and we knew it.

Conditions were dreadful, so I suppose I had mixed feelings about them. It hadn't been so long ago that they were the enemy, but they were so cowed, so beaten . . . and they smelled. They smelled because there was no soap, so they couldn't clean themselves. There was nothing in the shops and there were very few shops open. They were living in utter poverty and squalor. I didn't have any qualms about what the British and American bombers had done. We felt we were in the right fighting the evil Nazis. Of course I never met anyone who claimed to have been a member of the Nazi party, but having said that, all those Germans were ordinary human beings.

I was on detachment in Hamburg docks overseeing the storing and shipping of flour, sugar, potatoes and other dry sack goods by rail and road to army depots throughout West Germany. One day, the sergeant came to tell me that a hundred or so German labourers were refusing to work because they felt their lunch was inadequate. It certainly was. I couldn't have eaten it. Fortunately, I could speak German so I gathered them all together and promised them that if they returned to work I would go and see the colonel in charge of the depot and see if I could improve their rations. I did so and the colonel made sure that the workers' lunch rations improved. Thereafter, instead of receiving grim, sullen, unfriendly looks as I moved around, I was greeted with warmer looks and occasional smiles by most of the German workers. What the original stuff they had to eat was made of I do not know. It was an awful horrible dirty gruel stew and we had provided the rations for it. I could understand their attitude. It was hard work carrying sacks of flour, hard manual labour, and they did that all day and the food they were given looked and smelled awful. I had never had a smile from a German before those lunches were improved. We just passed each other and they didn't look at me, or at least when they did it was extremely unfriendly. I can't say I ever got to know the German population. I was part of the British Army of Occupation.

Things started to get better for the Germans in 1948 when they exchanged the old Reichsmark, which were worth about a ha'penny, for the Deutschmark. There was a limited allocation of this new currency for each person. After that things appeared in the shops and people started to look a little more prosperous. I suppose that was the start of the famous German economic miracle. I came back to a Britain that was still rationed, that still had bomb damage, where people didn't have much and for whom life was still very austere, but it was nothing remotely like what I'd experienced in Germany. Unless you saw life in Germany in 1947 you couldn't possibly understand what it was like out there.

For most National Service soldiers aged eighteen or nineteen in the late 1940s and very inexperienced in life, postwar Germany was a totally new experience. They were far from home, no family or girlfriends, in a strange environment where the young German women in their twenties and thirties hugely outnumbered the men. To marry a German girl permission had to be obtained. More than once young soldiers came to me with this request. Usually the girls were much older, frequently they were widows with children. The soldiers I am talking about were eighteen or nineteen, but even at that age they were relatively so much better off than anyone in Germany at that time. They were therefore the lifeline to a better standard of life for these German women.

Permission was given sometimes, maybe to someone more senior, someone older and more experienced. Usually the soldier making the request was posted within forty-eight hours to a unit hundreds of miles away. They were devastated and distraught. I can recall at least two young soldiers in tears when told they had to go. I can only hope that in later life they appreciated that these postings were for their longer-term benefit and that future marital happiness came their way.

I personally never said no, I had to refer the request upwards, but I knew what the standard drill was so I knew what the result was going to be. It was very hard on these young lads but looking back on it I think the army was probably right. The German women were quite desperate and the British lads were very inexperienced so I would endorse the general principle. I'm sure these lads were genuinely in love but it was done for their own good.

When the Berlin Airlift came, the only way to get into Berlin at that time was via Short Sunderlands and they took off from the docks. The Short Sunderland was a large squat plane that took off from rivers and landed in a lake in Berlin. Lots of provisions therefore were shipped down to my depot and the German labourers, supervised by the British, loaded these provisions onto the Sunderlands to relieve Berlin. The Germans were keen to help because they were so frightened of the Russians. I think we were all conscious that this could lead to a war. The Russians were now the baddies. I was in Hamburg so I didn't think I would be in a shooting war, but it was certainly a nervous time, a very tense time indeed.

At the end of my two years I decided to sign on. I was thinking of joining full time because I so enjoyed army life. I enjoyed the camaraderie and the sports, particularly rugby – I was a decent fly half. I think I approached them for the short service commission. I enjoyed mess life and I was used to the discipline. I was torn between wanting to go to university and wanting to stay on. I went in for the regular commission board, which I failed – only just, apparently, they said come back again. They didn't tell me why I'd failed. They said I hadn't quite shown the material they were looking for but I could try again in six months. I thought then that a bird in the hand in Cambridge was worth two in the bush. I went up to Selwyn College because King's Canterbury had a lot of connections there. After that I got glandular fever and I actually left Germany in a hospital ship. When I got better I served out my time in England. I think that failure with the regular commission put me off deciding to throw in my lot with the army.

I look back on those National Service days with great fondness and I wouldn't have missed it for the world. It turned me from a boy into a man and mixing with such a wide variety of people was very beneficial. When I went up to Cambridge, and indeed when I went into commercial life, I was back to mixing with middle-income, middle-class people. I thought the army was splendid for me, though I recognise not everyone thought that way. We had no choice about doing National Service but it did 95 per cent of us good, I'm sure.

JOHN DIXON

1948–1950

RAF Radar Operations

As far as I was concerned, if the Russians had actually started a war I was in no way fitted to fight it even after my National Service was finished.

I was born on Tyneside in 1928. My parents and my grandparents all came from there. In the 1930s my dad, like tens of thousands of others, lost his job and when he finally found another one it was as a Co-op insurance agent in north Cumberland, which was a very depressed area. We moved from the suburbs of Newcastle into Abbeytown, near Wigton, which was a village of some 250 people. Fortunately, both my younger sister and I won County scholarships to Wigton Grammar School. Melvyn Bragg went there about eight or nine years later. Without those scholarships we could neither of us have gone. I was a bright lad who could please teachers but I was in the sixth form at fourteen and I started to flounder. When we returned to school after war was declared in 1939 we learned that the headmaster and his wife, who were both committed pacifists, had committed suicide. It was horrible.

My dad had been an observer gunner in the Royal Flying Corps during the Great War. In 1940 when we were facing the prospect of invasion our neighbour's son came back from Dunkirk. My dad took one look at him and said he preferred to be in the armed forces when the Nazis invaded. They took him back and he went into the Ack-ack, although my mother wasn't very happy about it because we were in north Cumberland and the Nazis weren't going to invade up the Solway Firth. In 1943, however, the army cleared out all the older men so that they could promote the younger ones and he was ignominiously asked to leave the armed forces at the age of forty-seven. It was ridiculous in a way because in his work on his insurance round he was cycling over a hundred miles a week in all weathers. My dad was not happy at the decision.

I got my Higher School Certificate in 1944 when I was sixteen but I stayed on another year to try for university entrance. I had the chance of a place either at St Edmund Hall, Oxford or Emmanuel College, Cambridge. Oxford accepted me but I said I was going into the forces because I'd been interviewed in the autumn of 1944 and we hadn't finished the European war. However, Teddy [St Edmund] Hall took me early at seventeen in October 1945. I was always the youngest in college and in 1946 I was suddenly surrounded by ex-servicemen. They never talked about their service and treated me entirely as their equal. They wanted to forget about the war because it was hard for them to get back into the swing of being students again after what they'd been through.

I graduated in the summer of 1948. I'd already got all sorts of proficiency badges in the army and air force cadets – I'd done that at school – so they interviewed me as a potential officer when I said I wanted to go into the RAF but I said I thought National Service was a waste of time and later I was glad that I hadn't gone up that road. I was allowed some leeway as to when I was called up and in the summer I was helping on my girlfriend's family farm in the Lake District, so I asked if I could go in after the harvest had been gathered in September 1948.

I was called up to RAF Padgate near Warrington where I got kitted out for basic training. I think that was my only experience of a system which was totally hierarchical and in which all I had to do was to obey. Even school hadn't been like that. The camp was run by drill sergeants and corporals and the whole aim was to break down any resistance. I had never met that kind of bullying before and I was taken aback by it. We had to keep the billet spotlessly clean. I was made billet orderly so I was responsible for seeing that the blankets were folded properly. I made one of the men who, up to that moment, had been a friend re-fold his blankets and he wasn't too pleased.

I was twenty years old but I wasn't a mature twenty. There were working-class lads of eighteen who had seen much more of life than I had. In the next bed was a Brummie lad, and there were two lads from Stornoway who stayed together and one from Glasgow I talked to occasionally, but I didn't get close to any of them. You couldn't spend time getting to know each other because you had no slack time. You were always doing something – polishing, sweeping, cleaning, folding, marching. Every bit of your life was filled up. At Oxford, all my tutor would ask was if I'd like to do an essay on Shakespeare's tragedies and next week I'd bring him back a two-thousand-word essay, so to be regimented by the RAF like that was alien to me. An officer tore me off a strip when I failed to salute properly whilst carrying a rifle on parade, but it didn't make me respect him. There wasn't a lot of talk about sex in the billet but there was a lot of swearing, which I was quite used to in a boys' school.

I knew that I was going on to RAF Yatesbury in Wiltshire for radar training and that was so different from the basic training at Padgate. Yatesbury was like an enlightened school in comparison. I made a friend there – a young lad who had just got a Cambridge Open Exhibition in English – and we started reading *Sons and Lovers*, which had just come out in Penguin. Unfortunately he got posted somewhere else and that was the last I saw of him. I was at Yatesbury for about six weeks whilst they trained me to become a radar operator. I had no idea where I was going on to and they had no intention of asking me where I wanted to go. You were just told. In fact I was posted to a little radar station in Worth Matravers on the Dorset coast near Swanage.

RAF Worth Matravers had been at the epicentre of Britain's clandestine airborne radar research establishment during the war and it was still in the forefront of radar technology. The operators sat in front of a cathode ray tube and our master transmitter at Worth sent out a pulse that appeared at the beginning of a trace on the tube. Then, after a time delay, the slave transmitter either at the West Prawle station in Devon or the one near the Needles in the Isle of Wight sent out a second pulse, and that would appear further along on the trace and you had to keep it accurate to within one or two microseconds. If that was done it would allow planes flying in Europe and beyond to use it as a navigational aid. It had been used for the Thousand Bomber raids over Germany. In 1948 there was no war and it wasn't being used at all but we had to keep it going.

There were only about 100 or 120 men on the station. I started off in what was known as the effing cooks' billet, which was a bit smelly, then someone said 'Why don't you come and join us in the jazz billet.' I did, and that changed my life. That billet became the centre of life for a group of friends because we had so much free time. We did our work and then – unlike basic training – there was nothing that we were told to do. We worked the equivalent of four days on and three days off. Sitting at that cathode ray tube and talking to someone a hundred miles away, trying to keep the time distance right on their transmitter, you could even play chess with them. Quite a few of them were very interesting people.

In this billet there were a few people improvising jazz. Now I'd been a choir boy and was interested in string quartets because I played the violin growing up, but I was fascinated by jazz. One of them, Baz, said there was a trumpet in the NAAFI and why didn't I play second trumpet? So we got a big tin from the beach and put it on top of the stove in the billet, filled it with water and put the trumpet in. When we pulled it out it was absolutely full of gunk. It was horrible. Baz took me off to an empty billet near the perimeter fence and I started to learn the basic notes.

We played chess, we went for walks and rambles over the cliffs and we played and listened to jazz. Now, of the men in the jazz billet maybe a third had been to university, a third had done what we would now call A levels and the rest had left school at fifteen. The watches were run by an acting corporal – I became one after I'd been there a year – who had a little room at the end of the billet, but the door was always open and that was it. It was completely egalitarian – the opposite of Padgate. Three or four of the men were doing correspondence courses to prepare themselves for life when they left National Service and one of the lads who had left school at fifteen asked me if I wanted him to teach me German. So I found some books in a bookshop in Swanage and he had his own school textbook, which was called *Heute Abend*. That was quite typical of what happened in the billet.

There were some regular RAF men who had been grounded. When they found out they had been posted to Worth Matravers they were appalled, because for them it was the back of beyond. It couldn't have been a worse posting. They remained extremely aloof because they had no background in radar; the only one that did was Warrant Officer Legg, who knew all about it. If anything went wrong with the transmitter he was the one to fix it.

As far as I was concerned, if the Russians had actually started a war I was in no way fitted to fight it even after my National Service was finished, though the Cold War was certainly hotting up at the end of the 1940s. We got all sorts of anti-Soviet propaganda, which I found difficult to take because all through the war the Russians had been our gallant allies. Now they were our bitter enemies, so I was suspicious of what I was being told. Without them I knew we would never have won the war. I was a member of the Liberal Club at Oxford and I suppose I believed in the United Nations. I was very idealistic. My dad was Labour of course and he helped the Labour candidate get elected in 1945, so he was thrilled with the result.

I was demobbed at Easter 1950. Looking back I would be prepared to support a form of National Service that really was a national service. I still think I was right in that interview when I was still a student to query whether what I was going into in 1948 was really national service. To me a real national service would be learning things appropriate for youngsters of that age which they would be equipped to do. I don't rule out learning to fight but I'd be much more interested in some kind of community service. I think the way it worked, it was only coincidental that it had a beneficial social effect.

GEOFF ROCK

1948–1950

1st Infantry Division Royal Army Ordnance Corps

The British never trusted the Arabs. We always assumed that given half a chance they'd rob you.

I was born on 2 April 1930. The little old house I was born in has been pulled down now. It was next door to a sweet shop. I went to the main school in the town; it was a church school and that's closed down as well now. I was at school during the war, of course, and I left school a week before I was fourteen because Easter was early that year. Everybody left at fourteen then.

I was in church that Sunday morning when war broke out. At eleven o'clock the service was just ready to start and I remember the vicar announced it. Afterwards we all went off to fill sandbags. The Herefordshire Regiment left that same day from the drill hall. My grandfather served in the Boer War and my father served in the Great War. He was mustard gassed and it burned his arms badly but he never talked about it. He was too old for the Second World War so he went into the Home Guard. I used to run messages for the ARP, Air Raid Precautions, but I had to register for the forces when I was seventeen; I was trained, you see, so by the time I went into the army I was nearly ready.

When I left school I went to work for George Morris the builder, a well-known firm round here. I signed an old-fashioned deed of apprenticeship and I'd be paid very badly – much less than a pound a week. I'd gone to the Cadbury's factory first to start an engineering course but I hated it. I went to see the headmaster and he said I was the biggest fool that ever lived for turning down a chance to work for Cadbury's. During the war when the men were away you could get a job anywhere.

I had my medical in Worcester and then they called me up to go to Aldershot. I'd never been that far away from home before. My mother was worried but I was excited. I had to change trains in Didcot and when we got to Aldershot there was an army lorry there to pick us up. I remember we had a bath and got kitted out. We had to sign a bath book, you know, to make sure we had a bath at least once a week. It was all new and exciting. The lance corporal in our barrack room asked if we had any money. He said he'd look after it for us but I remembered I'd been told about this and that it was a scam, so I kept my money on me. I had about two shillings. It was so strange being in that hut with all those other fellers. I was a bit homesick. The first few days were the worst because they didn't allow you home for a month or so. They cut your hair short and the uniform didn't fit and it itched. It was very hard for that first seven or eight weeks. Once you got into it, it was all right but you never had enough time. If you had to do physical training they wanted you outside in your gym kit in five minutes.

The lads in that hut came from all over. There was a lad from Preston, a couple from Liverpool. I wasn't put off by the accents because we'd had evacuees down here during the war. The food was rough and ready. We didn't have plates, we had mess tins, and I couldn't believe we had to have our dinner and our pudding in the same mess tin. We were mostly eighteen, I don't remember too many who had been deferred. You met the vicar's son and the policeman's son. There were a lot of boys who could hardly read or write and the army educated them. There were Scotsmen there, and then there was all the religions. I remember the sergeant major one day saying he'd never seen such a league of nations. There was all sorts – Jewish, Catholic, Protestant, Greek Orthodox – all in the same tent and never any trouble. The Jewish lads didn't have to eat pork but if we had pork they ate it and that was it. There was no arguing.

The vicar's son hated it. He struggled a lot during the basic training because it was so hard. He was very intelligent and a marvellous sportsman but he just didn't believe in the army, though he didn't want to be a conscientious objector. After basic training he was all right and I think he ended up in the Education Corps.

Every Thursday there was a parade, after which we got paid. It was the deductions that frustrated me – seven shillings for barrack room damages even if there'd been no barrack room damages. They called you up and you saluted and you got your money. There wasn't much and you had to buy blacking and Brasso with your own money.

It was the ironing I found most difficult. Sometimes the iron would be broken and then you'd lay your trousers under your mattress and sleep on them, but if you turned over in the night, when you took them out they'd be creased in the wrong place. People helped each other though and by the time of the passing-out parade we were a unit.

Nobody wanted to go to the Middle East because there was nothing to do in the desert. We didn't mind if we were sent to Hong Kong or Singapore, that sounded exciting, and we didn't mind going to Austria or Germany. After basic training we were sent to a holding regiment in a transit camp in Aldershot and then we were told we were going abroad. We were given fourteen days' embarkation leave, but when we returned we still didn't know where we were going until a notice went up on the board and I could see that I and another chap had to report to a unit in Feltham in Middlesex. When we got there we were told we couldn't leave the camp after 7 p.m. because we were going the following morning. They put us on a train for Liverpool and that was when we pretty much knew we were going to the Middle East. That must have been June 1948.

It was on the *Empire Ken* that I met my best friend. His name was Malcolm Feinberg and he came from the East End of London. Lovely bloke. The army has to cater for all religions but he wasn't very Jewish – he was just one of us. We used to pull his leg about being Jewish – 'How did your grandparents miss the gas chamber?' Things like that – we didn't mean anything by it.

We stopped at Gibraltar first, then we arrived in Tripoli. It was a Saturday morning, I can remember it like it was yesterday. We couldn't get into Tripoli harbour. We had to be transported there in landing craft. It was hot, so hot. It was terrible and we hadn't been issued with tropical kit or anything. The *Empire Ken* wasn't a proper troopship. It had been converted. You were so far down in the bowels you had to shut the portholes at night because the water would come in, and that made it even hotter.

When we got off the landing craft there was a sort of welcoming party – English people anyway – the Salvation Army was serving tea to the troops. By this time I knew that I was attached as a guard to the bomb disposal team of the Royal Army Ordnance Corps and when I came off the landing craft I heard my name shouted. I turned round and it was a military policeman and I'd been at school with him. I was so pleased to see him.

Tripoli was all horses and carts then, very colourful. We had several Arabs doing skivvy work in the camp. You got to know some of them but most of them you didn't. One of them had three or four wives, I remember. One of his daughters had a very bad toothache and he was desperate to get something to ease the pain because they had no medicine, but we couldn't give him anything because we'd be court-martialled for it. These Arabs lived by the side of the road in makeshift tents and they had nothing really, that's why they stole everything they could. They'd pinch anything. I suppose I felt a bit sorry for them, especially the kiddies; but the only ones I ever spoke to were those who came into the camp and the local shopkeepers. Some of the shops were Italian run and they certainly seemed a class above the Arabs. They used to pray all the time, you know. The British never trusted the Arabs. We always assumed that given half a chance they'd rob you. We were warned you shouldn't walk back from the town to the camp by yourself. There were gangs of Arabs who attacked British soldiers. If you missed the transport, though, then you were in trouble. They just didn't like us.

There were a lot of things about life in Libya that surprised me – like finding there was nothing to sit on when you went to the toilet. It was just a hole in the ground with two pads at the side for your feet. The local women walked behind the men. They wore things round their heads and the men wore these long things. Till they were married they had to wear the veil, didn't they? They used to wash the camels in the sea.

Most of the time we were guarding the ammunition dumps. The troublemakers – the ones who were stirring up the trouble in Tripoli – were always trying to steal it. They were Arabs. There weren't many Jews in Libya, I noticed. I talked to Malcolm Feinberg about it – the Jews and the British had been fighting each other but we didn't talk about that. We talked about getting out of Libya. I missed the English weather and football. We played football against the Arabs – we hammered them. Mind you, they played without shoes.

The food was mostly dried stuff but we had some bacon – I don't know where that came from. The main meal was at night because it was too hot to eat at midday, though we had to parade in the heat. They said we could go to Cyprus if we paid for the transport but we couldn't get home. At Christmas though, the officers served the men breakfast.

The officers were quite strict. There was no familiarity but there weren't many bad ones. If you were in trouble there was always one of them you could see. I was there for nearly two years. Looking back on it, now that I'm older, I realise that it was an experience I wouldn't have missed for the world.

I played a lot of football in the army – I was a wing-half or an inside-forward – and I played the cornet in the band, so I reckon the army gave me a lot of opportunities. They offered me the chance to stay on – I could have taken on a three-year engagement and the pay was better. But I never wanted it. We came back from Tripoli and docked in Southampton. I had to go into the reserve after I was demobbed and I was called up again when Suez started, but it all happened so fast I never went anywhere.

I think the army was the making of 90 per cent of the men who went into it. It taught you to appreciate home and gave you a completely different outlook. If they could do that today there would be no kids hanging around on street corners. It turned me from a boy into a man. I think National Service was a wonderful thing. It was one of the best things they ever brought out. I never put away a pair of dirty shoes now. I always clean them before I put them away.

DENNIS WARWICK

1948–1950

RAF Clerk, Personnel Selection

What I remember most was all the swearing, which I hadn't been accustomed to. It was an eye-opener, as was the discussion of sex which was much more crude than I'd known.

My parents were both born in a village south of Wakefield. They married in 1929 and I was born on Good Friday, 18 April 1930. I was sent to an elementary school in the village of Wrenthorpe and then my parents moved back to the south of the town to a better area called Sandal. My dad was a vertical borer in a factory that made machinery for coal mining. My mother had been a domestic servant until she married and after that she didn't work. She'd been the only servant in a house belonging to a coal merchant and she was responsible for everything – the cooking, the cleaning, looking after the children and so on. I'm sure she was a very intelligent young lady and so got on very well with the family. She was also wanting to be away from her own family – she had one sister and nine brothers and I think she was very glad to get out of that household, so she went into service as soon as she left school at the age of fourteen. She did say once to me that she got a scholarship to the grammar school but her parents wouldn't let her go.

My father started life as a gardener but then moved into his trade, for which he had to complete an apprenticeship. His job meant he was seen as a skilled man and fortunately during the Depression there was still a need for coal mining machinery, so he kept his job. I'm sure there were difficult times but as far as I know he was never out of work during the 1930s. When the war started he was in a reserved occupation. He'd been born in 1904 so he did things like air raid warden work, but he kept his job because the factory started making parts for tanks.

My first memories are of living in a one-up, one-down terrace house. I can remember being in a cot in the corner of my parents' bedroom. As I grew up I continued to sleep in the same room. We didn't have an indoor toilet, we had to go down and across the yard to use it. We used torn-up newspaper not toilet paper.

My father hadn't been interested in the church but my mother had. We went to Evensong. The working class go to Evensong because somebody has to get the Sunday lunch ready at home. It's the middle-class folk who go to Sunday morning service. We didn't have modern cookware. Getting the coal range ready and cooking Sunday lunch was a long morning's job. Middle-class folk had servants at home to do it for them. We couldn't just come home from church and get meat cooked ready for lunch like you can these days. Dad worked five and a half days a week and if he had the chance he'd prefer to be in the garden. Saturday afternoon was for rugby league.

By the time the Butler Education Act of 1944 came in I was already at Queen Elizabeth Grammar School, Wakefield. I'd got a Storey Scholarship which paid all the fees, so my parents didn't have to pay anything. I settled there very quickly and I enjoyed it. The boys in the top form at the prep school were from a very different social background from the one I knew. There were some gifted boys at that school – Kenneth Leighton who composed a lot of church music, theatre and television directors Ronald Eyre and Peter Dews, David Storey's brother Tony.

The two big goals at school in my day were to be in the first XV at rugby and get a scholarship to Oxford or Cambridge. I only played once for the first XV – I was a centre but I wasn't quite good enough – and they never gave me the chance to try for Oxbridge. They had obviously decided I wasn't good enough for that either. They did enter me for King's College, London though I wasn't successful, but I was given a reserved place at Bede's College, Durham to read geography. This was late 1947 or early 1948. By this time I'd made up my mind that I wanted to become a teacher. I don't think my father understood that I had more possibilities of work than he had. I suspect he would have preferred me to become a draughtsman in the offices at his work so I'd be one up from him, because I'd be in the office and not on the shop floor. My mother never expressed any views but she wanted me to be close at home and working to bring some money into the household. They neither of them blocked my desire to go to university though.

I was still at school for the 1945 General Election. Wakefield was a Labour town and my dad was a Labour man but my mother was a Tory. My dad was a trade unionist, but my mother's family had been brought up in rural domestic settings so they looked to their lords and masters to tell them how to vote. The family wasn't at all political. I don't think I had a political discussion with my father ever, even later in life.

All the boys in my class at school were already in National Service because I was the youngest in the class, and I stayed on an extra year when they went off. That's when I got my chance in the first XV at rugby. We lived in a rugby league world, so getting used to rugby union was new. It was one of the ways the grammar school tried to make you into a middle-class boy if you'd come from the working class like I had.

I left school in the summer of 1948 and saw Bradman and the Australian cricket team at the Headingley Test match and later at the Scarborough Festival at the end of the season. Then I was called up in October, having decided I wanted to go into the RAF rather than the other services. I think I thought the RAF was more glamorous. I never thought about the possibility of seeing action where I could be killed. Soon after I got in, the Berlin Airlift started and then there was the Malayan emergency and Korea, but I seemed to miss all that and I was never concerned.

Some people ahead of me had got away with a year of National Service but I expected to serve for about eighteen or nineteen months, which is what I did. I was really looking forward to doing it because it meant I could get away from home. I passed my medical in Leeds though they thought I might be a bit colour blind. They asked me then which service I wanted to be in and I said the RAF. I was posted to RAF Padgate, so when the brown envelope dropped through the letterbox it had a rail warrant to Warrington. My mother was never very emotional, so when it was time to leave home she just said cheerio. I never saw my parents emotional. I never even saw them kiss each other – ever.

We were only in Padgate for a short time while we were kitted out and sorted out. Then we were sent off to do basic training at West Kirby in the Wirral. All your civvies were bundled up into a kitbag. Basic training was hard and it was a shock to the system – all that square bashing. Thirty of us were allocated to a hut and we had to stand by our beds and make sure we made them properly in the morning, and if we didn't we had to remake them. We had a tough NCO assigned to our hut and he was pretty nasty. I remember one Saturday night some lads had gone out and a few of us were in the hut complaining about the corporal when he appeared suddenly; he'd obviously heard and we had to spend the rest of the night cleaning the floor of the hut. He was like that all the way through – never easing off as we got near the end.

The hut was a great mixture of people from all social classes. What I remember most was all the swearing, which I hadn't been accustomed to. It was an eye-opener, as was the discussion of sex which was much more crude than I'd known. Most of them weren't from grammar school and many of them had left school three years before and got jobs, but I did meet plenty of people who had been to grammar school and were going off to university like I was. I don't recall not being able to understand anyone but people from the south were speaking a rather different dialect from me. It was always difficult to get on with people who had southern accents.

In that first few weeks when we were doing our basic training I think we had one weekend off. When I went home in my uniform my dad said I'd never looked better in my life and my haircut was really good! Basic training was tough but I was very fit as a result. We were doing a lot of square bashing but I played some rugby in the free moments that we had and on the weekends we could ride the electric trains from West Kirby into Liverpool.

At times during basic training they gave us tests – intelligence tests, spatial tests, IQ tests of one sort or another. I became a clerk in Personnel Selection – I was responsible for learning about all the tests that the RAF gave to their recruits and those who were leaving to see what sort of trade they might go into – so I should remember them all. I must have done reasonably well in the tests they gave me because I was pretty much given a free hand to choose what I wanted to do. I don't recall being pushed by them in any one direction but I saw this post of Clerk Personnel Selection which looked interesting. It was good training for teaching so I was then shunted off to the Air Ministry in London to see if they thought I was suitable. Presumably they did because I was sent to Imperial House in Kingsway. I remember being awestruck by London when I saw it for the first time, particularly the underground trains.

After training as Clerks Personnel Selection in Hornchurch I went back to Imperial House on Kingsway for six months and then volunteered to go overseas. I was living, would you believe it, in a luxury block of flats in Regent's Park. I really fell on my feet there. I enjoyed the work at the Air Ministry – it was statistically based. We got the test results and we worked from those. We worked on hand calculators and we all lived in Regent's Park, so the office got on very well together.

One night I went to a dance at the YWCA off Tottenham Court Road and met a young lady with whom I became very friendly. Her name was Pam Arlott and eventually we became engaged. She lived in Tolworth in Surrey and I started to spend my weekends there. We kept up a regular correspondence when I was posted out to Aden and when I returned she met me off the boat train at Waterloo station.

I'd never been out of England, so when there was a chance to be posted overseas I took it. It was August 1949 when the ship left Liverpool and I was off on my adventure. There were, I think, four possibilities as to where you could be posted – Iraq, Malta, Aden and somewhere else. I'd studied geography at school so I knew about the Nile and the Delta and the Suez Canal and all that sort of thing. I didn't know where I was going until after we got off the boat at Port Said in Egypt. One thing I did know was that despite being in the RAF I'd never have much to do with aeroplanes. I'm not sure I ever saw one during National Service except at RAF Hornchurch, where there was an old biplane at the gate of the camp.

Once we'd got off the ship at Port Said, we went by train down to the camp at Abu Sueir. That was a transit camp for those who were going on to their postings. The only contact we had with the locals was with the people who came into the camp to clean. I knew they were an alien lot. I didn't get the feeling we were going to be great friends. I suppose by today's standards I was probably racist in the way I regarded the local population. We called them wogs. We all did. I was told there was a possibility of going by air but in the end we went to

Aden, going down the Red Sea and into the Indian Ocean on a troopship.

I was always very keen on the church so I quickly got in touch with the Padre in the camp. Padre Nowers was very kind and he would invite me to stay with his family. There was quite a good congregation that went to the local church. It wasn't a problem but I did realise that there weren't many others who were as keen as I was to go to church. I didn't feel threatened by them but I was different in that respect. It was a really nice community that gathered round the Padre.

Very quickly I learned that there was very little work for me to do in Aden. I was posted to the education officer, Squadron Leader Harding, and he said to me in effect that I should find myself something to do, so I saw this old manual typewriter and I taught myself to type. I was soon on to five finger typing and touch typing and getting my word speed up. That was, without doubt, the greatest accomplishment of my entire National Service. I'm not as good as I used to be but I can still do it.

I was there to test people, mostly regulars, who were coming to the end of their service and wanted to know what sort of trade they were best suited for. There were various aptitude and intelligence tests. It was late October 1949 when I got there and that's pretty much all I did for the rest of my time there. It was a very overmanned service. There was a chance that the Berlin Airlift might expand into another war and I'd be involved but it never happened, though I was worried about it at one point.

Letters came once a week. My father wrote quite often, my mother didn't. Pam wrote about her parents and what was happening at home. My parents weren't too happy about me getting engaged to Pam because she was a southerner. They met her but they didn't like her very much. Her father was a caretaker in a school so there wasn't a class gap, but they didn't fancy the idea of us living down south because I was an only child.

I did a bit of teaching at the primary school where the children of air force regulars went. I joined a drama group and I was introduced to music, plus I kept up with my maths. There was an office I could go into where I could listen to music and I had plenty of time to do that.

I was signed out of the camp at Aden on 6 April 1950 but I had to be shipped back home and that took at least a fortnight. Then I went to a place in Bedfordshire to be officially demobbed, so it would be well into May before I was out. Then I went down to Tolworth to stay in a room in Pam's parents' house and while I was down there I looked around for a possible job. Amazingly a prep school headmaster in Surbiton wanted an assistant teacher for the summer term and he hired me at five quid a week. I gave my would-be mother-in-law rent for the room but it meant I learned a bit about private schoolboys. I played cricket for the local cricket team and we went to church in Tolworth, so I was twenty years old and I was set up.

I was grateful to National Service because it took me away from home, and it forced me to experience a much wider world and to interact with a whole range of different people I would never have met if I'd stayed in Wakefield. The negatives were that corporal and doing my turn in the kitchen during basic training. One day you'd be filthy with coal dust and the next you'd be wet through with sweat, washing and drying. I remember being very agitated that there were no dry tea towels and how was I expected to dry the cups with a wet tea towel? It's funny the things you remember.

National Service was a very positive experience for me. I remember it with fondness. I was growing up and seeing the world and when I got to Durham University you could immediately tell who had already done National Service and who hadn't. We were so much more mature and aware of the world in which we lived and our knowledge was based on much wider experience than those who had come straight from school, but there weren't that many of them.

Pam and I stayed engaged right through till I graduated from university. It was a good relationship for quite a long time, but by then it obviously wasn't working out and eventually she wrote and said it was over and done with. Many, many years later, maybe 1996, I got a phone call here in this house from Pam. She'd just lost her husband and she was wondering what had happened to me. Bear in mind I hadn't heard a thing from her since she'd sent back the engagement ring over forty years before. I found out later that she died soon after that phone call.

STANLEY PRICE

1949-1951

Green Jackets, Royal Army Education Corps

I had thought that drowning was the worst death I could think of so I wasn't going to join the navy, and the other one that terrified me was being up in an aeroplane and burning to death. In the army you hope that you'll charge, the buggers'll shoot you in the middle of your head and that will be that.

Due to the odd mixtures in my background, my introduction to the army was not auspicious – both my parents were Irish, but of a small sub-species, Irish Jews. My father had qualified as a doctor in Dublin and then came to London to find work. Because of this he thought it a good idea that when I went for my medical and was asked what I wanted to join I should say the London Irish Rifles. It was a regiment he'd heard of during the Troubles in 1916. I put this to the officer who interviewed me at my medical. He looked baffled and went to look up the

regiment in a reference book. He came back to tell me frost-
ily that the London Irish Rifles had been disbanded in 1922.
I think he put me down in his book as a smart-arse.

They say you can't ever forget your army number, and
they're right – 22344998. I was given that the minute I
reported to Bushfield Camp, the training depot of the Royal
Green Jackets Brigade near Winchester. Because I had three
A levels I was destined for the RAEC, the Royal Army
Education Corps, but had to do my basic training with the
Green Jackets, which comprised two very smart light infantry
regiments, the Rifle Brigade and the King's Royal Rifle
Corps. I discovered that many of our officers had titles and/or
double-barrelled names. Worse than that was to discover that
the Light Infantry marched at 140 steps a minute as opposed
to the Guards' traditional 120. The result of this was rashes on
the inside of one's thighs from the wretched, scratchy and
heavy material of British army trousers. It made one long to
be in the American army. We'd all seen their smooth uniforms from a hundred Hollywood films. If you reported to
the medics with your rash they simply said, 'You should be
grateful it's not the clap.'

Our second day at the camp we lined up at the quartermaster's stores to hand in the civilian clothes we'd arrived in. We had
parcelled them up in brown paper and addressed them home to
our mothers. We queued in alphabetical order. In front of me
was a pair of twins, the Gordon-Lennoxes. The first of them
handed his parcel over to the corporal in charge, who looked at
the address and said to the quartermaster, 'Blimey, look at this –
a bloke sending his clothes home to a boozer.' The Gordon-
Lennoxes' mother was the Duchess of Richmond.

I imagine that most National Servicemen's memories, traumatic ones in some cases, are of basic training. In the name of discipline and fitness we were subject to the most extraordinary verbal and physical battering. We got used to being screamed at on the parade ground in the most abusive language most of us had ever heard. I cherish the memory of a sergeant major giving the order to 'Right dress'. We whipped our right arms up to our neighbour's shoulder and shuffled our feet so we were in a perfect line and snapped our arms down again. The sergeant major pointed a finger at me and screamed, 'You, if you're fucking right dressed, my cock's a kipper!' He then marched smartly to the end of the line and looked down it. At least he was an honest man. 'Good God,' he shouted, 'my cock's a kipper.'

'Bull' was another appalling discovery, a weird ritual for keeping one's rifle, uniform, boots and bed space constantly in perfectly straight, clean, polished or ironed order. Hours and hours were wasted on this as the penalties for being 'sloppy on parade' or failing room-inspection were severe. There were times when the only thing that kept up morale was humour. When we were bulling kit, or on long route marches with a heavy pack, or sat frozen in the back of a truck, there was an eternity of filthy recitations and bawdy songs to keep us all going. 'Eskimo Nell' was the most disgusting, but I liked 'We're Off to See the Wild West Show' and its extraordinary collection of animals – the Woofum Bird who 'disappeared up his own arse 'ole, from which safe but insanitary position he hurled shit and derision at all his tormentors'. Not to mention the Gezola Bird: 'This 'ere monstrous creature has a triangular arse-piece and shits bricks and mortar – 'ence the Pyramids.' There was a kind of obscene poetry to it. After fifty or more years the words still come back, even when you don't want them to. 'Then up spoke my cousin Bert, quick as a flash he was – and witty too – "Fuck off," he said.'

For the first month of infantry basic training the whole intake were in it together: public and grammar school boys, tough nuts of the Geordie, Scouse and Cockney varieties, most of whom had left school at fourteen or fifteen. Class distinctions were very obvious. Their language and accent gave everyone away. At the toughest end of the scale, 'fuck' came in nearly every other word. A corporal once said to me, after I'd answered some question, 'Don't talk cuntish,' as though it was a dialect like Cornish or Kentish.

The toughest and scariest were undoubtedly the Newcastle Geordies and the Liverpool Scousers. I'd never met people like that before and I had trouble understanding what they were saying. They were tough because they'd come from tough backgrounds. There was a fair amount of thieving going on – they'd steal your cigarettes, your army belt, anything. Someone joked that when you take your boots off at night you should nail them to the floor to prevent them being taken. You deal with it by making friends, and your mates protect you and you protect them. You don't die for your country; you die for your mates.

After the first month our intake was divided into sheep and goats. Inevitably the goats were nearly all from public and grammar schools, with more of the former than the latter. After all, the Green Jackets were a very smart brigade. In my barrack room was an exclusive lot who called each other by the names of their schools. There was Eton, major and minor, Harrow,

Chouse (for Charterhouse), Wykie (from Winchester), Salop (Shrewsbury). I was a bit of a problem to them with my education so divided between schools in England and Ireland. I'd done the sixth form at the Perse School in Cambridge; to them it was a very minor public school, and I became a very plebeian Percy. In those days it wasn't racism that was the problem (we weren't yet mixed enough racially), it was the subtle gradations of the British class system that still bedevilled us.

To add to the distinctions of school and college were those of rank and regiment. There was a lot of snobbery involved when people started to ask you which regiment you'd been in. Someone took me to the right-wing Pitt Club at Cambridge and I looked in the visitors' book and there in 1951 or 1952 you had to write down your name, your title, your school and your regiment. Regiments stack up like the schools: Eton and the Guards – Coldstream, Grenadier, Scots, Welsh and Irish. After that was the Household Cavalry – the Horse Guards, the Greys and Blues and so on. The next level after that lot was my lot – the Light Infantry, the Duke of Cornwall's Light Infantry, the Black Watch if you were Scots, the King's Royal Rifle Corps, the Rifle Brigade. Then you came down to the county regiments – the Royal West Kents – and then the service corps – the RASC, REME, RAPC. The bottom was the Pioneer Corps. There was a strange class division in the army best summed up by a regimental invitation which specified 'Officers and their ladies', 'Non-commissioned officers and their wives' and 'Other ranks and their women'.

In the evening in Winchester you stayed in the barracks and polished your kit or you went to the NAAFI and drank dreadful tea and ate buns. NAAFI stood for No Ambition And

Fuck-all Interest. You couldn't get out and even if you could we had no money. The pay was dreadful. You put it in your sock or up your arse or somewhere secretive because otherwise it would go.

You soon found out that to get the right crease in your trousers you ironed them, and you put brown paper over the trousers so you could iron them very heavily without burning them. The boots were the worst thing because they were wrinkly and you had to get the wrinkles out of them. You put a thick layer of black boot polish over the toe caps and then you used brown paper and a hot iron again to press the bloody wrinkles out of the boots. There was always a know-all around to tell you how to do it. If it wasn't right at inspection you got three or four days confined to barracks. That was fairly barbaric looking back on it, but they felt it created discipline. If they could discipline you to do these things, when it was time to go over the top and they said 'Charge!' you bloody well charged.

Of course, when you were in basic training as a private there were cruel and sadistic NCOs who persecuted you. We were doing a bayonet charge at straw dummies. A little Geordie sadist was in charge and gave the order to fix bayonets. He told us to imagine sticking them into 'the enemy's belly, twist them round and pull out his guts. And I want you to scream as you do it.' I charged and used my bayonet as instructed, but I'd recently seen *All Quiet on the Western Front* and I didn't scream. The NCO noticed. He called me over and asked why I didn't scream. I thought it best not to mention *All Quiet on the Western Front*. I just said that as everyone else was screaming I didn't see the need. 'I fuckin' ordered you to scream. Go back and do it again – on your fuckin' own – and this time fuckin'' scream.' I did it again and fucking screamed like a maniac, but I saw him put my name in his book.

I had made a deal with myself before starting basic training that I was going to do everything they told me to do, because keeping your head down was the best way to get through it. I did it all except that one time. What stopped me screaming, I suppose, was that I still retained the idealised sense that this bayonet charge was just barbaric. But you have to forget attitudes like that when you're in the army. I wasn't proud of not screaming.

Corporal Moate was a bastard, he was just waiting for someone to do something wrong so he could punish him. I'll never forget his name.

When it came time to go off to Wosbe I was in the last group to go. I still blame Corporal bloody Moate. I was living alone in a barracks in Winchester which I suspect had been condemned in 1924. It was bleak, and it went on for about six weeks because all my mates had already moved on and I was in a holding company waiting for my transfer to Mons. It was terribly gloomy and I was given dreadful jobs to do like painting coal white and scraping stains out of wooden floorboards on your hands and knees with a razor. After two or three weeks of this I was getting very low. If the guys I'd been through basic training with had been around I'd have got through it. I was miserable and I suppose that the guys who couldn't fit in felt like that all the time.

I had no skills. There was no point in putting me in something electrical or mechanical. I had supposed I would just go into the infantry like everyone else. I had claustrophobia so I couldn't go into the tank regiment. The smartest regiments were the cavalry but for me that was scary, the idea of being trapped in a tank. I had thought that drowning was the worst death I could think of so I wasn't going to join the navy, and the other one that terrified me was being up in an aeroplane and burning to death. In the army you hope that you'll charge, the buggers'll shoot you in the middle of your head and that will be that. I wanted to become an infantry officer and when Korea started they said that everyone who had a good O level in maths, if they went to Officer Cadet School they'd go into the Artillery. That's what happened to me.

The only place I didn't want to go was Korea. I knew enough about world politics even at eighteen to realise that against three million Chinese you're on a beating to nothing. I'd have gone anywhere else. After Mons and training as an artillery officer I would have been posted to an artillery unit somewhere in the world and I had no control over that, so I could have gone to Korea. I didn't enjoy the trigonometry and I didn't think I'd make a very good artillery officer. If I had to fire a gun or throw a grenade I'd have done it because I'd been a sportsman and I was used to running around. Calculating trigonometry was a nightmare and I was in charge of four 25-pounder guns. I was scared of letting people down, of getting people killed. My commanding officer realised this just in time. He wanted us to win in Korea and had me transferred to the Education Corps. He didn't realise that at the time they were not giving National Service commissions. After much going back and forth I was eventually sent on the sergeants' course at Beaconsfield.

That was where I met the most inspirational character in my life so far. Major Lord Wavell MC ran the Education Corps at

Beaconsfield. He had one arm and was an extraordinary man. He made everything OK. He was a great soldier, the son of Field Marshal Lord Wavell who had been Viceroy of India. He made us more than Education sergeants. He gave us a sense of what life was about and he did it in the army and in uniform. He created a very good feeling. Everyone used to think the Education Corps were a lot of sissies so they were nervous of their image. During Education Corps training the NCOs were not RAEC men, they were Coldstream Guards, Irish Guards and so on, because they overcompensated to make sure we knew we were soldiers as well as teachers.

Conventional army stuff was first thing in the morning. Bugles at reveille, 7 a.m. – quite civilised – then you'd be on parade and you'd do a bit of marching. Then they'd order you to fall out for whatever it was you were doing and you went to an instruction class where you learned how to teach maths or history or the war poets. After lunch you'd do a cross-country run or march, or Wavell might say, 'I want to see you at a youth hostel near Keswick in the Lake District and I'll give you thirty-six hours to get there from Beaconsfield.' I was a smart Jewish lad, because it was pissing down so I hitch-hiked to London, spent a nice night at home and borrowed the money from my dad to take the train to Keswick like a *mensch*. Of course I hadn't realised that Wavell was one step ahead of me, because when I looked out of the window as the train was drawing into the station at Keswick I saw military police lined up waiting for smart buggers to get off the train so I stayed on the train, which went to Carlisle, and got off there where there were no MPs. I hitched back to Keswick and got in at some awful hour but I got away with it. I thought I deserved a decoration. In terms of leading men and showing initiative, why not?

Sometime after demob, I learned that Major Lord Wavell had won his battle to rejoin the Black Watch and be listed for active service despite his handicap. On Christmas Eve 1953 I heard on the radio news that he had been killed in Kenya leading a patrol against the Mau Mau.

When I eventually passed out as a sergeant there were some great postings going – the Caribbean, Hong Kong and so on – but the sergeants who still had over a year to do got those. I only had about five months left to serve at that stage as I was allowed an early discharge to go to Cambridge. National Service had gone up from eighteen months to two years since I joined and in the end I was sent to an Army Ordnance Corps depot at Bicester – a crappy posting, but it was near Oxford and not too far from London where I'd just found a very desirable girlfriend.

My duties at Bicester were divided between teaching illiterates and trying to help the sergeants and sergeant majors, war veterans in their thirties and forties. They were faced with passing the newly introduced army exams, academically on a par with O level. If they didn't pass they'd lose their rank, which probably entailed losing their married quarters as well as reduced pay. It was grotesquely unfair – and an embarrassment all round – for them to become dependent on a twenty-year-old sergeant to maintain their status and livelihood, and for me to mix with them socially in the sergeants' mess but still have to teach them in the classroom.

I did about twenty months in the end. Those of us who would have lost our places at college were allowed out early. I also had to do three years in the Territorial Army and that usually meant two weeks' camp a year. I found that more stressful than the army and I was glad I'd done the army first. When you're having a great time at university the last thing you want to do is return to army discipline, foul food and a scratchy uniform.

I have to say though that the experiences of National Service made more impression on me than anything else that has happened in my life since. When you come out of the army you feel much tougher than when you went in. If you can survive that you can survive most things. I know for a fact that there were many National Servicemen who did not survive National Service. It was nasty but if you go into that situation with certain handicaps it's going to be accentuated by that sort of treatment. It was like a nervous breakdown. National Service didn't produce anything different inside you. It merely accentuated all the weaknesses and the problems you started National Service with. At that age it was a long time. If you're twenty, two years is 10 per cent of your life. It certainly sharpened my sense of humour and my sense of observation. I know they say we should bring it back and make society more homogenous but I don't agree, though I think some form of community service might not be a bad idea. However, there is no doubt that it brings people together. You don't fear other people so much because you've met them. Growing up a nice middle-class Jewish lad it was a great release to get out and be with ordinary people.

JOSEPH STRODE

1951–1953

1st Battalion, The King's Regiment

One of the jobs of the King's Regiment was doing the guard on Spandau prison where they kept Speer and Hess and that lot. I remember seeing Speer, Funk and von Neurath ... They had allotments you know ... it was odd watching [Hess] with a wheelbarrow when you remember what he used to be.

I was born on 6 November 1930 in a little terraced house on Springfield Street in the centre of Liverpool. We lived there till 1939 when the war started and we all got bombed. A bomb landed in our backyard so we had to move out of the house and spend the night in the local school whilst the bomb disposal squad – the suicide squad, we used to call them – took the bomb out.

My dad was a docker so he wasn't called up. I remember

coming back after one raid and my dad was lying there still drunk from the night before and covered in soot. He'd been drinking, came home, passed out and didn't wake up when the bombing raid was on. The soot got dislodged and came down the chimney and covered him and he still didn't wake up. He looked like Al Jolson.

I left school at fourteen and got a job at Bent's Brewery, helping the engineer to maintain all the machines. After that I got a job on the railway because my dad knew someone who worked there and they sorted me out. It was a government job, which is why I didn't go into National Service when I was eighteen. If I'd gone in then, in 1948, I'd have probably missed the Korean War – but I didn't. All the friends I had went into the army when they were eighteen and I wanted to get in there. A matter of a couple of weeks after I packed the railway job in, I got my call-up papers. I fainted at the medical, which wasn't a good start. We were standing in a line and I started sweating. Anyway, I got through and they sent me off to Chester to do my basic training.

My mother was distraught when I left. She had nine children but one of my sisters, Jane, was killed, run over by a bus in St Anne's Street. She was only fourteen years old. I was about the fourth oldest and I was twenty when I went into the army. I went in with a lot of lads from Liverpool. We got to the station at Chester and we all got into the back of this three-ton lorry and as soon as we got off at the barracks the shouting started: 'Get off', 'Do this', 'Do that'. We got kitted out but the uniform was horrible. I'm left-handed so the rifle drill was really difficult because I had to learn to do it right-handed. I was allowed by the school to learn to write with my left hand

but the army made no allowances. I remember saluting an officer with my left hand and he just looked at me and said, 'What
army are you in?'

'The British Army, sir,' I said.

'Then you'd better learn how to salute with your right hand.'

The barracks were all Lancashire lads, though we weren't all
from Liverpool. We were attached to the King's Regiment,
which was a Liverpool regiment. There were lads from the
Lancashire Fusiliers and South Lancs as well as the King's
Regiment doing their basic training together and then when
we finished after eight or ten weeks we'd go back to our original regiments. I wanted the King's because it was a Liverpool
outfit and I had an uncle who'd been in it. I was in A company
of the 1st Battalion The King's Regiment.

My uncle had told me that the first thing to do was to volunteer to play a sport, even if you were no good at it, because
otherwise you'd be peeling spuds. I used to play outside left.
Everton was my team – Dixie Dean and Tommy Lawton and
Joe Mercer and Cliff Britton. That was a great side. I was into
all sports and that got me through.

Basic training was tough. After lights were turned out there
were a few sniffles but there were other sounds too – there was
the crackle of chocolate from someone who'd just got a food
parcel from home. I hated the NCOs – we all did. Kit inspections were bad because if you didn't pass you wouldn't get your
weekend pass to go home. I did well though, I really did, and
after basic training I was made up to corporal. We were a
mixed bunch in the barracks. There was always someone who
couldn't march in step.

At the end of basic training I was sent back to the King's

Regiment and since the regiment was out in Berlin I knew that's where I'd be going. That's where the majority of my barracks went – to the British zone in Berlin, which was entirely surrounded by the Russians.

I was looking forward to it. I thought it would be an adventure. The Germans were still a beaten lot in 1951 when we got there. The ones we saw were the cleaners who cleaned the barracks. We were in charge of them and they'd lost the war, so that's all we cared about really, and they were obliged to us because we'd given them a job, a good job, cleaning and cooking. We didn't do patrols, we did a lot of guard duty at the barracks and every Friday we had to go on a regimental cross-country run. We had an RSM, Matt Deutsch, in A Company and when we had to parade in the square before the run he positioned A Company right next to the gate so we'd be the first ones out and in the lead on the run. The military police were stationed halfway along the route and they used to stamp your hand, so when they inspected they'd know who had skipped it and you had to go back out and do the whole run with the MPs next day. It was all right out there but you had to do what you were told all right.

One of the jobs of the King's Regiment was doing the guard on Spandau prison where they kept Speer and Hess and that lot. I remember seeing Speer, Funk and von Neurath and I think there were two more. They had allotments you know. Hess used to come out – it was odd watching him with a wheelbarrow when you remember what he used to be.

I'd only been in Berlin a matter of a few months when we were all summoned to the cookhouse. The lieutenant colonel came down and said, 'I've got brilliant news for the regiment.

We have been selected to represent the British Army in Korea.'
I think he meant it. They were all army barmy, them lot. It
depended on how long left you had to serve. If you had less
than six or eight months or something like that you didn't go,
but I had eighteen months. We came home first for a week's
embarkation leave.

We were in hammocks on a troopship called the *Devonshire*.
It was like the *Bounty*, it was that old. I used to sleep on the
deck because it was better than the hammocks. People were
seasick and throwing up. We were on that ship for six weeks.
It stopped at Mombasa to take water on and at Colombo in
Ceylon. They let us go ashore at Colombo to stretch our legs
and we got caught in a monsoon. Then we got to Hong Kong
and we stayed in a barracks near the little walled village of
Fanling, and that was where we did our battle training. I think
it was there that I was volunteered by someone else to do the
job of a silverman – I was in charge of all the regimental silver
and I was also a batman to Lieutenant Colonel Archibald
Snodgrass. I didn't get a promotion or more money or anything
like that, but it was a good job really.

You couldn't help thinking you might not make it. I mean
when we got to Korea there were men who never came back
from patrols. I was lucky. I went out on patrol only a couple of
times. When you're in the army you have no idea what's happening, you just obey the last order you're given. I had no idea
whether we were winning or losing the war. We were there to
relieve the Northumberland Fusiliers, because they were going
home as soon as we got there. As a soldier all you want to do
is get there and get home again in one piece. There was a feller
from round here, he was in the Parachute Regiment – I think

his name was Jack Gibbons – and I saw him in Korea. I said, 'What are you doing here?' and then a few days later I learned he'd been killed.

I had no idea what that war was about. Nobody explained it. I just wanted to get out of it alive. I knew we were fighting the North Koreans and then the Chinese came into it. What I do remember is the winter of 1951–2. They said it was the coldest winter ever, it was thirty below out there, and when we got to a camp in Japan on R&R they burned all our clothes and kitted us out again because we were in such a state. I've got photographs of the helicopters bringing in the wounded. It looked just like that TV series, *M★A★S★H*.

I think I was fortunate in that by the time I got to Korea it was the tail-end of the war and a lot of the sting had gone out of it. We just did patrols into the valley. You could get yourself killed all right but it wasn't like the open warfare of the early days on other fronts. They were using napalm, you know, and we were being shelled quite a lot. We used to have 24-hour packs – tins of soup and cigarettes and toilet paper – and we lived on that sort of thing for quite a few months, living in a sleeping bag. I've kept some of the stuff I had back then. Here's a pamphlet that the Communists sent over. They were trying to, you know, stir up trouble. They'd send over shells that would explode and all these pamphlets would come out.

Is equality guaranteed in the USA? Why are there restaurants from which Negroes are strictly forbidden found in America and why are you alone plunged into the most dangerous front line of the battle? Are you going to die a dog's death to preserve the privileges of the white Americans? Signed General Political Bureau of the Korean People's Army.

Here's another one. 'In countries of socialism and people's democracies there is no racial discrimination of the Negroes and the freedom and equality of men are fully guaranteed.' Here's a magazine just called *Peace* dated November 1952. 'Peace Conference points the way to the end of the Korean War.' It's a kind of a digest. It came out of a shell burst. 'Mothers dread the possibility of their boys being sent to Malaya or Korea to fight in a rich man's war, to come back maimed or not to come back at all.'

I never thought about all that stuff. What was the point? You had to go into the army whether you liked it or not and the army sent you where it wanted. There was nothing I could do about it. 'Ours was not to reason why, ours was just to do and die.' We never talked to each other about it at the time but now, looking back on it, we seem to have spent all our lives supporting the Americans – just like we are now. Here's a card from Korea which I must have got at Christmas 1951. It says:

Merry Christmas.
Whatever your race, color or creed
All plain folks are brothers indeed
Both you and me want life and peace
If you go home the war will cease.
Demand Peace! Stop the War!
Greetings from the Chinese Peoples Volunteers Korea 1951.

Here's another one I kept:

British Officers and Soldiers,

It is 28 months since the Yanks dragged Britain into this war. Nearly ten thousand British lives have been killed or wounded in this period. Actual number of casualties in this period 9,393. The Gloucester regiment has suffered particularly heavy losses as a result of American selfishness. Now British soldiers have been committing the most terrible crimes against prisoners of war. They want you to share their responsibility. All over Britain the people long for peace yet this so-called United Nations delegation which is run entirely by the US without a single Britisher on it has been sabotaging the truce talks. They are forcing you to face another grim winter in Korea. Is it not true that almost every letter you get from home mentions how prices are going up? – food, clothing, fares and almost everything else. The Ministry of Labour has reported there are almost 517,000 unemployed in Britain. Where is Britain getting as a result of tailing behind the Yanks? – the American big business millionaires who want to grab the whole world by the pocket. Is it not quite plain that only peace will put a stop to further unnecessary casualties for all you lads. That only peace will save your folks from the grave burden of armaments expenditure and peace will give you the chance of spending Christmas along with your dear ones. Even US airmen have lately been refusing to fly in the Korean War. Friends! Don't fight for the Yanks any more! Without you they cannot keep up this war!

Merry Christmas from the Korean People's Army and the Chinese People's Volunteers.

Well, it was their country I suppose, so fair dos. I thought General MacArthur, the American who was in charge of the UN operation, was a bit of an idiot, though he'd been fired by the time I got there. I stayed in Korea for the rest of my time in National Service although we did get those R&R days in Japan. I thought the Japanese people were lovely – all that bowing and they loved their families. I think they were indoctrinated in the war. I mean, look at those kamikaze pilots – I like the one about the Jewish kamikaze pilot who landed in his father's scrapyard.

When we were in Japan me and this other feller, Dempsey his name was – he was a bit of a lad – stayed one night in a hotel, and the manager comes up to us and says do we want a girl because he can sort it all out for us. Anyway, next morning we had to pay and we didn't have enough money, so he said that Dempsey had to go back to camp to get the money and I had to stay there – as a sort of hostage, I suppose – and we had to hand over our paybooks. You couldn't do anything without those paybooks. So when we got back to Korea we had no paybooks so we didn't get paid. That went on for about three or four weeks, so we paid someone to forge new ones. Then we got sent for and the officer confined us to barracks for three weeks. He said we could have got five years in jail if we'd done forgery outside the army. I was not very happy. There was no jankers as such. We were on jankers because we were in Korea.

The war was still on when I left but by the time we got back they'd signed the Treaty of Panmunjom and it was over. We'd been living in terrible conditions and I was so happy to get back to being a human being and doing what I'd done before – dances and girls and going to Goodison Park to watch Everton.

When we went home we caught a train from Southampton to Liverpool. I don't know how she found out, but when I got off the train there was my mother waiting for me on the platform. She threw her arms round me and I was dead embarrassed like but . . . She used to wear my medal as a brooch.

I was unemployed for a bit when I was demobbed but my father had been a docker and in those days it was like a family business, and that's why I finished up on the docks – I was there for thirty-odd years. I can't say I enjoyed being in the army but it stopped me being an idiot.

NORMAN McCORD

1951–1953

RAF Flight Controller

*The [bus] conductor asked what he'd got on his lap
and Drew said it was a bomb he was taking to the
RAF. The conductor asked a little uncertainly, 'Do
you really think you should be sitting on the bus
with that thing?' Drew admitted that on the whole
perhaps he shouldn't be, so he got off at the next
stop and walked the rest of the way carrying this
unexploded German bomb.*

I was born on 14 April 1930 in the mining community of
Boldon in the northern part of County Durham. My father
was a hewer in Boldon colliery. My mother, who had been
in domestic service earlier in her life, had first married a
chemist shop sort of chemist who had died shortly after the
marriage. She had then married my father, and with the small
inheritance she had from her first husband he left mining and
they acquired a small corner shop selling general merchandise

to the high-density terrace housing where they lived in North Shields. Very *Coronation Street*. My father was much broader in his speech than my mother. It was her idea that I should take elocution lessons briefly.

I was born when my father was still working in the mines and I suspect it was my arrival that was responsible for my mother persuading my father to leave the pits. I remember nothing of the Jarrow March or growing up in an area of economic deprivation, because by the time I was aware of what was going on around me, even the North East was on the road to recovery.

On the Sunday morning when war was declared I was out with my father when the sirens sounded in North Shields. There was a special train that took all the children from North Shields to a station close to Wooler. We were equipped with a gas mask, suitcase and had a label tied to us. The allocation was done at the other end so my mother didn't know where I would end up. I was picked out by the wife of the garage proprietor in Milfield. I went with someone else from the same street in North Shields to the same place, where we shared a room. The garage proprietor and his wife were very kind. They had twin daughters just a little older than us. They were not very well educated but they had an encyclopedia which I devoured. We didn't have books around our house very much.

I recall very clearly the election of 1945. I was bitterly disappointed. I thought the electorate would show its gratitude to Winston Churchill and it didn't. My explanation for the result was ingratitude. My father approved of the Attlee government's nationalisation plans wholeheartedly – particularly the nationalisation of the mines. He believed that the mines were being given to the people. And the National Health Service was clearly a very good thing, although we were very satisfied with our GPs under the previous system. We were poor but we paid a small regular sum to the GP – who drove a Sunbeam Talbot car, I remember. And lots of people did that, which entitled them to free treatment.

We had Empire Day at school every year and we all thought the empire was a marvellous thing. It was a force for good throughout the world. When Britain chose to give her empire away we were rather saddened – the colonial peoples had all the blessings of British colonial rule and look how casually they dismissed them.

My year was the first year that my school submitted candidates for university entrance scholarships. They put a dozen of us in for the entrance scholarship examinations for King's College, Newcastle. I won the Senior Open Arts Scholarship. I was constantly reading books in the local public library. I never went to see Jackie Milburn playing for Newcastle United – I've never been in the slightest interested in sport.

I knew I would have to do National Service and I had the choice of doing it before going to university or after I graduated. I chose to go after. I thought I ought to keep the impetus of academic life going rather than wait for two years and I wasn't sure they would necessarily hold the scholarship for me on my return, but when I got to King's College, Newcastle I discovered that in my class there was only one other who had come straight from school. All the other students were ex-servicemen and that made me feel very young. On the other hand I knew I was better at academic work than they were.

I was an ATC Cadet when I was at school, No. 346

Tynemouth Squadron Air Training Corps – most of us were in the Cadets though it wasn't compulsory. I was doing my bit. If you joined the ATC and you gained your proficiency badge you were guaranteed service in the RAF when you were called up. You also had a special service number. Mine was 3414463. People who hadn't been in the ATC were 285 or something like that to begin with. At school we did two evenings a week in the ATC, from 7 p.m. to 9 p.m. Curiously, one of the early airfields I was on was at Milfield, where I'd been evacuated, and it was from there that I had my first flight. It was on a De Havilland biplane. I even got a flight in a two-seat Vampire.

Coming to the end of my time as an undergraduate I had to go to a drill hall in Newcastle where I had my medical and took a number of aptitude tests to see how well I could judge angles by eye. Later I realised that this was to test how well we could play with the radar screen. I went in, I think, in early autumn, September or October 1951. When the brown envelope came through the door it had a rail warrant to Warrington inside it and a letter telling me to report to RAF Padgate. It was the first time I'd left home because I'd lived at home during my time at university, though I think it was more traumatic for my parents than it was for me because I just accepted it as inevitable.

I was at Padgate for a week where we were kitted out, then from Padgate I was moved on to RAF Weeton which is a training camp near Blackpool. I was there for eight weeks of basic training with one weekend off in the middle to go home. All the aggression of basic training I just accepted as something that was inherent in the system. The barking and shouting start right at the beginning. The hut inspections and the drill, and the rifle drill . . . I was an appalling shot, so when we went onto the rifle range it was a problem, because my left eye is better than my right and I had to turn my head at a strange angle to try to line up a straight shot. I could manage the drill all right but I was never going to become a marksman.

I was on perfectly friendly terms with the other people in my hut, though I found the broad Scots accent a little difficult to understand. We went to a dance at the Tower Ballroom and one of the men from the same hut proclaimed, 'Drink has no effect on me at all,' before promptly falling flat on his face. I made no lasting friends in that hut but no lasting enemies either.

Obviously there were some people who didn't like the basic training – they were miserable and sluggish, slow to respond to orders – but we were all mutually supportive. We all loathed our drill instructor, the corporal whose job it was to bully you. All the shouting was deliberate, of course. There was a fellow who was given the job of cleaning the parade ground with a toothbrush. He was an extremely rebellious young man, though, and I wasn't rebellious at all. I thought I was part of the armed forces defending the United Kingdom of Great Britain and Northern Ireland and if my superiors wanted the beds made a certain way I was quite happy to oblige. I struggled with sport as part of the programme of basic training but class-room training – lectures and learning by rote – was no problem. Even the spit and polish of the boots was no problem. When I went home during the break in basic training I told my mother I was enjoying myself, but I would have done that whether I was or not.

At university I'd been a member of the King's College Army

OCTU, the Officer Cadet Training Unit. At the end of your undergraduate career they'd assess whether you would be suitable for making into a National Service officer and if so, which branch would be most suitable. When I was called up it was understood that I would be on the path that led through basic training to Fighter Control training to OCTU. So I knew where I was going to be sent at the end of basic training, because there was only one Fighter Control training station and that was at Middle Wallop.

The first aircraft that you learned to control was an Airspeed Oxford which flew at about 120mph, then you graduated to Spitfires. I repeatedly saw groups of three or five Spitfires taking off from the grass airfield at Middle Wallop. They became our fighter and target when we graduated from Oxfords. When we were doing Oxfords they gave us the occasional flight in them so I flew over Stonehenge. Spitfires were the fastest aircraft you controlled during your training.

If you passed your flight control course you then became an officer cadet. I think that as a National Service pilot officer I was paid thirteen shillings a day. I had to pay my mess bills out of that, including the basic two shillings a day that you had to pay anyway before you paid for what you bought. It doesn't sound much but I had never had any money growing up anyway. I was at Fighter Command training for eight weeks, then there was leave, and then in the spring of 1952 I went for three months to the Officer Cadet Training Unit at Spitalgate near Grantham. One of the more interesting requirements of an officer was to buy a hat, so that if I were in civilian clothes in Grantham and I was saluted by an airman who recognised me I could raise my hat to him.

At the end of the OCTU experience there were sixteen of us left at Spitalgate. The adjutant called us all in and said there were eighteen vacancies in the branch, and he told us to sort sixteen of them out between ourselves. Eventually I was attached to the Ground Control Interception Station at RAF Seaton Snook, which is halfway between Middlesbrough and West Hartlepool. It was then an operational station not a residential station. Seaton Snook was being constructed whilst I was living as a lodger at a neighbouring RAF station, RAF Thornaby on the outskirts of Stockton-on-Tees. Thornaby itself was so overcrowded that I literally had to stay in private lodgings. In fact the overcrowding was so bad and the organisation so shambolic that when we had our parades we had to do them on the road outside. They were not, shall we say, distinguished examples of the RAF at drill. Thornaby was our residential site for the first few months I was there and we never took part in the Thornaby parades.

We were sitting targets. I was given three extra duties because of some dereliction I had performed. All the regular officers were only too pleased to catch out a National Service pilot officer so they could be given duties they didn't want to do themselves. There were officers left over from the war who wouldn't have been commissioned in peacetime who were very rude to us National Servicemen and that grated on us.

My job was to sit in front of a radar screen which showed where the fighter and target aircraft were. I'd have a microphone in my hand and I'd tell the pilot of the fighter what to do. If it was a daytime interception the fighter pilot would see the target a few miles away but at night you were dependent on your flight controller. Once the pilot didn't believe a word I was saying because his screen had gone down, which he didn't realise, and he passed within 500 feet of the other aircraft. For safety reasons you worked on a 500-foot height separation and I'd got it spot on.

The other memorable incident had far more unhappy consequences. I could see the plane on my screen drifting off course and the pilot never acknowledged my calls. There was nothing I could do. I watched it helplessly until it drifted off the screen altogether. I learned later that the young pilot had crashed into the Cleveland Hills and been killed. I gave my written evidence for the inquiry and that's all they asked of me; I never heard anything more until two years ago I discovered that this young pilot had left in a hurry and grabbed the wrong helmet from the rack. The helmet had slid down and cut off his oxygen supply, causing him to lose consciousness and crash into the hillside. That was a maturing experience for me.

In late 1953 the annual air defence exercise took place. By this time the air force was re-equipping with more advanced aircraft like Canberras. The Vampire fighters attached to the Royal Auxiliary Air Force squadrons couldn't cope with them. If you were trying to control a Vampire against a Canberra it was almost like having to hold the target. At the end of this exercise, which was spread out over a few days, there was a great jamboree and all the piston-engined bombers in Germany were gathered together to carry out a raid on northern England. It was a huge wodge on the radar screen coming across the North Sea. All the fighter squadrons in the north were scrambled to meet this threat. There were three squadrons of Meteors at RAF Linton-on-Ouse in north Yorkshire which were given to me to control. Of course, the wing commander took over virtually as soon as they were up in the air but it had been quite an honour for me to be given that particular job.

One Easter weekend at RAF Seaton Snook when there was only a skeleton staff around the place I was duty officer. We had a telephonist called Leading Aircraftman Drew, who was living in lodgings in the nearby community of Seaton Carew. On the Saturday he was making his way to the bus stop in Seaton Carew to get the bus to Seaton Snook when he was accosted by the village policeman, who took him to a garden and pointed at a metal object on the ground and asked him to take it with him to Seaton Snook. He told Drew that it had been found on the beach and he thought it would be better taken to the air force. Drew was an obliging chap, so he picked it up, walked back to the bus stop, got on the bus, went upstairs and waited for the conductor to issue his ticket. The conductor asked what he'd got on his lap and Drew said it was a bomb he was taking to the RAF. The conductor asked a little uncertainly, 'Do you really think you should be sitting on the bus with that thing?' Drew admitted that on the whole perhaps he shouldn't be, so he got off at the next stop and walked the rest of the way carrying this unexploded German bomb.

He came into the guard room and told the story and the duty policeman summoned the duty officer, who was me. I got on the phone to Catterick, which was where the nearest bomb disposal unit was based, and they said they'd send someone on Monday. Not being willing to order someone to do something that I wouldn't do myself I asked the duty policeman if I could borrow his gumboots and his torch. I knew there were some disused buildings at the far end of the big aerial field and I thought I'd leave the bomb there for the weekend. It was very muddy out there and halfway across the field one boot got stuck in the mud, and my stockinged foot came out and waved in the air. I put the bomb down and then the back of the torch fell off and it went out. Fortunately it all ended happily. I laid the bomb in some straw in the building, and the bomb disposal unit came up on the Monday. They confirmed it was a live bomb and it could have gone off at any moment. There was no inquiry or anything like that.

The rest of my two years was spent there in West Hartlepool. I did have a posting to the Canal Zone in the run-up to Suez – it wasn't Nasser, it was when King Farouk was deposed by the army in 1952 – but it was cancelled before it became operational. I was given my tropical equipment grant and my tropical injections but as soon as it was cancelled I had to pay the money back. I was however happily protected against yellow fever and the like in the north-east of England. When I finished my two years I had three and a half compulsory years to do in the Auxiliary Air Force unit based in Newcastle, so I carried on my work as a fighter controller there and, though I didn't have to, I stayed in the Auxiliary Air Force until it was closed down. It was two evenings a week and an annual camp.

By that time I had gone up to Cambridge as a research student when I received a letter half-requesting, half-ordering me to attend a camp at RAF Boulmer, which is near Alnwick in Northumberland, for six weeks during my long vacation. I was now a flying officer and I managed to save just enough out of my wages to go on an archaeological holiday by myself to Algeria and Tunisia, which was great fun. I was of course an impoverished student, so I always welcomed the chance to go back to the life of a flight controller as an RAF officer during the vacations. It paid rather better than working on a building site.

Interestingly, I was pretty much obsolete by the time I had finished because everything was changing so fast. The piston-engined bombers which I understood were being cut and cut and cut and the jet bombers were coming in.

My work as a flight controller was extremely interesting and I was very tempted to stay on, so obviously my experience of National Service was very positive. There were experiences, like the young pilot who crashed into the Cleveland Hills, that were character building. That call sign is engraved on my memory for ever. If I had gone to Cambridge after I had graduated from King's College I could have had an extremely miserable time there. Because I had met so many people during National Service, some of whom were also going up to Cambridge, I had friends there before I arrived. That made a difference, as well as the maturity I had acquired.

I have to add that I have probably suppressed a lot of the unpleasant things that happened to me in the air force. I am remembering the things that I like to remember. I think I was one of the lucky ones.

PART 2

THE MIDDLE
1952–1957

Nothing became Attlee's Labour government quite like its leaving of office. After six years of monochrome austerity, legislative worthiness and social bleakness, its farewell performance took place on the South Bank as the Festival of Britain crowned the summer of 1951 in a blaze of triumph. The Labour government of 1997 tried hard to copy its success with the ill-fated Millennium Dome but failed miserably. The 1951 Festival was conceived initially as a centenary celebration of the 1851 Great Exhibition, but its real purpose was to release the creativity of British architecture and design and at the same time to give the suffering population a glimpse into the lifestyles of the future. It succeeded triumphantly.

The years since the end of the Second World War had become frustratingly difficult at home and abroad. In 1949 Russia had exploded a nuclear bomb and China had been 'lost' to the Communists. The world which was supposed to have been made safe in 1945 was suddenly unsafe again and the National Servicemen who by the terms of the last National Service Act thought they would serve only eighteen months now found their term of servitude increased, because in June 1950 Britain was at war again. Admittedly the country was 'only' part of a United Nations police action, while Korea was a long way away and there would be no repeat of the Blitz, but the country was fighting an enemy one of whose partners now had the ability to detonate a nuclear strike.

In one sense the nuclear proliferation of the 1950s and 1960s made armies less vital. If the last war had been the People's War, then the people were beginning to realise that the next war would be fought by the scientists and that conventional soldiering was likely to become obsolete. As Geoff Bennett, who was in Germany in 1954, points out with appropriately mordant Lancashire humour, the Russians, if they'd been serious about invading Britain, would probably have rolled straight over the Lancashire Fusiliers and the British Army on the Rhine and been at the Channel ports in a couple of days. In the event of a nuclear war conventional armies were entirely superfluous. The British Army of the Rhine had been formed in 1945 as an occupying force in the British sector of what became West Germany. As the potential threat of Soviet invasion increased, BAOR became more responsible for the defence of West Germany than its occupation, even if both Geoff Bennett and Hugh Hudson felt their presence there to be largely for show.

Such pessimistic thinking didn't, however, bring a halt to the fortnightly call-ups and National Service continued in Britain unabated. As youngsters like Joseph Strode and George Johnson were sent off to fight in Korea, Hugh Gaitskell, the Labour Chancellor of the Exchequer, had to find more money for the war from somewhere. To the dismay of some he found it in the newly formed National Health Service. The introduction of charges for false teeth and spectacles was such a travesty of the principles that had led to the foundation of the NHS that

Aneurin Bevan, by now Minister of Labour, John Freeman, later known as the austere interrogator on BBC Television's *Face to Face* but in 1951 Parliamentary Secretary to the Minister of Supply, and Harold Wilson, President of the Board of Trade, all resigned in protest. Labour was imploding. By the autumn of 1951 Ernest Bevin was dead and Stafford Cripps was a sick man. The optimism of July 1945 had been shattered by years of continual crisis. It was time for a change and Labour supporters knew it.

The surprise was that the 1951 election produced a result that was so close and that Labour actually won the popular vote, increasing its own vote as it did so. A few weeks after the Festival of Britain was closed to the sound of booing and a widespread feeling of sadness, a General Election was held in which the slender Labour overall majority which had resulted from the election of February 1950 was turned into a narrow Conservative majority. One of the first acts of the new government was to tear down the buildings on the South Bank which had been erected for the Festival, apart from the Royal Festival Hall which had always been designed as a permanent legacy. The Conservatives had a different version of Britain and most of the public took to it rapidly because prosperity was on its way, government controls were to be lifted, and the shops were slowly being stocked with goods that people wanted and could afford to buy.

There followed a struggle for the soul of the British people which, as we can see from our vantage point in the twenty-first century, was won decisively by the consumerists. That high-minded ideal of British public life, a Britain supported wholeheartedly and best represented by the BBC, came under increasing attack from the forces of American consumerism. In 1955 the BBC's monopoly was broken by the arrival of ITV, which of course meant that the power of a new and greatly influential means of advertising was now linked to the rising tide of affluence and the easing of controls on hire purchase. As the first ever commercial was aired on British television – it was for SR Gibbs toothpaste and it ran only in the London area, controlled by Associated Rediffusion – the BBC reacted in the most violent manner possible. On the Home Service, Grace Archer died in a fire in the Brookfield stables as she tried to rescue her horse, Midnight. The episode attracted eight million listeners, made front page news the next morning in every newspaper (except *The Times*, which still carried classified advertising on its front page) and led to the BBC switchboard being jammed for forty-eight hours by heartbroken listeners. Based on the experience of one of my friends' parents, some Archers listeners never recovered from the shock.

All rationing ended in July 1954 when meat finally came off the ration. The war had lasted for six years. Rationing had survived for nine years after its end. It had been a long time coming and even its end was inglorious. R. A. Butler's budget for 1953 increased the sugar ration from ten ounces to twelve in order, he was delighted to proclaim, to allow the nation to make sufficient cakes to celebrate the forthcoming Coronation.

The radiant new queen was to be the symbol of Britain in the 1950s. Her father had died in February 1952, when Princess Elizabeth and her husband were visiting Kenya, just before George Penny arrived there to deal with the consequences of the Mau Mau uprising and the fallout from the trial of Jomo Kenyatta.

The funeral of George VI was observed, as you will see in his story, by the film director Hugh Hudson, who was then at Eton and who was part of the school's contingent that lined the streets of Windsor to pay tribute as the King's cortège made its way to burial at St George's Chapel on the Windsor Castle estate. The photograph that made its way around the world was of the new Queen, in a black coat and hat, slowly descending the steps of the BOAC aircraft that had brought her back to Britain from Kenya, where she had received the news of her succession. Waiting, bareheaded, on the tarmac were Churchill, Attlee and Anthony Eden. The miserable days of February 1952, the death of a king still much admired, belonged to the age of monochrome.

By June 1953 the film of the new queen that was shown in cinemas and news theatres was in colour. It was the high summer of 1953, when Lock and Laker bowled out the Australians at the Oval and England regained the Ashes, amid national celebration, for the first time since they were lost in 1934. The Coronation itself took place on the day when news reached the country that a British expedition led by Sir John Hunt had conquered Mount Everest – even if the summit had been reached by New Zealander Edmund Hillary and Sherpa Tenzing (aided by their supply of Kendal mint cake) – although the weather on the day turned out to be cold, wet and thoroughly unpleasant. Julian Mitchell, who was in the House of Lords stand, remembers, perhaps with a degree of dramatic licence, that it was so cold he could see snow flurries being blown along the Thames. Still, the weather failed to dull either the spectacle or its reception.

My family was but one among a million who decided to buy

a television for the first time in order to invite envious neighbours in to watch it with us. My brother, being a very smart young boy of some eleven summers, claims that he persuaded our parents to buy it a month early so that he could watch the 1953 Cup Final, the famous 'Matthews final', which was the first time the Cup Final had been seen on television – though it was only the second half that was transmitted at that stage. We were all, however, Elizabethans now, possibly New Elizabethans, as the country listened to Ronald Binge's ubiquitous 'Elizabethan Serenade' and looked forward optimistically to a future that would be as great as the age of Gloriana had been in the sixteenth century, when the Cup Final on television wasn't of primary interest and beating Spain didn't require keeping the Barcelona midfielders Iniesta and Xavi subdued.

The planning of the ceremony included much agonising over whether the sacred moment of the anointing of the new monarch should be shown and indeed whether close-ups of the Queen would be permitted at all, and if so of what size. It was reported that over twenty million people watched the Coronation on the 2.7 million sets in use at the time. Television, which raised the royal family to new heights of popularity, had come to stay in their lives.

The rapid spread of television in the early to mid 1950s was matched by a flow of new consumer goods into the shops. It was as if affluence came hurrying on the heels of penury. Shops which had stocked up on fourteen-inch televisions which rested on table tops suddenly found that demand had switched to the new free-standing seventeen-inch sets with doors designed to camouflage the screen and turn it into a piece of living-room furniture. Changes in the composition of the

Retail Price Index illuminated Britain's changing patterns of consumption. The weighting given to food was reduced; candles, lump sugar, rabbits, turnips and similar items were rejected in favour of nylons and washing machines, camera film, telephone rentals and second-hand cars.

Much of this new demand was the result of R. A. Butler's 1953 budget, which cut sixpence from the standard rate of income tax and slashed purchase tax by 25 per cent. Yet economic affluence came at a social price. Considerable anxiety was expressed at this time about the youth of Britain. The terms 'juvenile delinquent' and, more pithily, 'cosh boy', the latter named after the preferred instrument of attack of many of these violent young men, began appearing in an increasingly frenzied press. There is no reason to suppose that the level of petty crime, even of a violent nature, committed by teenagers was significantly higher in the early 1950s than in previous years but it was seized upon by the press, and a film like *Cosh Boy*, made in 1953 and directed by Lewis Gilbert, exploited this public perception.

The eponymous anti-hero, played by James Kenney, becomes infatuated with the respectable sister of one of his gang. She is played by the young Joan Collins and she already has a nice boyfriend, but once the cosh boy has his way with her, her clothes and make-up undergo a radical transformation – and not for the better. When she confides that she is carrying the cosh boy's baby he wants nothing more to do with her, so she seeks an ending appropriate for the times by hurling herself into the Thames. Meanwhile the police have traced the cosh boy and arrive at his home just as his new stepfather is about to cure the problem of juvenile delinquency by administering corporal punishment with his belt. The police decide to let this thoroughly responsible piece of parenting continue undisturbed before hauling the whole gang off to Borstal.

Cosh Boy, though not exactly an outstanding feature film, is a very useful social document as a reflection of early 1950s urban Britain. This is the country the next contingent of National Servicemen left behind when they were called up. It was on the cusp of a huge cultural change led by two forces in particular – commercial television and rock and roll music. The film *Blackboard Jungle*, starring Glenn Ford, was released in 1955, and soon became notorious not for its story of a belea-guered teacher in an inner city school but for the music played over the opening titles – Bill Haley and the Comets singing 'Rock Around the Clock'. When it was shown to British audi-ences in 1956, many young people got up and jived in the aisles, to the consternation of the government. In an attempt to prevent this behaviour from spreading into full-scale rioting and looting, the Gaumont circuit that was distributing the film decreed that it could not be shown on a Sunday.

However, the moral panic that had gripped the nation, or at least the popular press, could not be halted so simply. 'Rock Around the Clock' was immediately spun off as the title song of another feature film under its own name, a fairly lame excuse for reprising it in a much worse picture. The tide however was irresistible: if 1953 had been the year of the twin triumphs of Queen Elizabeth II and a domestic Ashes victory, 1956 was the year of Elvis Presley and an Ashes victory. This time even Jim Laker's 19 wickets for 90 in the Old Trafford Test match could not deflect a young person's attention from the riveting music and public persona of the swivel-hipped young man born in

Tupelo, Mississippi. Yet as far as our National Servicemen were concerned, Elvis might as well have stayed below the Mason-Dixon line, because once they were in uniform there was very little rock and roll in Catterick or RAF Padgate.

It's a common perception that the 1950s were a decade of conformity, of family solidarity, in which conservative values – to say nothing of Conservative values – still dominated a Great Britain which had willingly returned to the social and cultural values of the 1930s. It was the 1960s – which began in 1963, according to Philip Larkin – that are popularly supposed to have been the decade in which families started to split up as each individual relentlessly followed a selfish course in pursuit of their own satisfaction. The family stories which follow indicate immediately how far that general perception was from the truth. Bernard Reynolds speaks movingly of the traumatic collapse of his parents' marriage which tore apart the world inhabited by his siblings and himself. Ian Rees tells of his time in the National Children's Home in Wales and his feelings as a young boy who knew that his mother had given him away shortly after his birth. It may be that the conspicuous consumers of Great Britain who voted for Harold Macmillan in large numbers, watched *The Grove Family* on BBC Television and listened to *Life with the Lyons* on the Light Programme were a middle-class construct and a smaller percentage of the population than had previously been supposed.

Hugh Hudson's eloquent denunciation of the snobbery of Eton and his relief that National Service allowed him to mix with men from working-class families must surely have informed the manner in which he so brilliantly directed *Chariots of Fire*. All the prejudices of the upper class which he, along with Colin Welland, the screen writer, and David Puttnam the producer, brought to light in their successful portrait of the stagnant, stratified British society of the 1920s were clearly much in evidence in the Eton of the early 1950s. Problems of class were revealed by the way in which National Service operated, but if the government hoped that by artificially mixing classes during basic training they might reduce the problems of class conflict they were to be seriously disappointed. As all the officers who passed the War Office Selection Board (Wosbe) reveal, once that initial period of enforced social mixing was over the officer class disappeared behind the walls of the officers' mess. What is interesting is that apart from Hugh nobody else appears to question this pattern. They may have casually thought that it was somehow undemocratic, but they knew that this was the way the armed forces had operated for centuries and two years of National Service was not going to overturn it. Class divisions were endemic in British society. Why should it be any different in the armed forces?

Teenage pregnancy, illegitimate babies, adultery and divorce were by no means restricted to the working class. Nicolas Hawkes tells of the collapse of his parents' marriage and his mother's subsequent remarriage to J. B. Priestley. It is clear that his mother suffered significantly from the attitudes of the archaeologists who were her professional colleagues and Nicolas himself understandably did not enjoy the ensuing public discussion of his family's private affairs in the newspapers. At boarding school at Bryanston he was automatically a target for jibes, though it appears that most of his schoolfellows behaved well. Nicolas's story is fascinating because he is the first to suggest an attitude to the local population among whom the

National Servicemen found themselves that was not the result of years of imperial rule, and it is clear that his months in Ghana as a National Service officer around the time of independence was crucial in shaping his future life. Here is an indication that immersion in schoolboy adventure stories about empire did not automatically lead to an imperialist posture and might encourage a view of indigenous populations that could be reconsidered in the light of experience.

This second part of the book encompasses the single most important military campaign of the whole National Service period. The actual Suez campaign was of brief duration – less than a week from start to finish of the ground war. Its impact on Great Britain both at home and abroad bore no relation to the brevity of the fighting. All the men in this section who were in uniform in the autumn of 1956 were aware that if the war continued for any length of time they were almost bound to see fighting. Ironically the man nearest to Suez, Brian Sayer, was in an RAF camp in Jordan completely surrounded by the Iraqi army. For as long as the war continued they were helpless. If an RAF plane had taken off from the base in order to help British forces fighting in Egypt, the Iraqi army would have destroyed Brian and the rest of the camp in a matter of an hour. Nothing happened. British forces in Jordan were unable to come to the aid of the British task force. The Americans, angered by their ignorance of the collusion between Britain, France and Israel, put immediate economic pressure on sterling and Britain had no choice but to agree to a ceasefire. It was a public humiliation and a highly visible indication that the days when British world power derived from her overseas empire had passed for ever.

Eden's belief that Nasser was another Hitler and had to be stopped as the world had failed to stop Hitler before 1939 was not widely shared, not only by other countries but by most of his own. Suez was a watershed in British history because it demonstrated how weak Britain had become on the world stage. Marches and rallies in Trafalgar Square denouncing the action were matched by debates on television in which the anti-government forces pressed home their outrage, fuelled by sections of the press including the *Observer* and the *Manchester Guardian*. It was particularly galling for many people to hear official British voices speaking of the need to stop Egyptian aggression when, at virtually the same time, Britain had done nothing as Russian tanks rolled into Budapest and crushed the Hungarian Uprising.

What becomes clear from the answers to my questions about Suez was that most of the National Servicemen knew very little about what was going on. Indeed, as probable participants in the war, had it developed that way, they knew less about the origins and detail of the Suez Crisis than anyone at home who watched or heard the news or read a newspaper. By and large the National Servicemen had no access to information, which was clearly the way that the military authorities wanted it. Brian Sayer, a quiet thoughtful man, was slowly starting to realise that not all the 'wogs' were the sort of people he had been conditioned to look down on, but his experience in the news cinema in Amman, when the Jordanians acclaimed Nasser's demagogic denunciation of Western control of the Suez Canal, is a very good illustration of the way in which the British armed forces were thinking in October 1956.

Between the ages of eighteen and twenty, or for those who

deferred between the ages of twenty-one and twenty-three, young people were gradually starting to see themselves as the world saw them. National Service, like any kind of college, gave all conscripts after the helter-skelter of basic training the time to begin this process. I don't want you to imagine that they all had profound thoughts about themselves and their place in British society. I would simply like to present these men as they really were in the years of their National Service and to let them speak for themselves and tell you who they were, and how those two years changed them.

ROLL CALL

GEORGE PENNY	1952–1954	LANCASHIRE FUSILIERS
BERNARD REYNOLDS	1952–1954	REME 17/21ST LANCERS
IAN REES	1952–1955	GREEN JACKETS, KING'S ROYAL RIFLES
GEOFF BENNETT	1953–1955	LANCASHIRE FUSILIERS
GEORGE JOHNSON	1953–1955	ROYAL ARMY SERVICE CORPS
JULIAN MITCHELL	1953–1955	ROYAL NAVY
JOE TROTTER	1954–1956	ROYAL ARMY PAY CORPS
HUGH HUDSON	1954–1956	ROYAL ARMOURED CORPS
JOHN SNOAD	1955–1957	RAF PHOTOGRAPHER
HAROLD RHODES	1955–1957	ROYAL ARMY MEDICAL CORPS
NICOLAS HAWKES	1955–1957	ROYAL HAMPSHIRE REGIMENT, 3RD BATTALION GHANA REGIMENT
BRIAN SAYER	1955–1957	RAF DRIVER/MECHANIC

GEORGE PENNY

1952–1954

Lancashire Fusiliers

During basic training I rang home ... and I broke down, I just burst into tears. [My dad] told me to buck up like people did in those days – 'Stop your crying. For God's sake just buck yourself up,' he said. I was very homesick ... there were quite a few other lads who felt just as frightened as I did.

I was born on 3 October 1931 in Seaforth, Liverpool. I grew up in the Kirkdale area of Liverpool, in a street which people always called 'the posh street' because all around it was a bit rough. My mother was very strict about how I had to behave and how I had to speak properly but that was unusual in Kirkdale. I don't think I was posh but I think others round there might have thought I was. My mother worked in Kirby in a munitions factory and my dad went into the navy in 1941. He'd been a store manager for Dunlop rubber company before that.

We were a very close family. My mother had seven sisters and my father's mother lived not far away either. My parents were strict church-going Protestants and they influenced me in that regard. My dad was discharged from the navy in 1944 because he had duodenal ulcers and was hospitalised. It took a long time for him to recover and when he did he tried to work on the docks, but he didn't last long there and he was soon back at Dunlop. My mother worked at Dunlop in Walton too.

I left school in December 1946 and became an apprentice joiner at Harland & Wolff in Bootle, doing shipbuilding repair, and I was there till I did National Service. My first wages was fourteen shillings a week, which wasn't much even then. I had to give it all to my mum and she gave me back my pocket money, which was about five shillings. I'd been doing a paper round as well, so I was doing OK. And then, as soon as I turned twenty-one, along came National Service. My dad had been in the navy and I'd done five years working on ships, so I asked to go into the navy, but I got sent to the King's Regiment so that was that.

I wasn't looking forward to it. To tell you the truth I was frightened. Even at twenty-one I was frightened. My dad said to me, 'Don't let us down.' I passed my medical A1 and I was sent to join the King's Regiment at Formby Barracks near Southport. That camp isn't there any more – it's a housing estate. Anyway, during basic training I rang home and I was talking to my dad on the phone and I broke down, I just burst into tears. He told me to buck up like people did in those days – 'Stop your crying. For God's sake just buck yourself up,' he said. I was very homesick and we couldn't leave the camp at all for the first fortnight, and we were getting up at five in the morning. There were quite a few other lads who felt just as frightened as I did. They were mostly eighteen and I was one of the oldest in the hut. I'd wanted to go into the navy so I really didn't want to be there, but after a week or so you start to get used to it. The food was OK and you started to make friends. I remember my army number all right. 22741332. Once it goes in you never forget it.

We should have had twelve weeks' training at Formby but we were sent home for embarkation leave after ten weeks. When I first went there I was put into the Manchester Regiment. We were supposed to go to Korea at first with the King's Regiment but a few days later we were told we were going into the Manchester Regiment and we were given silver fleur de lys badges for our berets. The King's Regiment was a silver or golden horse. Now we were going to Malaya with the Manchester Regiment.

During basic training I got pneumonia, so I was taken to hospital where they gave me that horrible gentian violet on my tongue which tastes shocking. Anyway, after a while I was sent back to finish off basic training. I did all that crawling on your belly and through the water and then we were told we were going to Malaya and we got two weeks' leave. I felt good going home, showing off the uniform and all that. Then we went back to Formby and we found out that we were joining the Lancashire Fusiliers and that we weren't going to Korea or Malaya. We were going to Kenya.

I have to say the Lancashire Fusiliers was the best regiment in the world. We'd all read about the battalion being sent from

Aqaba to Kenya in late 1952 or early 1953 to deal with the Mau Mau uprising. At the beginning of March 1953 we were taken on trucks to the Liver Building and dropped off, and then we made our way to a troopship called the *Lancashire*, which had been the last ship I'd worked on when I was at Harland & Wolff. And when I got on who should I find but my cousin, who was working on it as a plumber. We were a month on that ship and that made it more enjoyable. We went to Port Said on the Suez Canal and stopped there for a day and a half – there were some antics went on there. Then we went on to Aden and then over to Sudan, and from there we went down to Mombasa. We disembarked there and got onto a train, but what I mostly remember is seeing women walking around bare breasted. The train took sixteen hours to get from Mombasa to Naivasha station and there we were met by trucks and taken to Naivasha camp. It was near to the lake, which was beautiful – so much wildlife.

We'd heard on the ship that conditions were frightening – the Mau Mau were using bows and arrows as well as rifles, you see. Jomo Kenyatta was the instigator. As soon as we got there all we had time to do was to throw our stuff into the tents and then get on parade. It was spring weather so it wasn't too hot at that point, though when it rained it rained in torrents. The day we arrived we were taken to a patch of land which we had to weed, and we did that till about eight o'clock at night. It was hard work but we got British food and the chef had worked at Dunlop.

That first night we were called out to go and guard a prison camp where they kept the Mau Mau who had been captured. There was certainly no abuse of the prisoners going on that I could see, no atrocities like we saw in Iraq with the Americans. We never talked about the Mau Mau till we were in action with them. We talked about football. I'm a big Liverpool supporter – and there were quite a lot of Evertonians there as well. We did ask ourselves what the hell we were doing out there but then we were called out to deal with a Mau Mau riot, so you didn't ask yourself that question any more. The commanding officer told us to look after ourselves, help each other if we could, but not to get involved with the Africans because you didn't know who was Mau Mau and who wasn't. I never saw any atrocities but we knew that they were going on. They had these horrible things, I think we called them mashies, and when we caught one with one of them he just claimed he was using it to cut grass. You didn't know whether to believe him or not but they were terrible things. If we wanted to wash in the stream when we were out on patrol we all had to guard each other.

We went out one night, up to our necks in a river. We knew that the Mau Mau had gone into a village and slaughtered the whole lot, children and everything, about 150 of them. The sergeant told us to go down and get washed and as we were washing we heard gunfire. We didn't know what was going on and the next thing is we saw a figure coming through on her own. It was a woman and she had a little girl with her. The sergeant fired blindly, thinking there was Mau Mau there, and killed the little girl and badly wounded her mother. I'd been a scout and I tried to wrap something round her skin like a tourniquet. She ran off into the bush. I doubt she lasted the day though. We never saw her again or heard anything about her. I shouted at the sergeant, 'What the hell were you thinking of, killing a little girl like that?' and he shouted back, 'I'll put you on a charge.' Anyway the commanding officer came up to me later and said, 'It's all right, Penny, I've told him to drop the charge.'

We had occasional skirmishes with Mau Mau but never any direct confrontation. We were just police really. The camp was great, plenty of sport – football and cricket – and some great lads, all from Liverpool. We got on with it really and though there were some who never adjusted, most of us did. I was pally with about eight lads and we kept up after we were demobbed. There was a bit of swearing but that didn't bother me – I'd heard it all on the shop floor. There wasn't that much talk about sex, apart from odd references to 'I fancy that one' and so on.

When we went back to Nairobi, we got the freedom of Nairobi and paraded with fixed bayonets in a big field – the whole battalion was there. We'd finished our term of duty and the Black Watch took over. I was in Naivasha from April to September 1953 but the lads before us who had been in Aqaba were the ones who had seen most of the battles with the Mau Mau. There was a bit of a battle with us actually, because the previous lot had mostly been Mancunians and we were mostly Scousers. You know how it is. We mixed all right with the Regulars though.

When we left Kenya we sailed on the *Dunottar Castle* to Southampton. There was no leave so we went straight on the train. We knew we were going to Germany next but first we went to Barnard Castle in County Durham for two or three weeks. We sailed to Germany from Harwich and the battalion was based in Iserlohn. The camp was excellent. I went into the

Orderly Room office and I finished up my time there. I was made up as a lance corporal and I got more money for that but I was essentially in administration. I went from A Company to B Company. If you kept your nose clean you got on OK, and I suppose I was flattered because there were a lot of things in the Orderly Room that were secret that I knew about: troubles in Egypt or Malaya, things like that. Don't forget we had no newspapers or news on television or the wireless. We got parcels from home but they sent the *Dandy* and the *Beano* and cake. That's what we all liked.

I got on fine with the Germans and I got on fine with the officers. In fact I even baby-minded for the Orderly Room commander. His kids were around nine and eleven and I think that's why I got my stripe and my job in the office. My pay must have been around two pounds, but I made a bit more sewing for the other lads who paid me for it because I was good at it. I left at the end of September 1954. They offered to make me a sergeant if I signed on for another year but I said no because I'd just had enough. And besides, I wanted to go into the Merchant Navy.

When I came out of National Service I had to join the TA at Tranmere Road in Liverpool. I was part of the engineers then because I was a tradesman. I was wondering if I would be called up when the Suez crisis started but I wasn't. When I came out I found I had to start all over again. I couldn't get into the Merchant Navy, there was a lot of back-handing going on there. A bloke said he'd get me in if I gave him a hundred quid but I wouldn't do it. I went back on the ships as a joiner in dry dock and after two weeks I was made redundant. I thought, 'That's it,' so I went into buildings and started to learn my trade as a joiner on building sites. I was a joiner for the rest of my working life. Even now, at eighty years of age, I teach children how to do models at the local school.

BERNARD REYNOLDS

1952–1954

Royal Electrical and Mechanical Engineers, 17/21st Lancers

When you went in through the gates [of Belsen] there were mounds of earth and you were told that's where bodies were buried, ten thousand here and eight thousand there ... and there wasn't a sound, no birds, nothing at all. Everything was deathly still. You came back out through the gates and suddenly you could hear the birds chirping again. It was that no sound that told you it was a camp of death.

I was born on 12 March 1931 in Hereford hospital. I was the eldest in the family – I had three brothers and a sister – and we lived in a two up, two down with an outside toilet and no electricity. We had gas lamps downstairs and we used candles when we went upstairs to bed. You didn't think much about it – you don't as a kid, do you? That was just the way it was in those days.

My dad worked on building sites but there wasn't a lot of work around in the 1930s so he went into the army in the King's Shropshire Light Infantry. During the war my mum and my dad broke up and when I was eleven, along with my sister I was taken in by my auntie. She was the one who really brought me up. The other boys were brought up by my grandmother. My mother went off with another chap, she left us and that was it. I wasn't very happy about it. I only saw my mother a couple of times after that but I saw my dad regularly when he came home after the war. He lived in Weston-super-Mare.

Anyway, my auntie and uncle were wonderful to us. Between the age of eleven and fourteen I used to work with my uncle evenings and Saturdays at his garage. I think I got half a crown a week. I was good at maths at school and when I left at fourteen I had the chance of three jobs. One was with the GPO as a telegram boy and there was also a chance to go on the railway in the office. Then there was my uncle's garage, which is what I did because I was used to it. I took an apprenticeship there as a motor mechanic, which meant I could defer my National Service until I was twenty-one, so I didn't go into the army until April 1952.

I was called up to Blandford Forum in Dorset for basic training but my medical had been at St John's in Worcester. I wasn't looking forward to it because I'd got married just before I was called up. We'd been courting for four years. It'll be sixty years next year. Neither of my parents came to the wedding, which upset me a bit, but my uncle and auntie and my grandmother were there.

I knew I was going into the Royal Electrical and Mechanical

Engineers from the start, which I was happy about. Basic training was six weeks – I think it was longer for the infantry. It was a bit of a shock, I can tell you. We got picked up in three-tonners when the train arrived at Blandford station and they took us to the camp. The first thing we had was a small-pox injection, because there was a smallpox outbreak at the time. Then we had our hair cut. Then we had to collect all the kit and you were weighed down by it. They found us a really ropey barrack room which we had to clean out. I think they probably did that on purpose to get you started.

It wasn't the first time I'd slept away from home because I'd been on cricket tours before, but this was nothing like a cricket tour. This was the first time I'd met people from different parts of the country – Brummies and so on. The ones I couldn't understand were the Scottish, the Glaswegians and that, and the Geordies weren't easy either.

The NCOs were bastards, but that was their job really, wasn't it? There was one big Yorkshireman, he must have been about six foot three, and he had lots of problems. The corporals really bullied him. He was bit slow, you see. Another chap was so bad at everything they kicked him out in the end. He was hopeless, he couldn't see much because his eyesight was so bad. How he got passed A1 I have no idea. I felt very sorry for him. There was no point in back-squadding him because he was so com-pletely hopeless.

You were up at six and in bed at midnight and every evening it was all bull, so you had no time for anything except clean-ing boots, polishing studs. The inspections were rough, really rough. You had to lay all your kit out on a blanket and it had to be in the right order and it had to be spotless, but they'd always find something and they'd tip it all out and make you do it all again. One or two people in the barracks got it in the neck every time, it seemed. I didn't get it but I saw it happening all the time. What could they do about it? They just had to start all over again. I was probably lucky because most things went OK for me. I learned how to march in step – that took a bit of time. The discipline smartened us up, I suppose. I hated it at the time but afterwards, thinking about it, I suppose it did me a power of good. Don't forget that sort of discipline was expected in those days. The food was horrible but you had to eat it just to keep going. In basic training you didn't even have time to go down the NAAFI, and you got shouted at all the time. Once you got past basic training the shouting pretty much stopped.

After Blandford I never saw anyone I did basic training with again. I went down to Taunton for an eighteen-week mechanical course of technical training. I had no problems hitch-hiking home from there at weekends in my uniform. It took about four or five hours. Sometimes I only got a thirty-six-hour pass, not forty-eight, so by the time I got home it was time to go back again. Once I got dropped at Bristol and I had to walk all the way across the city to pick up something on the other side. I wanted to get back to see my wife Pam – she had a job as a secretary to the agent for the local Conservative MP. We had a rented flat round here. It was really hard leaving her. We'd only been married a few weeks but the army didn't care if you were married or not. You got twenty-eight shillings a week minus the barrack-room damages – though there were none – and then I gave Pam about a pound. All I had left was about six shillings, which was just enough for the NAAFI where you could get eggs, chips and beans for sevenpence. At the end of the week I had nothing.

I finished at Taunton in the autumn of 1952 and I was sent to Arborfield near Reading. It was a transit camp and you waited there till they posted you overseas, but it was also the place where the REME training centre was. While I was waiting to be told I was going to Münster I was a regimental policeman there for a couple of months. I might have been sent to Kenya during Mau Mau – that's where my brother went – or I could have gone to Egypt, I suppose, but in the end it was Germany. I was attached to the 17/21st Lancers, a tank regiment out there. I was responsible for the Scammell recovery vehicles. I had to sign for it and it was worth about five thousand pounds.

I remember the first breakfast we had when we left Harwich by boat. We had bubble and squeak and the Yanks had everything – pints of cold milk, everything you could think of. They started handing us chocolate bars. They were generous people, the Yanks.

Münster was a nice city but there was still a lot of bomb damage, even though the war had been over for seven years. We didn't really have much interaction with the Germans. I found them very aloof, maybe a bit resentful. I think that's what we'd have been if it was us who had lost the war. If you walked down the street they would look the other way. They wouldn't even look at you. It was the madmen though, Hitler and that lot, who were the real villains. The barracks we lived in had been built for the SS and they were very nice – only six or so to a room and the toilets and washing facilities were first class. And the roads, those autobahns. I'd never seen anything like it. We had no motorways then in this country.

The Coronation was on when we were out there. We heard it on the tank radio – and that's where we heard the Stanley Matthews Cup Final and winning the Ashes at the Oval. I remember that better than the Coronation. I played quite a lot of cricket for REME and various divisional sides. Most of the REME sides were made up of officers who had been to public school. One of them had been captain of the first XI at Eton and in the nets I bowled him three times on the trot. That was wonderful. He didn't fancy the quick stuff on matting wickets laid on top of concrete.

I went to Belsen while I was out in Münster because quite a few of us wanted to see it. It was about a three-hour drive from where we were based and we were taken there in a three-tonner. The British had renamed it Hohne. When you went in through the gates there were mounds of earth and you were told that's where bodies were buried, ten thousand here and eight thousand there . . . and there wasn't a sound, no birds, nothing at all. Everything was deathly still. You came back out through the gates and suddenly you could hear the birds chirping again. It was that no sound that told you it was a camp of death.

I was promoted to lance corporal and one day Captain Wood had me in and said he'd make me a sergeant if I signed on for an extra year, I think it was. I didn't think about it for a minute. I was married and I wanted to go home. I had a job waiting for me at my uncle's garage. If the army was offering me a chance to see the world I didn't want it. I came home and played cricket for Herefordshire and watched Lindwall bowling at

Worcester. I was demobbed through Aldershot. I was there about a week but I'd been counting the days before release for months. Pam and I wrote to each other almost every day. Those letters were very important.

IAN REES

1952–1955

Green Jackets,
King's Royal Rifles

I hated the parades. That quick marching. I was no good at it, you see, and once or twice I passed out, fainted. They were going too fast for me. They were running all the way and I couldn't keep up. You had to carry all that equipment on parade.

I was born in 1934. I don't know who my parents were. I was brought up in a children's home in Bridgend in Wales from 1934 till 1948. I was warned against finding out who my parents were. I was taught how to respect my elders and speak the truth and all that. We had church in the morning and school in the afternoon. I never forgot that upbringing, the way I was taught, and I've always appreciated it. Mind you, you got the cane if you were in trouble. I got it when I was twelve for a dare. Four of us walked the seven miles to Maesteg and stayed out all night and the police caught us. We scrumped apples and found a workmen's hut to sleep in. I didn't resent the punishment – a few strokes on the hand. That's the way it was.

I had to leave the home when I was fourteen – that was the regular age you left, same as the school leaving age. At that time I wanted to be a cook so they sent me up to a hostel in the West End and I was looking after myself. The Master – that's what we called the man who was in charge of the National Children's Home in Bridgend – took me down to the station in Cardiff, then somebody from the Children's Society took over from there and took me to the hostel where I was designated to stay in London. I think I was paid about two pounds and ten shillings but I had a room to myself.

Children were adopted from that home in Bridgend but not me; nobody wanted me. Somebody looked at me but it didn't work out. I stayed at that hostel in Latimer Road for two years but after that I moved into lodgings in Camden Town. Nobody helped me out, but I got a job as a packer with a big firm that sold dresses and I took care of myself. I had a bit more money – maybe three pounds ten or four quid. Rent was about thirty bob a week and though it didn't leave much, everything was a lot cheaper then.

I knew National Service was coming and there was nothing any of us could do about it. Shortly after my eighteenth birthday I got a letter telling me I was being called up and I had to report to the barracks in Winchester. I had to go for a medical in the West End, but they always pass you A1, don't they? I took a train from Waterloo to Winchester and when I got off I was in the army. They met you at the station with a lorry and they took you up to Infantry Depot O at Winchester Barracks. I remember Corporal Coram – he was a right so-and-so. I suppose he thought he was doing his job – instilling discipline. He became a sergeant before I left. Everyone hated him of course.

We had inspections once or twice a week. You always knew when they were coming but they were murder. Everyone standing by their bed. He loved all that. He had to find fault with someone, didn't he? He loved to throw your clothes around after you'd laid them out so carefully just before the officer came round. Some people slept on the floor because they'd laid their kit out on the bed proper and they didn't want to mess it up. One time I had a small crack in my mug and he threw it out of the window, so I had to go and buy another one. That's the way it is in the army, isn't it? The way I was brought up I was used to the discipline. The lads who came from families found it harder. I didn't have a family, did I? I only got jankers once when I overslept.

I hated the parades. That quick marching. I was no good at it, you see, and once or twice I passed out, fainted. They were going too fast for me. They were running all the way and I couldn't keep up. You had to carry all that equipment on parade.

The basic training was somewhere between six and eight weeks. You had to have such a shine on your boots, didn't you? You had to burn them off and rub them all down so you got a good shine on them. Bullshitting they called it, and it was really hard doing that. There was a lot of bribery going on – you know, people paying someone else to do their bulling. Most people were from London, maybe from Kent or Essex, but nobody from up north or anywhere like that, so I was the only Welshman and that was because I was living in London when I was registered for the call-up.

At the end of basic training you just got posted to wherever your regiment was based. I was put in the 2nd Battalion and they were in Münster, so I was sent to Germany, not far from the border with Holland. Anyone who was put into the 1st Battalion was sent to Sennelager in Westphalia. It was 1952 and the first time I'd ever been out of the country. It was exciting and a lot better than being sent to Korea, which was what I was really worried about. You heard a lot of stories about what it was like in Korea. You didn't want to go there and until we were told we were going to Germany we didn't know, did we? We took a train from Winchester to Waterloo and then across London for the night train to Harwich, a boat to the Hook of Holland and then a train from there to Münster.

I'd been working for Jews in the dress shop and of course I'd heard what they'd been saying about the Germans. The Jews I worked for were very good to me but I didn't take much notice of what they said about the Germans, though I suppose I was a bit down on them. We could go out in the evening in Münster but we didn't have much to do with the Germans really. I suppose we were there to keep them in line by show-ing them that we were still around, but the enemy was the Russians not the Germans. The Germans did all the cleaning round the barracks and most of them were quite pleasant.

I became a batman to a nice officer, Second Lieutenant David Bedford. I kept in touch with him for years but he's dead now, God bless him. He asked me – it was a volunteer thing, but it meant I earned more money because he paid me. He'd come from Winchester College – a really lovely man. His family lived in Winchester and they were rich, I suppose, but he had no airs or graces. I came from the canteen after breakfast and brought him a cup of tea, made his bed, got his room tidy, laid out his equipment, made sure it was clean – things like that. It was a pretty easy job. I once tried to do a corporal's course but I soon found out it wasn't for me. The officers had a job and I did my job and that's how it was. I wasn't a very good speaker. I was very shy and I couldn't go out in front of the class and speak.

I enjoyed the army life. I thought it was good, that's why I went into the reserves for five years. It taught me about friendship and comradeship. I'd signed on for an extra year before I even got to Germany. I was on my own so why not? The first time I got leave I had nowhere to stay because I'd had to give up the lodgings I'd been in, so I stayed at the Union Jack club in Waterloo. I was on my own, I didn't know anybody, I was lost really. I decided to stay in the army because it gave me a home and you got extra money, maybe thirty bob or so.

I left in 1955 but I was back in again in 1956 because they called me up for the Suez crisis. I had to go back to Winchester, then we were taken to Woolwich and flown out to Libya. The sea was beautiful but it was too hot. We waited there for a few months, but nothing happened apart from me getting sunstroke and spending three or four days in hospital. We stood about in the desert for a bit then we came back by boat.

I didn't want to sign on as a regular. By the time I'd done my three years I'd lost my enthusiasm, but there again I was coming home to nothing. I had to find lodgings and a job. I came out with two weeks' money.

GEOFF BENNETT

1953–1955

Lancashire Fusiliers

It was now nearly ten years after the war. It was no longer about the Germans. The BAOR was there in case the balloon went up when the Reds attacked, but we all knew that the only way we were going to stop the Russians was to nuke them. It was said that the Russians would have been at the Channel in seven days or less whatever we did. From East Germany right through us.

I was born in 1931 in Rochdale. I was at Bury Grammar School from 1942 to 1950 and I did seriously consider joining the army at the age of seventeen, but in the end I decided to do my National Service and try to get to Sandhurst from there. I'd joined the school CCF at the age of thirteen and I enjoyed it very much and I thought this wouldn't be a bad life. I loved the unit, the corps, the comradeship that came from that. Also, I used to read reports in the press about how absolutely superb the British soldiers were and I thought I'd like to belong to that lot. When I got to seventeen, of course, the National Service Act meant I was going to go into the army anyway. There was no choice. So now I had the opportunity to try it for a couple of years. You can't go into a bank and say I'll try it for a couple of years. But you could in the army.

When I was thinking about going in at the age of seventeen I certainly had thoughts of seeing action, but when I actually got my call-up papers that was no longer the case. I thought I was being trained to do a job – kill people – that I didn't really want to do. If I was told I had to go out and kill people I'd have done it but I didn't have to. It was 1953 before I went in because I went to university first and deferred. Oxbridge liked you to do National Service before coming up but redbrick was the other way round and I went to Birmingham to read Classics.

When the time came my situation was almost unique. I had been in the University Training Corps for three years, and the system was that if you'd done that you could go before the officers' selection board. If you passed, fine, but if you didn't you could have another go when you got called up. I actually went before the selection board before I was called up.

The system was that you were put into squads of eight and given a number and told that at no time would you be inspected except when you were told you were going to be inspected. That was rubbish, because when we were eating people were walking round looking at us and you knew you were being observed. If you ate your peas with a knife you were out. That all took place over forty-eight hours at Barton Stacey in Hampshire, not too far from Aldershot.

At the end of the forty-eight hours you were lined up and given an envelope. Inside this envelope there was a piece of paper with three options. Option one said you were recommended for officer cadet training; option two said that you were not recommended for officer cadet training; option three was not recommended at present but brought back in six months' time for further assessment. The last two were crossed out and I was recommended for officer training, so when I was called up I'd passed the selection board and done all my basic training, which was a peculiar situation.

The Korean War was just finishing and the difference between the eighteen-year-olds who were waiting to go to Korea and the twenty-year-olds who had just come back was huge. The first lot were boys and the second lot were men. The ones waiting to go might have felt differently privately, I suppose, but to all outward appearances it looked like they were going on a jaunt. The men coming back had really been through it. They'd been at the sharp end all right. They didn't talk about it much, but that's frequently the case with soldiers who have seen too much.

In the University Training Corps we did basic infantry – handling the Bren gun, the rifle, basic drill, PT – and we were a team. Once we had to do a five-mile bash and everyone had to finish in a certain time. If we didn't, if just one man lagged behind, we'd all failed and we'd all have to do it again. We ended up carrying the equipment and weapons of one of the soldiers with two people dragging him along. We did get him in – just. What did go against us was that he hadn't done it properly.

I graduated from Birmingham University in June 1953 and

when I got my call-up papers I had to report to Oswestry in Shropshire. Generally speaking, and for reasons I never found out, when people from Rochdale went into the Gunners that's where they had to report. When I got that slip I was furious, because I'd wanted to go to the Lancashire Fusiliers who were based in Bury. I went to Oswestry and I said, 'This is stupid. I want to challenge this call-up. I want to go to the Fusiliers.'

They said, 'Oh, but this has come from the War Office.'

So I said, 'Who do I write to, to get it changed?'

I heard them talking in the inner office. 'There's this kid outside who wants to complain!' They came out and they said, 'I'm sorry, there's nothing we can do. But I can give you an address to write to.' So I did. I got no reply of course.

During basic training there were boys who were almost in tears because of what they had to do. For a start getting up at half past six was a shock to the system. Some of these lads couldn't cope, so they got up at half past five to get their bed space correct, to get their windows cleaned. That was the only way they could cope. Simple things like sewing on a button they couldn't do. Many of them had obviously never cleaned a pair of shoes properly.

There was one boy who was completely out of his depth. We were given buttons to sew on our greatcoats. We had to take off the general service buttons and sew on artillery buttons. He was struggling, and this was basic drill, I'd been doing it for eight years. This boy whined, 'Bennett, can you help me?' I looked at what he'd done and it was a mess. A day or two later we had a room inspection and his bed space was also a mess. The inspecting sergeant tore a strip off him and this boy started to beat the sergeant on the chest and then burst into tears. To his credit the sergeant took no further action. He realised that this poor lad had got to the end of his tether. He was transferred to the Pioneer Corps. They do all the dirty work – digging drains, digging roads and so on. There were quite a few who couldn't really cope, but they struggled on with the jobs they had to do.

Eventually someone realised that I'd been infantry trained in the CCF and the University Corps. I was called into the office in Oswestry and they told me I was going off to the Officer Cadet School at Chester. So I was only in the Gunners for three and a half weeks before I went off to Eaton Hall near Chester and the OCS. Training at Oswestry was specifically for training gunners, people who would fire 25-pounders, and all the ancillaries, the technical assistants, learning to use the theodolites that the gunners use. OCS was directed specifically at training us to be officers, so we were put into command situations.

I was commissioned in January 1954 as a second lieutenant in the Lancashire Fusiliers – which is what I'd asked for – and I was sent to Germany. I just missed action in Egypt and Kenya, and in Cyprus, because I was in the middle. The battalion had been in Egypt in 1951 with all the trouble there and had gone down to Kenya the next year to deal with Mau Mau, so having done those tours they came back to the UK and then went off to Iserlohn, which was near Dortmund. That's when I joined them. Cyprus blew up in 1956 just after I left.

We didn't have much trouble with the Germans. We got on well enough. I had a smattering of German. We didn't mix with them much at all. There were certain pubs that were out of bounds because the Germans didn't want soldiers in them. They wanted their own pubs for themselves and we had a bar in Iserlohn where our soldiers mostly went.

It was now nearly ten years after the war. It was no longer about the Germans. The BAOR was there in case the balloon went up when the Reds attacked, but we all knew that the only way we were going to stop the Russians was to nuke them. It was said that the Russians would have been at the Channel in seven days or less whatever we did. From East Germany right through us. We felt we were the best battalion in Germany, the smartest, the most efficient, and we didn't think much about the reality that if the balloon had gone up we'd have been wiped out. I knew that either the Russians would go through us or we'd be nuked, but we never consciously thought of that. We didn't think of ourselves as being in the front line, but we were certainly close enough to it.

We were well treated on a daily basis. We had good equipment in the BAOR because of the proximity of the Russians and the food was good – and the accommodations were terrific, because they were the barracks that had been built for the elite of Hitler's forces. Our officers' mess had been the German sergeants' mess – the officers had their mess somewhere in the town – but ours was like a luxury hotel where we were waited on for all our meals.

The soldiers who played football for the battalion in Germany played at a much higher standard than I'd ever played at, though I did do athletics. In our battalion the big thing was boxing and they won the BAOR boxing competition. When it got to the boxing season, all the best boxers were posted to

Headquarter Company and they did no training at all other than to train for boxing.

There was a big, big gap between officers and men. In the 1950s the officers' mess was totally distinct from the rest of the barracks. I had a servant. I pressed a bell and a chap came in. I ordered a drink and that went on your mess bill, which was paid at the end of the month. I was paid about thirteen pounds a month and the average mess bill must have come to about ten pounds, which included laundry and that sort of thing but also the band fund and the silver fund and all the rest of the funds we paid into. It was odd initially, coming from the modest background I did, but you soon got used to it. In fact I had two servants when I was an officer; one was a Scouser and both were Lancastrians. It was the way things were done. There was no point in anyone complaining. I met a few of the public-school Oxbridge officers. In the battalion there was no difference between them and us, but where I did notice it was at Eaton Hall, where you had Etonians and Harrovians and Wykehamists and all that. What you noticed about them was they were not so much arrogant as full of self-confidence. They were, I suppose you could say, 'splendid chaps'.

Yet at the same time we were almost an anachronism. We had a PMC, President of the Mess Committee, a stickler for etiquette called 'Squeaker' Briggs. He came into the mess one day to find a few women who had arrived as the girlfriends of the Belgian basketball team, who were playing against the battalion. He was appalled. 'Corporal So-and-so,' he shouted, 'I shall take my tea in the back office.' The very idea of women in the officers' mess appalled him. Whoever had organised the match ought to have asked for his approval before bringing women into the mess. On Monday, Tuesday, Thursday and Friday nights we had to dress in formal blues for dinner, seven thirty for eight o'clock. Wednesday and Saturday were supper nights and we could wear a dinner jacket. On Sundays we were permitted to wear a lounge suit for supper. A number of people thought this was all very anachronistic but I thought it was great. I conformed to all the rules, I really belonged to that mess and I enjoyed it all.

Every fourth Friday was a band night, when the band came and played for us, and once a month we had a guest night when we had a few guests in. Every now and again the families of the older married officers were invited to share Sunday lunch. One Sunday I was on my way to lunch in smart blazer and neat trousers, regimental tie and clean polished shoes, and I was brought to a halt by Squeaker Briggs. 'Bennett! Where do you think you're going?'

'I'm going to the mess for lunch, sir.'

'Then go and get properly dressed and put on a suit.' He was obsessed but I didn't resent it.

A lot of the National Servicemen that I knew didn't want to be soldiers, of course. All right, they had to do it for two years and they accepted it. Yes, there was a lot of bad language from the soldiers, but we swore a lot in the mess too, though I rarely swore at a soldier. They would use the f-word as five different parts of speech – noun, adjective and so on – but it never bothered me. I remember I did swear at a soldier once. I found him asleep so I kicked him to wake him up. 'You're a fucking idle bastard!' I said.

An hour or two later he came up to me. 'Sir, could I have a word?'

I said he could. He said I was right but I shouldn't have called him a bastard. He was a Scouser. I was amazed he was so sensitive.

There was always one incident or another. We had four Scousers and, though it was never proved, they beat up the brigadier's driver. There was some background to it but they were deeply unpleasant. Three of them spent some part of their National Service in the glasshouse but mostly discipline was maintained because you knew you'd be in trouble if you didn't obey orders.

There was a chap called H——. If you went into action you certainly wanted H—— around but in peacetime he was a mess. He came to me once asking me to get him a pass, an extension from ten thirty to midnight. All soldiers had to be in barracks by half past ten. We officers could stay out all night, and sometimes some did, as long as you were back in again by the time of first parade the following morning. Anyway I just told him to put the request to the sergeant major. He said the sergeant major wouldn't give him one and wouldn't give him an explanation as to why not.

So I said, 'All right, I'll try,' and I went to see the company commander, Jimmy Wickham. I shouldn't have done it really, but I said H—— wanted a pass and the sergeant major and he didn't get on and he wouldn't give him one. So I got H—— the pass and gave it to him and of course he was found in Iserlohn drunk at three o'clock in the morning, no hat on and no belt. He was desperate for that extra bit of freedom and that's how he used it.

He was brought up before the CO. 'I'll get twenty-eight days,' he said to me.

I said, 'You've not even been tried yet.' But he did. He was sent up to Bielefeld, that was the nick, the equivalent of Colchester in Germany. But he told me he wouldn't do the twenty-eight days. He was going to get 10 per cent or three days off for good behaviour and he'd spend twenty-two days awaiting confirmation of sentence after a special plea. He lay on his bed for twenty-two days and did three days' hard work.

I'd been in Germany about six months when I was called in by the CO. He said there was a vacancy in the barracks on Bolton Road in Bury because they needed a trained subaltern at the depot and I was the only National Service officer with enough time to do so I spent six months there and then I went back to Germany. I didn't feel fraudulent coming home like that. It was just another job.

I met someone years later who had known the Bury Barracks. He said he knew a few sergeant majors who would have stopped the first bullet if they'd ever gone into battle (in other words they'd have been shot by their own men), which threw me, but what I'll always remember is he said, 'The ones we couldn't stand were the young officers who had been to university and wore one pip on their shoulder and they all thought they were it.' And he was right.

I certainly felt that National Service opened up for me a spectrum of mankind I'd never seen before. You'd talk to a Fusilier you thought was a bit thick with not much to offer, then you found out he was interested in cricket or pigeons. Many of them had surprising hobbies. I was constantly surprised by these guys who hadn't been to university, hadn't been to a grammar school. I came out of National Service with more confidence, but I suspect I also came out with a certain amount of arrogance. It suited me well enough as a schoolmaster – If I said jump on your way up you'd ask me, 'How high?' Not all schoolmasters could do that, even those who had been in National Service.

I liked the army. I liked the way it created order out of chaos. Regulations. Certain standards that you had to work to. I always thought that National Service was necessary in the late 1940s and throughout the 1950s because we couldn't build up a regular army of a sufficient size to meet our commitments all over the world – apart from the Korean War there was trouble in Egypt and Malaya and Mau Mau in Kenya, and Cyprus was coming up, and of course because we were part of NATO we had to have troops in Germany.

I certainly look back on my National Service with great fondness. I had no animosity towards it. I knew that I had it to do, so I might as well get on and make the best of it.

I was due to leave in August 1955, and in June or July the CO called me in and asked if I would consider extending my commission and taking a short regular service commission. I can't remember if I said no or said I'd think about it, but by then I'd had enough. I certainly felt that I didn't want to be tied down. I felt that outside the army there was a wide variety of things I could do, although to be honest when I did leave I had no idea what I was going to do next.

Author's note: Geoff Bennett eventually returned to Bury Grammar School, where among the thousands of boys to whom he taught Latin over the next forty years was the author of this book. I suspect that my Grade 6 Latin O level was a poor return for his efforts. I am sure my refusal to join the school CCF was taken by him and other masters who had served in the armed forces as a signal that the country was going to the dogs and nothing would have done me more good than to have been put through basic training. I can still hear the sound of his marching boots as he came down the corridor towards our form room on Tuesday afternoons when he was smartly dressed in uniform once more. Mr Bennett evoked no nickname. He was one of those masters you didn't mess around with. *Ave, O magister. Morituri te salutant.* Or, recalling *Monty Python's Life of Brian*, as Graham Chapman has to write out a hundred times on the Jerusalem wall, *Romani ite domum.*

GEORGE JOHNSON

1953-1955

Royal Army Service Corps

The food all the time we were at that camp was terrific. You had a choice of turkey, chicken, ham, duck, fillet steaks. Usually it was mince with mash, just horrible food. When I heard we'd be getting American rations I thought we'd gone to heaven.

Everyone remembers their army number – except me. I know the last four numbers, 0844, because that's all they use in the army, even on pay day. I was born on 1 August 1934. My parents were from Liverpool but my grandparents came from Ireland and one from Manchester. I was the eldest of three kids.

My dad was a merchant seaman. He did long trips – he'd be away from home for two years then come back and be home for quite a while. That was a normal merchant seaman's life. My mum worked in Rootes, a munitions factory in Speke, during the war but I wanted to be a merchant seaman like my dad. My mum wasn't keen on losing me but it was all I ever wanted to do when I left school at fourteen. I got a job on a tanker but what I'd really wanted was a passenger ship. I was on the catering side and they threw me on this tanker and I was away for Christmas and I hated it. I jumped ship in Holland because I was so unhappy, but then I found I was an alien without a passport, which wasn't too great. I had no money and I lived on my wits for ten days until I gave myself up to the British consul. I was just desperate to get home but because I was an alien without a passport I ended up in jail. That was the reason I had to go into the army.

When I got home from this ten-day journey round Holland I was only there for four weeks before I was in the army. It was that quick. The medical was in Pownall Square in the centre of Liverpool. I was called up on 28 May 1953, a few days before the Coronation. I regretted jumping ship because I wanted to get into the Royal Navy but they wouldn't have me. I went to the recruiting office and I told them that my uncle was a commander. I could see they were impressed and they took all my details but when they came back they said I was too late. They said my name was on a pair of boots down in Aldershot. That was it.

The letter with the rail warrant said I was to report under the clock at Lime Street station. I knew I was going to the RASC but I'd also fancied one of the Scottish regiments – as a kid I'd been a solo drummer in a bagpipe band for the Boys' Brigade but they wouldn't wear that. I didn't want to join the King's Regiment because I didn't want to be a foot slogger. I wanted to be something different.

I was sent first to RASC in Aldershot. As soon as I got

down off the three-tonner that took us from the station to the barracks, they started yelling at us. I just used to laugh. They used to go mad at you and I kept getting pulled in for laughing at it. I knew you had to conform. You might as well get through it the easiest way you could and that was by conforming, doing what you were told. I used to bull other fellers' boots and get their snout for it. It didn't bother me at all. I quite liked the army in the end. I don't think I ever had to do a guard duty. I was always stick man, the tidiest man on parade, and that's why I never did a guard duty. I can brag about that.

I was told you should never volunteer for anything in the army but I was the reverse. I put my hand up for everything. The reason I became a corporal–batman was because they looked at my record and saw I was a volunteer and that's why I got a good job. I volunteered for the paratroopers' course as soon as I finished basic training and moved over to the Maida Barracks, but I got injured. I'd never worn boots before in my life and they gave me the most terrible blisters. It really got me down. You just got on with it because if you reported sick you had to take all your bedding and equipment and carry it all with you. It was too much trouble.

I'd been in the Merchant Navy so I didn't find life in the army hut too bad, but there were others who couldn't conform and they struggled. It was homesickness for them but I'd been away at sea. I laughed and joked a lot and tried to help that way.

During the paratroopers' course I was put in the boxing ring with an evenly matched opponent and you're supposed to batter hell out of each other. Before you get into the ring you walk down past the officers. I was walking with a marine commando who was six foot two and I'm five foot six. Anyway they took one look at us and they rematched me with a lad from Glasgow with a flat nose and a cauliflower ear. I didn't like the Scots anyway but I knocked the living buggery out of him – through fright. I just never got on with the Scots but apart from them I got on with anyone.

There were some public-school lads in basic training but they were soon whipped out and went off to be officers. I was never particularly bothered by that. One guy I was sitting with on the first exam was very clever and very well spoken. Before he left to go to Wosbe he came to see me and shake hands. He said, 'You're a great guy, George, and I hope we meet again.' When we were doing the paratroopers' course at Maida Barracks, a sergeant in the MPs came in to see me and it was him.

When I'd finished basic training and the paratroopers' course I went to a transit camp. When I got there this guy came over to me and said, 'You're a Scouse, aren't you? There's a Scouse in the nick and he's dying for a smoke.'

I said I'd go round and see him. I went and I threw five Woodies in, and a voice came out and it said, 'I'm bloody sure I know your voice.' I thought his voice rang a bell too and it turned out to be Billy, one of my school mates. We met up a week later when he finished his jankers and we hitch-hiked home together. It took us about thirteen hours to get back to Liverpool and after seventy-two hours back we came to Aldershot, but the train broke down so we were five hours late getting back. Billy says to me, 'George, don't laugh when we get in because I'll laugh if you laugh and then I'll be on jankers again.'

When we got to the gate the provo sergeant came out and he started shouting at us, 'You're late!' but he had no roof to his mouth, this sergeant, and when he started shouting we both started laughing at him and we both got thrown in jankers. Billy was one of those who could simply never conform. He was always in trouble. He ended up doing six months extra.

When I was in the transit camp there were two of us in our hut who had turned nineteen and it was us two who were sent to Korea. I was originally going to go with the rest of the hut to Egypt but because I'd turned nineteen it was Korea. One night I was in London ready to board for Egypt, then the next night I was in Liverpool on the *Empire Halladale* bound for Korea. I never even had time to see the family. I knew a docker who was on board and I wanted to get off the ship and slip home to the Dingle – that was where I lived – so I borrowed his mac and cap but I had my army boots on and when I got to the bottom of the gangway the River Police shouted, 'Aye, aye, there's one of ours there!'

On the way out to Korea, the first port of call was Port Said, then Aden, Colombo and Singapore. We stayed in a transit camp in Singapore and it was about New Year. There was a Scottish regiment there and you know what they're like at Hogmanay. It was like a battlefield – bottles flying, fellers being taken away on stretchers. I was hiding with a couple of Micks. I couldn't get on with the Scots at all.

Korea was my first posting but the real fighting was over. The first night in Seoul we were told we were all going to see a Korean executed. He'd been a spy. We watched this feller blindfolded and then shot. That was our first day. The war wasn't on but we still got medals for going.

My first port of call in Korea was Pusan, but after a few days I was sent on to a detachment in Seoul, which is nearer the 38th Parallel. We were living in a bombed-out school because there was nowhere else to live. They were in tents prior to that. It was freezing. It's cold there nine months of the year. More troops died of hypothermia than gunfire before they got the parkas and the proper gear.

Early on in Korea we were at an army transit camp and we were queuing up for food, and someone says because it was such a big transit camp they served American food. Now the army food was terrible, just awful. The food itself might have been OK but the British army cooks were terrible. So a guy's been served and he passes me and I call out, 'What have you got there?'

And he says, 'Turkey and ham,' and I think, 'Who's he trying to kid?'

Then the next one passes and I ask him and he says, 'I think it's duck.' Duck?! We get to the head of the queue and sure enough it was a turkey roast that was on that night. The food all the time we were at that camp was terrific. You had a choice of turkey, chicken, ham, duck, fillet steaks. Usually it was mince with mash, just horrible food. When I heard we'd be getting American rations I thought we'd gone to heaven.

I was a driver and I started off driving wagons, but I got to the stage where I was driving an officer about. In the RASC you did everything. I drove about four officers but the bloke who got me made up as a batman-driver was Lieutenant Ridell. Not many people liked him but he looked at me, looked at my background and said, 'You're just the type we want.' I drove him around for a few weeks and then I was moved on, but many years later when I was working on the *QEII* I met a priest from Liverpool who coincidentally knew all about Ridell. Apparently he left the army and became a priest, rose through the ranks and was sent to the Vatican. The Pope wanted to give him a really important job in Rome but Ridell said he wanted to help the poor in Africa, so he was sent out there. When he got out of the helicopter in some village he stepped on a landmine, and that was it.

You were only allowed to be in Korea a certain time because of the intense cold, so I did the last six months of my National Service in Malaya. They'd made the mistake of keeping me in Korea for thirteen months when I should only have done nine and when they found out they whipped me out almost overnight – I never got the chance to get a nice fat tip from the very nice officer I'd been driving. He owned fifty-seven chemist's shops somewhere down south.

I actually thought I was being demobbed early because I'd done longer than I was supposed to do. Anyway, when the ship docked in Singapore I found out I was being posted to Malaya. I spent the next few days as a guard on a train going up to Kuala Lumpur and getting shot at by the Communist insurgents – that was the first time I'd been involved in any shooting. They told us nothing about what was going on out there, but it was a war and it was exciting. Lads going out into town for the weekend, one or two of them might be shot or stabbed. It wasn't an old-fashioned battle; it was snipers and that sort of thing. Very different from Korea, where nothing happened and I had the time of my life.

Malaya was frightening. On that train to Kuala Lumpur for eighteen hours I was handed a rifle with live ammunition. Every carriage had a guard with a gun and you were open to the world. It was so scary. In Malaya, driving an officer around, I was supplied with a loaded handgun. And I lost my stripe because I wasn't substantive. Also I didn't read orders properly. I turned the wrong way when I came out of the camp to get to the motor transport yard, which was 150 yards away, and I was up on a charge immediately.

Malaya was very different from Korea. Discipline was far more strict because it was a war zone. We were back to heavy square bashing again. I volunteered for the boxing team to try to make my life easier – you got better food and extra money. The Ordnance Corps in the British Army always had the best boxing team. I only had one fight and I was knocked out in twelve seconds. In fact my entire team got knocked out – that tells you how good we were.

I was counting the days till I got out towards the end. I couldn't wait to get back to sea. I came home from Singapore on the *Devonshire* and we docked in Liverpool in June 1955. From there we had to go to a camp somewhere in Surrey, Kew Barracks, and I got my demob papers. I've kept the report on me: 'An honest soldier and trustworthy. This man has proved himself to be a good driver. He has plenty of initiative and common sense. I would recommend him to any future employer.' You needed that kind of reference to get a job in Civvy Street.

I qualified as a B3 driver and when I came out of the army I did a year as a heavy goods wagon driver, then I was a chauffeur for the chairman of the Watch Committee until I went back to sea. I had that bad record of jumping ship and it took a while to clear that up.

I could say that I loved every minute of National Service but I didn't. Obviously, though, it didn't do me any harm.

JULIAN MITCHELL

1953–1955

Royal Navy

The officers in the army went off to Mons, but we were with everyone else and they despised us, they stole everything that wasn't nailed down ... the only person I couldn't get on with was one of the engineers, because he had such a strong Geordie accent I simply couldn't understand a word he said – though nor could anyone else.

Mitchell, Charles Julian Humphrey, Midshipman RNVR. Ship at the time of issue: HMS *Untiring*. There's a picture of me with hair, which I haven't had for many years, and here's my naval identity card and there's my submarine underneath. Naval identity card no. 202213. Flag officer submarines. The number you want from me went straight out of my head as soon as I became an officer. The navy was really only interested in officers.

You joined the RNVR at school and you had to do two or three weeks in a school holiday. I was determined not to go in the army. My brother had been in the army. He'd been at Catterick and he described being surrounded by people from Newcastle. First he couldn't understand a word they said and second they stole almost everything.

I was born in 1935. My father's family came from Portsmouth. He was in the navy during the war and I come from an interesting seaman-like background. My great-great-grandfather was a notorious smuggler in Portsmouth and I'm sorry to say he was sent to the House of Correction, as they then called it, for smuggling tobacco, so there's always been the idea of sailing in the family. Apart from one summer holiday in Cornwall I didn't spend my childhood messing about in boats like *Swallows and Amazons*, despite the fact that my father had been in the navy. When I was about ten or eleven the idea was that I would eventually go into the navy and that meant I would go to Dartmouth, but luckily that was abandoned. I hated the CCF at school. I found it really boring. I wanted to go into the navy because I was looking for an easy option.

My father was a lawyer in the City and I grew up all over the place. We lived in Bishop's Stortford initially and he commuted into the City, but then war came and he went into the RNVR and ended up as a commander at the Admiralty helping to plan for the postwar world. He went back into the City but he decided he wanted to live more grandly than we'd done before the war, so we went to live in Gloucestershire. We were sent to prep schools and then to Winchester. Winchester was an army school because the 60th and the Rifle Brigade were based in Winchester and lots of boys went into them.

The war was very much still in our minds and it was assumed that some form of military life would go on for ever.

I really didn't want to go into the army. Everybody did National Service, but I thought there were better things to do than be chased round the parade ground, even if you got eventually to be an army officer.

I hate to say this but it's true – the public-school system had its own class system. Eton and Winchester and Harrow and Rugby thought themselves much superior to a lot of other schools and we were taught to think that. The preacher at the service on Sunday told us that we were particularly special because we were being educated at this great old school and as a result we owed something to society. The more special we were the more obliged we were.

Winchester was supposed to be a very brainy school. It wasn't particularly brainy at all unless you were a scholar, which I was not. They were middle-class people and they became surgeons and lawyers or they were in the wine trade – all very conventional so to go into the navy was quite unconventional. It had all sorts of advantages, one of which was you didn't have to stamp your feet on the parade ground. This went back to the days of sailing ships when one watch was always asleep below and didn't want to be woken by heavy boots trampling overhead, so the navy doesn't stamp.

The corps at school was technically voluntary but of course you had to join. I didn't enjoy it and I looked for ways of getting out of the duller bits – that's why I joined the naval section. There were only half a dozen of us and we sat in a classroom and tried to do knots and various other naval things which I never learned to do. The navy was a means of escape from the army for me and it seemed much more romantic.

When I left Winchester to do my National Service I

believed I was going to go up to Cambridge, but I had no plans beyond that other than knowing that I didn't want to do any of the things my parents had suggested to me. I wasn't hostile at all at that time to the idea of National Service. The notion of the soldier citizen goes back to the Greeks – if you are part of society you should defend it. If the citizens don't, the chances are the state will be overrun by barbarians. It wasn't until I got to Oxford afterwards that I began to question it all and become more radical.

We were certainly very unquestioning politically in those days. We were very patriotic, we'd won the war and we were endlessly in chapel; there would be a hush and then there would come an announcement that a boy had been killed doing his National Service, a boy that we'd known. The head boy of the school was killed in Malaya. That caused a great sense of seriousness which was probably lacking before – it gave us an understanding of the real danger. When I was doing my National Service I remember reading in the paper that one of my contemporaries had been killed in Malaya – shot by his own soldiers because he had a terrible stammer and he couldn't get the password out. Nice boy too.

We didn't really expect to see action but we weren't particularly alarmed by the idea. Some people in submarines when I was there did things secretly, like going as far north as Archangel where they listened in to Russian signals. They did it in the Baltic, in motor torpedo boats. Before I went into the submarines there had been a terrible disaster when HMS *Affray* went down with an entire class of sub-lieutenants, so there were dangers other than just warfare.

I was called up in September 1953 so I was here for the

Coronation. My brother and I sat in the House of Lords stand and it was so cold on 2 June 1953 I can barely describe it – freezing wind, and I swear there was snow blowing along the Thames.

The navy was my first experience of real life. At the time I went into the services I didn't know I was gay. I assumed that the boys I was sleeping with at school were just a passing phase. People talked about sex the entire time but being gay was not an issue for me. The first great shock that every public school-boy got was that the word 'fuck' was in every single sentence. We were aghast and when we went home we couldn't tell our mothers because they'd be very shocked.

We had a medical but that was just a day trip and they said I was A1, so I went back home again and waited for the call-up papers to arrive. There was no emotion really when the papers arrived. Everybody had to do it, my brother had done it. There was of course a certain fear of the unknown because I had no idea what was going to happen, but I took it more or less in my stride. I'd been head of my house at school and won various prizes for this, that and the other. I think I must have been very arrogant but in a sense that's what public schools did to you. You might not have been as self-confident as you looked but they certainly taught you how to look self-confident, and those who couldn't show that self-confidence suffered rather.

The National Servicemen who went into the navy were mostly supposed to become officers, though not everyone made it. We went to Victoria Barracks in Portsmouth, which has now been pulled down. It had long been condemned and half of it had been bombed in the war, and we were in constant danger of being hit by falling bricks. In our first dormitory (I'm not sure we called them dormitories), some people had already been to university, so the person who was put in charge was the oldest person, a man by the name of Sowerbutts. He was not at all pleased to have been put in charge. We Winchester boys thought he was rather northern and we were a little surprised to find ourselves under the authority of somebody called Sowerbutts. The class system was very much in evidence.

The navy wasn't nearly as awful as the army but you still had to lay out your kit in a certain shape or form. It was very stupid but it's actually quite important in the navy, because there's almost no room on a ship. Everything has to go into the smallest possible space. If you see these people who sail around the world, everything fits inside something else. I had a locker and everything had to go into that locker. So you had to lay out your kit in a special way and your trousers had to be folded seven times. I was really bad at that. I do remember the first morning getting up and cleaning my teeth with particular thoroughness, because I felt that everything might be inspected. I was pretty fit, so I had no problem with the PT, and I liked games. We did a fair amount of marching about but not too much.

One day a warrant officer came round to inspect and this was where the class system came out very strongly. He had worked his way up from the ranks to become a warrant officer. He must have been in his thirties and I can't remember his name now. He hated us because we were snobby and young and talking posh, so he was very rude to us all about our kit. He gave us a little talk about how we all thought we were so wonderful but we weren't. Nobody had ever talked to us like that before, in that class way. He told us we had no right to think of ourselves in that way. He was very neat, crisply dressed with very short hair. The hatred just gleamed from him. I don't know if he did that to every class – maybe we were just a particularly awful lot.

One thing about the navy I thought was absolutely marvellous. Everyone took turns at being in charge of the platoon and we had to go and salute the officer in charge, and because we'd been in the corps at school we were frightfully efficient and smart the way we saluted. They were terribly laid back and relaxed, and I was very impressed by that. The navy wasn't snobbish like the army. There was no equivalent there of the Guards.

The first six weeks was waiting to go to the equivalent of a Wosbe, but in the navy it's called a CW Board – Commission and Warrants Board. They started training us in very basic things, like Morse code. This was the equivalent of the army's basic training. We peeled potatoes and we were shown films about VD – I missed that, to my great disappointment, because I was on guard that day, but everyone else came back white-faced. We were on guard at night, walking round the barracks carrying a gun that had no ammunition in it because I suppose they thought we would shoot each other by mistake. We had no idea what to do if someone came over the wall. We weren't allowed out for a long time, which made us all feel like we were back at school. My brother said about the boys in the army who came from Newcastle that they had never been away from home before and that they would cry for their mothers. We had been taught not to cry for our mothers, so we didn't.

The exciting moment was the CW Board. I'm sure it was the same in the other services. They gave you a bucket and a ladder and a piece of rope and said somebody was trapped in a crashed aeroplane and you had to get them out before the avalanche started. They still do them. It was a bit like one of these television shows. Some people were really bad at it and got very flustered. Also we each had to give a talk for five minutes. I suppose they must have given us a subject – I met someone the other day I was in the navy with and he said he had to talk about armchairs.

What I do remember is that I passed but two of my friends didn't. This was a terrible blow for them, a bit like failing your eleven plus. I think they were sent back and had to be ordinary seamen, whereas those of us who had passed were sent off to HMS *Indefatigable*, which was a vast aircraft carrier with something like 1500 trainees on board. We were called upper yardsmen and we wore a special white thing round our hats so everyone could always see us and it was obvious if we were doing well or badly. The rest of them were people directly from HMS *Ganges* or the other naval recruiting places. We all lived in one hangar and we were under constant siege from the class war that was going on. On Saturday nights when people came back drunk, it all started off in dry dock in Plymouth where there were only something like a hundred lavatories for two thousand people – it was very unpleasant. There was a Sailors' Rest Home we could go to at weekends. That's where you could get a decent bath or a shower. Conditions were very poor.

Then we set sail for Portland and the training in the harbour there was very intense. Everything was divided by mess and one day a week you were a cook for the mess. You had to fetch the food from a central place, cook it, do the washing up and take the gash – gash is the naval word for rubbish – to the gash chute, which just dumped it into the harbour. It was very cold indeed during the winter months but we had lessons all the time about navigation, how you transferred people from one ship to another, refuelling . . . it was quite a cramming course, but I imagine the army was pretty much the same. Every day started with scrubbing decks. The petty officer had woken us by banging with a stick on whatever made the loudest noise, shouting, 'Hands off cocks, on socks.' We slept in hammocks, my first time for that experience – I don't think my back's ever recovered. We were in great rows of these hammocks and if anyone felt the urgent need to wank during the night everybody woke up.

In the navy – and I'm sure in the army – there were a lot of boys who had grown up in children's homes. They were extremely hostile to us who were going to be officers and there was one boy who got into trouble all the time because he would get drunk and start fighting us every Saturday night. That was class warfare at first hand, no mistake about that. The officers in the army went off to Mons, but we were with everyone else and they despised us, they stole everything that wasn't nailed down. We had to carry many things backwards and forwards and people were always losing soup spoons and God knows what, and if you did you were in trouble.

During those first three months on the aircraft carrier we had to keep a journal. Now I rather fancied myself as a writer and I got absolutely furious if some sub-lieutenant dared to criticise my prose style, but in general the officers in charge of us were very nice, very sympathetic. They could be critical if our shoes weren't polished to their satisfaction, but I don't remember anyone particularly sadistic apart from that one warrant officer who hated us. Their tongues could be quite rough, though, on occasions. Petty officers certainly held the petty power. They could stop your leave and that was important – there was very little to do on the ship, so we looked forward to going ashore on weekends. A lot of people got drunk and got into fights of course, but I wouldn't like to make it sound terrible, because it wasn't.

I volunteered for submarines because I didn't want to be on a big ship. Being on a big ship as a midshipman was the lowest of the low. Midshipmen in the navy are known as 'snotty'. In other words you're a useless young person whom everyone can despise, and on a big ship you never did anything interesting at all. If you were lucky you might be allowed to drive the admiral's barge but that was about it. We went out one day on a submarine and I got talking to members of the crew, and they told me that a submarine is so small that the men on it are a community in a way that a big ship can never be. From the point of view of a very junior officer you had real things to do, you had a proper function.

By the time I was finished I was the navigating officer of my submarine and I knew more about it than the two officers who were senior to me. I was also torpedo officer, though we didn't have any torpedoes, and gunnery officer, though the only guns we had were six pistols which we had to fire off once a month. We would go on deck and throw bottles from the boardroom parties and try to hit them with the bullets from those pistols, and I think that in all the months we did this we never once hit a single bottle. It is incredibly difficult from a moving ship to hit a bottle in the water. I don't think we ever hit one.

I don't think I learned too much about anyone else at the beginning, when we were all in this large hangar on board the aircraft carrier, but I certainly did when I got to be a junior officer on board a submarine. There were only three or four officers on this tiny submarine which carried maybe forty or fifty people altogether. That was when I got to know everyone on board; the only person I couldn't get on with was one of the engineers, because he had such a strong Geordie accent I simply couldn't understand a word he said – though nor could anyone else. That was when I really got the benefits of the social mix, because although there was a class system operating between officers and men, everybody's life in a submarine depends upon everybody else knowing what to do in an emergency. Now the cook's name was Rasmussen – he must have been Danish – and everyone knows that cooks are famously not the most highly educated of people, but he knew rather better than I did what each pipe that ran through the galley was for and what you had to do under certain circumstances. Everything was marked in different colours.

You were allowed to volunteer for where you wanted to go in the navy and I wanted to go abroad. I thought that if I were in the submarines I'd have a very good chance of getting to the Mediterranean or Australia or somewhere like that – there was a flotilla based in Malta and one based in Sydney. Guess where I was sent? Portland. I spent almost my entire National Service in Portland.

As a junior officer I was in charge of the correspondence and because of that I got to know a great deal about people's lives. One man had an illegitimate child and he wanted to marry a woman who wasn't the mother of his child. A lot of the problems were to do with pay. Most people had their pay sent to their wives, but his pay was docked to send to the mother of the child. One or two weekends a month we were allowed to go home, but he told his wife that he only had one weekend leave a month and on the other one he went up to London, got himself picked up by a gentleman in Victoria station, earned quite a lot of money over the weekend and got it sent home to his wife.

It was a friendly place. I was extremely lucky. I had very nice captains. A friend of mine aged eighteen or nineteen and also ex public school was an officer too. One of the sailors came up to him and said, 'Sir, I wonder if you could help me. My wife's gone frigid on me.'

We didn't sleep on the submarine, we slept on the depot ship. My captain and my first lieutenant on the depot ship were both married and they had married quarters on shore. They went off to see their wives and I was allowed to sleep in their cabins, but one of the warrant officers on the depot ship found out about this arrangement. He thought that all National Service midshipmen were scum so he made sure I went back to my hammock like everyone else. The warrant officer rightly felt that men like him weren't treated as proper officers. There was always a class thing going on. I imagine the RAF might have been more democratic because it was newer and therefore it didn't have all these old-fashioned traditions.

I was paid twenty-eight shillings a week and I kept it in a money belt which I always wore. There was a ritual involved in being paid. You took your cap off and put it down and the money was placed on top of the cap. The petty officer who taught us about this in basic training said, 'Whatever you do, don't keep your French letters in your hat because you don't want them falling out in front of the orficers.' None of us had even seen a French letter at that time.

One of my duties on the submarine was to pay the crew. I had to go to the pay office on the depot ship and count all the money and take it back to the submarine. I was always terrified I might have done it wrongly because if I was short I had to make up the difference myself. There was a rum ration but I wasn't allowed that until I was twenty. I wasn't allowed to drink beer but we drank ourselves silly on gin, brandy and whisky. In those days the navy got very cheap liquor and tobacco because it protected the British merchant fleet. A bottle of brandy was about five shillings. A man would come in from Benson & Hedges who sold alcohol as well as cigarettes and we drank in vast quantities. I had had the occasional glass of wine before but it was in the navy when I drank seriously for the first time. I remember standing on the deck of the ship and seeing two lighthouses at Portland Bill.

I read a lot of poetry when I was doing my National Service, and I spent a lot of time writing. The only two excitements we had were when we sailed up the Seine to Rouen to show the flag and once when we went to Ostende. On the first occasion one of our servicemen was drowned and nobody knew how it had happened. He disappeared and he was found dead in the Seine. We assumed he'd got drunk and fallen in. On that trip one officer gave us some very serious advice about what to do when we went to the local brothels. 'If you want to avoid the clap,' he said, 'you go up the backside.' And guess who was the only one of us on that trip to get the clap? Him of course. It was a serious offence to get the clap. It meant you lost money.

We would go out to sea, dive, stay dived, have lunch, come back up and go back in again. We played the mouse to the cats upstairs. One day we got lost. We were towing a buoy behind us, but the wire parted and it went one way and we went the other way, so the ship that found the buoy thought we had sunk without trace. We stayed in the same place, but when the wire snapped and we parted company with the buoy it went out to sea and they all followed it.

We were having lunch down below when we heard the sound of twelve explosions and that meant we had to surface immediately. We started to come up and the captain stopped at thirty-two feet and looked through the periscope. 'Good God,' he said, 'what's happening? There are ships everywhere.' It was such an emergency. It must have happened on a Friday because my parents were going down to the country and at Paddington station they saw some *Evening Standard* special about it. By the time they got home it was all over, but they certainly had a bit of a scare. I remember climbing up the ladder into the depot ship and someone was waiting for us white-faced.

We went to Rosyth once and I spent a lot of time in Edinburgh. Another time we went up to Loch Long. We were firing experimental torpedoes. They had compasses in them so they could turn round. Only they didn't. One of them ran ashore and blew up a transmitter.

Somebody was killed when we were practising with torpedoes using a new form of propulsion, hydro-peroxide or something – it exploded and a man was killed. What united the whole ship, indeed the whole flotilla, was the behaviour of the press. The man who died had been living with his young wife and child in a caravan somewhere on Portland

Bill. The press got in and took photographs of them and the hatred of the press was absolute. We really hated journalists. There was a very strong sense of community. We talked of ourselves as the cavalry of the navy, but it wasn't that. It was the smallness of the submarine and the fact that if anything went wrong we were all in trouble. We had to practise getting out of a submarine, so a huge tank was built in Portsmouth. I was hopeless at it and I knew if anything happened I was never going to escape.

These boats had been built during the war and were not meant to last, and this was nearly ten years after the end of the war. They worked on hydrochloric acid batteries, or on diesels when you were on the surface, and the combination smell of diesel oil, acid from the batteries, salt water and smoking – because everyone smoked all the time – meant that your clothes absolutely stank, and so did you. People would go home to see their wives, who were repulsed by the smell. That was very unpleasant, I must say. I am amazed by how much we smoked. It was almost compulsory. All the captains smoked, so we all did.

I never got out of Portland. Some of my friends went round the world, but I don't regret what happened to me because I got to know people. I would read poetry, or maybe the novels of D. H. Lawrence, and these chaps would come and talk to me about it. But it worked both ways because I learnt a lot about them. I remember being on watch one night and overhearing a conversation between two men who were discussing sex. One of them told the other how he told a woman he was wearing a condom, a Frenchie he called it, but then fooled her by taking it off before he came. I was quite shocked by that.

That kind of discussion was completely absent from my knowledge of life.

It was a real eye-opener to listen to men from all over the country telling me things about their lives which were so different from my own. A Cornishman would tell me about his life in Cornwall. We had a signalman, a Welshman from the valleys, and he explained why the Welsh hated Churchill because of the Tonypandy riots. That was a shock because Churchill was such a huge hero. It was not a sentimental education.

Portland itself was a most dismal place. HMS *Osprey* was there, which was where sonar training took place – that's the noise made by sound going through water with all those pings. I had a friend I'd been to school with on one of the frigates and he told me that one night one of the sailors tried to kill another one with a bread knife. That was an eye-opener for him. Drink was usually the cause of trouble.

Portland was quite nice in summer to go for a walk on, and Marie Stopes lived in one of the old lighthouses – so there was this phallic object with Marie Stopes inside it – but mostly it was a dismal town. When the depot ship was away once we had to stay in pubs there and that was awful. The pub keeper was a dreadful man – constantly drunk. Weymouth on the other hand was quite nice, particularly in the winter when all the crowds had gone. There was an excellent second-hand bookshop there and the man who ran it used to talk to me and recommend books. I was educating myself during National Service.

At that stage I couldn't decide whether to be an actor or a poet when I left university. I wasn't made fun of or victimised for such aspirations, not at all. I wrote my poems and sent them off to small magazines who returned them all fairly smartly. I was reading some poems by Alan Ross, who had been in the navy himself. My captain read the book and gave it me back without a comment. Those officers were a very decent lot. They were probably much too nice and maybe that's why none of them got very far in the navy. You could get to be a captain quite young, but to get on further than that was quite tough.

We had some excitement when *Above Us the Waves* was made and you can see me standing behind Donald Sinden in a few scenes. The cast were frightfully generous when they left – they gave us a dartboard.

There were always troubles with sailors who wanted to get out of the navy because they'd signed up for such a long time. They would cut off their fingers with a penknife or they would damage the engines. They would be sent off to prison and there would be stern words from the captain, and they would be described as ullagees, or maybe it was sullagees. It was a word everyone hated. That happened more on the big ships than the submarines. On the other hand you did meet people like the man on the *Indefatigable* who was a double-bottomed stocker. He'd been on that ship for years and years and never got transferred. He was like something out of a story by Herman Melville, like Barnaby the Scrivener. He was probably only about forty-five but he seemed to me like the Old Man of the Sea.

Britain's place in the world might have been slipping but the navy was certainly in denial about that. They saw Great Britain as one of the great powers of the world and the Royal Navy was integral to all that. One summer the American navy arrived in port. We were frightfully shocked that the officers and men called each other by their Christian names. We thought that was disgraceful. They had more advanced submarines than we did.

We were always training people from abroad and in the build-up to Suez we were asked to take out some Egyptian army officers – my job was to show them around. The crew were really rude to them, didn't like them at all, called them wogs. It was these Egyptians specifically they didn't like, not all wogs generally. One of the Egyptian officers tried to win favour by offering sweets round which were refused by absolutely everyone – I don't think they had a very good time with us. I think this might have gone back to the war, when a lot of Egyptians hoped the Germans would win the battle of El Alamein, but thinking back and knowing now that Suez was only a year away maybe there was a sense of apprehension. One must be careful about looking back and reading things into it with the benefit of hindsight.

I was very against Suez, but I'd been at university for a year by then and life was very different than it had been in the summer of 1955. Everybody could see that the British government was telling lies and if we wanted to control the Suez Canal we would have to do it by some other means. I went on the Aldermaston March and in the 1959 General Election I voted Labour, which was not how I had been raised. I was never an extremist. I was always rather cool. The change didn't really happen in National Service though. It happened afterwards at Wadham College, Oxford. My father wanted me to read law but I fought him and we settled on PPE, which I gave up after a year. Instead I read history, which I loved. I went to a college that was almost entirely without public schoolboys and when I met my new student colleagues for the first time they were horrid to me for being posh. I didn't think I was posh. I thought people who went to Christ Church were posh. That's where all the lords went. I wasn't radicalised at all until I got to Wadham, where I turned against the riding and hunting world. I found it all very tedious. I liked riding but I found Gloucestershire society pretty dull.

I realised at Oxford how badly my school had prepared me for life. It had prepared me well enough to be an officer in the navy but not for life in the wider sense. I had gone to a ghastly prep school that was designed to get people into Eton with the sons of lords whose fathers had been killed in the war. I felt out of it because I was much more middle class. You really wouldn't have noticed at my prep school the huge social changes brought about by the Attlee government.

I wouldn't say I was unhappy during National Service but I was bored. I never felt that I was particularly well suited to life in the navy. I felt I could do it – indeed it was suggested that I stay on. But most of the time I was bored being stuck in the harbour. It was like being at school. I couldn't wait for it to be over. My National Service was just an extension of school. I loved going to sea on a fine summer's morning, sailing along the Dorset coast, and I liked sitting on the bridge, so some of it I clearly enjoyed.

I was supposed to go back to the navy for three weeks in 1956 because I was obviously in the Reserve, but I got out of it because someone wanted me to crew a yacht going from the Isle of Wight to the Mediterranean. The navy said that was fine, though as it turned out we never got further than

Cornwall. After that I was never called back, even though I believed that I was still a temporary acting sub-lieutenant. In fact I had a third-class railway ticket to Fort William, to which I suppose I would have had to report, but I lost the warrant. Anyway, I thought my position in the Reserve went on for life, but apparently it stopped when I was about forty.

I'd been intellectually starved in the navy. I was frustrated and I suppose I resented those lost two years of my youth, but I did notice when I got to Oxford that those of us who had done National Service were far more mature than those who had come straight from school. They all seemed very young and we didn't muck about. We were much better students. The conversation in the wardroom had been very pleasant but rather banal – they were nice people but they didn't question anything. At college I met people who questioned everything, and so of course I questioned everything too. The grammar-school boys I found there had a much bigger effect on me than the working-class Geordies, Scotsmen and Welshmen in the navy because they were my intellectual equals.

JOE TROTTER

1954–1956

Royal Army Pay Corps

You were called out and told where you were going. The officer called my name out and said, 'Trotter, MELF.' I thought, 'Where the bloody hell is Melf?' Then I found out it was Middle East Land Forces and I thought 'Gawd help us.'

I was born in 1936 in the old City of London Maternity Hospital on the corner of Old Street, so I'm a true Cockney because I was born within the sound of Bow bells. My dad was a carpenter and my mother was a seamstress. Her family came from Wapping and my uncle used to take me to watch Millwall. I had two younger sisters. We lived through the Blitz, though we never went down into an air raid shelter – Mum didn't like them because she thought they were full of mice and rats. We lived in a basement and we used to get under one of those old kitchen tables when the bombers came over.

Dad was very political. He was a founder of the old Finsbury

Labour Party before the war so I was delivering leaflets for the 1945 election. Politicians used to give speeches on street corners in those days and us kids were encouraged to jeer them if they were Conservatives. My wife's mother always called Churchill a warmonger. Most of my friends went with me to the local secondary modern. A couple went to the grammar school and one went to St Martin's School of Art, but there was no stigma attached to going to a secondary modern.

I didn't have an apprenticeship when I left school so I had to do my National Service when I was eighteen. I did odd jobs for a signwriter, then I was a typewriter mechanic for a small firm in the City. I didn't want to be a carpenter like my dad but three years after I left school I was doing National Service. I had to sign on first at the local Labour Exchange, then some time after that you got a letter telling you to report to Tavistock Square for a medical. It was just like the film *Carry On Sergeant*, standing there without a stitch on, being told to cough and all the rest of it. I got the letter to report to Devizes in Wiltshire in August 1954. Apart from hop picking in Kent that was the first time I left London. I can still remember my army number as a private in the Royal Army Pay Corps. It was 23059598 and my rifle number was C1917.

I did ten weeks of basic training. I was told never to volunteer for anything, but when they measured me up for the uniform I was told to tell them the boots were pinching so I didn't get the pimply ones, because when you got to bullshitting you had to use a candle and a spoon and smooth them all down. If you complained and said they pinched you might be lucky and get a pair of reconditioned officer's boots, and they weren't too bad to spit and polish.

I met lads from Yorkshire and Sunderland. I had to ask the Geordies and the Scots to speak slower because I couldn't understand them. You go into different companies when you arrive for every intake. I was told to make the best of it because if you fight it you'll have a terrible time. When I arrived at Devizes station there was a lorry waiting and they called your name out and got you in the right one. Then when we got off that's when the shouting started – 'Get in line', 'If you cried when you left home you'll be crying more when you leave here' – all the old favourites. It was the educated ones who struggled most. One of them came from Bristol University but had a thick beard, so if he shaved in the morning he needed another one by lunchtime and they kept back-squadding him for it. He was on jankers all the time, working in the cookhouse or running round the square with his pack on. I felt very sorry for him.

We lived in a Nissen hut, with a stove in the middle of the room which had to be cleaned up but gave out very little heat. We didn't have lockers, we just had a peg where you put your spare kit. It was all about getting kit ready for inspection – how to press your trousers and so on. Some lads just couldn't do it. If you had a hole in your sock you had to learn how to darn it. You had to polish your boots and iron the laces. First few days there was a lot of crying because the lance corporals picked on the weakest ones. After that you just got on with it. I slept on the floor before the inspection because I didn't want to mess up what I'd laid out. They used to love tipping beds up so it went all over the floor after you'd spent all night bullshitting. They got us in a competition – one platoon against another – and you wanted to be the best so you had to work together. Some of those lance corporals were quite sadistic.

We had to learn how to do hospital corners and the sheet had a line down it, so that line had to be in the middle. Some fellows couldn't do that so you had to help them out. You had to do all this stuff with sheets and blankets which you had to fold and turn over so it all looked like a square box, with your greatcoat behind them and your battle dress behind that. When I was mayor of Islington people used to say I had the shiniest shoes they'd ever seen – I used to spit and polish them. My dad used to say to make sure I polished the back of the shoes as well, because when you went out of the door they might be looking at them.

It got easier towards the end of the ten weeks of basic training because you knew what to expect, and then you were building up to the passing-out parade. My dad came down for that. We got no time off; what time off we did have we concentrated on getting things right. We were paid twenty-eight shillings a week and we had to make provision to send money home (I think I sent seven shillings), and when I got caught not having shaved properly I was ordered to go down the NAAFI and buy a new razor and shaving soap – all of which of course I had to pay for. I kept my money in the map pocket of my trousers. I kept it wrapped up in a handkerchief so it wouldn't rattle when I was marching.

After the passing-out parade we did some overseas training in Devizes because the Wiltshire Regiment training camp wasn't too far away. You were called out and told where you were going. The officer called my name out and said, 'Trotter, MELF.' I thought, 'Where the bloody hell is Melf?' Then I found out it was Middle East Land Forces and I thought 'Gawd help us.' After the overseas training I had twenty-one days' embarkation leave, then I went to Ash Vale just outside Aldershot and got kitted out with lightweight uniforms and so on. I was there for a week, so at the end of the day I could get on a train to Waterloo and be home every night.

The Royal Army Pay Corps had a big pay office in Fayed in Egypt, so I knew I was going there. I was shipped out three days before Christmas 1954. It was the only time my mother got upset. Before we left we were in a holding camp on Goodge Street, so it meant I could get the number 30 bus home every night till we were taken to Stansted for the flight.

When we got out there everyone knew you were new because you had white knees. You worked outside stripped to the waist and you hung your battle dress out in the sun to bleach it. One of my first jobs was to repair the colonel's typewriter, but it needed a new spring and I couldn't do it. I know it wasn't a holiday but I went on a trip to see the pyramids while I was there.

The local Egyptians were lucky if they had jobs in the British army camps. The dobie wallahs who did the laundry, the cleaners who did the sweeping, at least they had a job rather than walking round the desert unemployed. It wasn't our fault we were shoved there. I was there till April 1955 when the British started to move out of the Canal area. Everything was loaded onto landing craft and we were all taken to Famagusta in Cyprus. From there we went on to Dhekelia, which was south, on the way to Larnaca.

When we got there we liked it. It was greener than Egypt and fresher, and there was fruit growing on the trees alongside the road. The lorries would stop and we would pick up water melons. Even the barracks were new maisonettes with tiled bathrooms. The NAAFI was modern and there were tennis courts and everything. I thought tennis was a cissies' game till I got there. They had to carry me off the court, I did so much running around. It was like a holiday camp.

The RAF had bases in Nicosia and Akrotiri out in the west of the island, but the Green Howards used to do ceremonials at the governor's house before the troubles started and that's where I met the film composer John Barry. All the corps were out there – the pay corps, the service corps, REME and so on. The regiments, like the Green Howards, had their own camps. When the Green Howards went home the Middlesex Regiment took over.

I was in charge of the post, bringing in the mail bags from the main Nicosia office, which was why I was made up to lance corporal. It was a security thing, looking after the money in those bags. I got another fourteen shillings, I think, but I had to increase the amount I sent home.

Before the troubles you could see Greeks and Turks sitting outside those little cafés playing backgammon. The married personnel were actually living in the town, like in Larnaca. We had to do foot patrols down there with a sergeant major or an officer and we would make sure the married couples were OK. We'd have dinner with one and supper with another. It was something you volunteered for. We were a peacekeeping force really. When the riots started in Larnaca a curfew was imposed and the various corps used to do their patrol so the Middlesex could have a rest. The trouble came from the Greek Cypriots, who wanted union with Greece, and then that was resisted by the Turks, who didn't. They had good jobs on the army base. We had cleaners who would do all the cleaning of the bathrooms and the toilets except before a big inspection, when we were back to cleaning the urinals with a razor blade and all that malarkey.

We got on better with the Cypriots than we had with the Egyptians. We could buy cigarettes for a shilling a packet and if we were invited for dinner in the town we'd take these packets of fags but all that stopped when two soldiers who weren't in uniform got shot one night. We couldn't understand why Archbishop Makarios was causing so much trouble because the Greek Cypriots we met were being treated really well by Britain and they were exporting fruit and veg there. We couldn't understand what benefits they thought they were going to get from union with Greece. The British deported him and the next day the riots really broke out. Colonel Grivas was the leader of EOKA, the Greek Cypriot nationalist military resistance organisation, and Sir John Harding was sent out as the British Governor.

I stayed in Dhekelia till July or August 1956. We came home on the *Empire Ken*. That was like a holiday because we didn't have to work and we were sunbathing all day. We stopped at Tangier to pick up fresh food and we were allowed ashore for a couple of hours, and then we sailed to Malta. As we pulled out there was a troopship pulling in, and the men in the regiment on that ship were on their way to Suez because that was starting to build up to when Nasser seized the canal and there was all that trouble. Eventually we got back to Ash Vale, where we saw the blokes who had been in the reserve being dragged back in ready to be sent out to Suez.

When I came back I was signed off by my local doctor, who was a friend of Dad. He tried to persuade me to become a carpenter like Dad but I still wasn't interested. I got a job with Viota in their factory that made cake mixture. I was a dispatch manager. Viota merged with Robertson's the jam people, who made the golliwogs, but they moved the production process up to Bromborough in the Wirral.

I think National Service was a good thing. It taught you a trade, it taught you discipline, and it taught you how to look after yourself. And everyone still comments on how clean my shoes are. That was National Service in a nutshell. And I still press my trousers, though I don't do it with brown paper. It wouldn't do today's lads any harm. But I think you always remember the good things, don't you?

HUGH HUDSON

1954–1956

Royal Armoured Corps

We had these sadistic sergeants – probably homosexual – unmarried often, though not always. These men had eighteen-year-olds under their control, completely green, from different backgrounds, and these sergeants were very cruel – not physically, but you got the feeling they took a sexual pleasure in their sadism, without a doubt. They were horrible.

I went from Eton straight into this other world. It was the armoured corps, the cavalry as they called it, but I went into the ranks. I went in January 1954, just before rationing completely finished, but things hadn't changed that much since the end of the war. It was all very austere still and the Conservatives were well entrenched. It was winter. It was absolutely freezing and I was sent to Carlisle Barracks, right up by Hadrian's Wall. Most of the boys I'd known at Eton went into the Guards but I wanted to go into tanks.

I'd been in the CCF at school but I can't say I enjoyed it much, I suspect it had been compulsory. I do remember we had lined the route during the funeral of King George VI. The funeral service was in St George's Chapel in Windsor Castle, so the cortege came from Paddington to Windsor by train, and being the school next door we lined the route.

I remember that brown envelope coming through the door containing the rail warrant and my heart sank. You know it's coming but you don't know when, except you know you can't get out of it. However, I have to tell you it was probably the best thing I ever did. I'd come from an elitist atmosphere, full of snobbery and untold riches – which my family didn't have. My parents were divorced so I lived with my mother and stepfather near Bath. I was only sent to Eton because my grandfather, who had been an MP in the nineteenth century, had put money away specifically for that purpose – my father was a poor farmer in Dorset and he had no money. He was a writer, wrote many books on Russia on which he was an expert. He was also a very powerful lay figure in the Church of England and later in his life became involved in ecumenical movements between Canterbury and Rome. He was a very good man.

I didn't see my father much, but it was his father who had put the money aside so that his grandchildren could be educated at Eton. That was where he had gone, as had his father and his grandfather and so on, so it was a family tradition – but I hated it. I didn't have enough money to keep up with the people at Eton who were part of the financial elite. That's why I've been a socialist all my life, and that's why I understood Harold Abrahams [the character played by Ben Cross in *Chariots of Fire*]. That's why David Puttnam was so clever in casting me as the director, because he knew that I would understand the class structure and Eton and Cambridge and all that. What Harold Abrahams was fighting against because he was Jewish ... well, I understood all that. I remember Jewish students at Eton being appallingly treated. I don't think the Holocaust had much impact on those people. If the Nazis had defeated us they'd have been sending all the Jews to the camps. I haven't got a single friend from Eton days.

To be thrown into the ranks was wonderful for me. National Service changed my life. It made me see another part of the world and I became good friends with people from a different class, people with a completely different experience of life from myself. The start though was a physical struggle because it was extremely tough. I was fit – you're always fit at eighteen – and of course I'd played an enormous amount of sport at Eton because a great deal of emphasis was placed on it. I was pretty average at most sports – cricket, football, Wall Game. I'm making a film about another Eton rebel – George Orwell, otherwise known as Eric Blair. He was a Colleger, in other words he was there on a scholarship, and on the whole intelligent people like him who became Scholars were looked down upon because it was sporting prowess that was important at Eton, as well as the elitism of it and the snobbery.

I left in the summer of 1953, went back to Bath and then to Carlisle in January 1954. Some people deferred by going on to university first but I didn't want to do that, I was waiting for that brown envelope. Nowadays people finish their schooling and are free to do what they want, but we weren't. We had another two years to go of service – or rather education, because for me National Service was definitely an education.

I could have gone to Kenya, I suppose, or Cyprus. I could certainly have gone to Suez. Our regiment was on stand-by for that and if it had gone on a little longer we would certainly have gone. The tanks would have been planed or shipped out.

We were at Carlisle for basic training, for about ten weeks or so, and then I think we were sent to Catterick. I could have gone into officer training but I turned it down. I didn't want to perpetuate what I had hated at Eton. I did not like what I had seen at school. I come from a very traditional family but I did not want to become an officer in Her Majesty's Army, I wanted to have the experience of meeting the rest of the world.

I was intrigued by these guys, ordinary people who would go out for a drink in a pub, look for girls, go to the local dance, try to pick one up. I had had a very privileged middle-class education and I was curious about this other world. If they had a negative image of my lifestyle I don't remember them saying it, because we were all thrown in together into basic training and it didn't much matter where you came from then. You helped each other through the endless bulling – polishing your boots so you could see your face in them. If someone didn't know how to make a crease in his trousers or make his bed the right way you helped them because that was the camaraderie you experienced. Beds had to be made a uniform way, like in a hospital, with everything tucked under and away, and some people couldn't manage it so you helped them. Some people couldn't iron or sew and you helped them. You learned all these things. I can still sew. I do it now. I can knit. I can darn socks. Actually I love ironing. I find it very relaxing. We learned all those things that normally men don't learn.

We were up very early, 6 a.m. probably, and we were woken

by reveille. Up. Doing whatever you had to do that day. If it was an assault course you'd be checking your boots, then you'd have to drive trucks, that sort of thing. As far as I was concerned I'd probably give myself about seven out of ten for attitude. Peeling potatoes though was hell. You had to put up with potato duty but there were a lot of them because we had chips with everything. There were mounds of potatoes. You needed the food, you needed the fuel for what you had to do.

It was complete bullshit and everyone complained all the time, but you had to do it. If you resisted you were excluded and put on a charge – sent to the guard room, extra guard duty. That was hell – up all night, freezing cold, then you were straight into whatever you had to do the next day. You didn't have a day off because you'd been on night duty. You had weekends off but not during basic training. It was horrible. Constantly cold, constantly hungry. We were issued with eating irons at the beginning and you kept them with you at all times. The uniform was awful too – the roughness of it, thick khaki, disgusting – awful underpants. Everything itched. Maybe there was a purpose to it, I don't know. Maybe it was planned that way to make sure that you did what you were told, so if you were told to go over the top of the trenches and get yourself machine-gunned by the Hun you would do it. That was the army at its worst. Bad decisions made by the brass at HQ getting young men killed.

It was bleak and sparse up at Carlisle and at Catterick. We had these sadistic sergeants – probably homosexual – unmarried often, though not always. These men had eighteen-year-olds under their control, completely green, from different backgrounds, and these sergeants were very cruel – not physically, but you got the feeling they took a sexual pleasure in their sadism, without a doubt. They were horrible. We had to do the most ridiculous things – painting stone, painting coal white, that kind of rubbish. I was often in the guard room on a charge of smoking on guard duty or sleeping on guard duty. The philosophy of the discipline was to reduce us all to one common denominator. It took all the stuffing out of you, and all the background, except of course I couldn't change my voice. I suspect I was much more plummy then than I am now.

People got badly picked on for their physical inabilities – their inability to march properly, their failure to handle the assault course. They'd been very rough and tough, mind you, at school. There were steeplechase runs that went on for ever, almost like a marathon. They were once-a-year events and they were absolute hell. I was forced to do those at school, so I didn't really mind the assault courses. The best preparation for a life in the army was a life at a public school.

After a year I realised that I might as well take the commission because you got paid better and life was a little more comfortable. My father had been in the cavalry and maybe I thought there was a little more glamour in being a tank officer. I certainly didn't want to march all the time and being in the tanks I could ride, but of course it was much more dangerous. A shell goes inside a tank and that's it, everyone dies. I didn't think much about dying at eighteen, though.

I went down to Mons for officer training. I wanted a short commission for a year and I only just made it, I think. I was made up to second lieutenant, or a cornet as it was called in those days in the tank regiments. Then we were shipped off to Germany for a year where I had a great time – it was really so relaxed then. It was quite a change after the start we'd had.

We were in Luneburg Heath in north-east Saxony on the German border. The nearest town was Hamburg and we were frequently patrolling the border just across from the Communists. There was a large expanse of no man's land and at the end machine gun towers and border posts. We had the tanks and our job was to demonstrate our force on this side, the West German side.

It wasn't the first time I'd been abroad but it was the first time I'd had any taste of foreign life. We were horrible to the Germans, terrible. We were supposed at this time to fraternise with the Germans and try to be nice to them, but there was a lot of hatred going on still and on exercises we paid absolutely no attention to the farmers, we drove across their fields, ripped up their crops and let off our blanks inside the courtyard of their farms, which blew all their windows out. We weren't supposed to do it – it was against the army code of practice. We were meant to treat them well, but we didn't. We were irresponsible and pretty horrible. I didn't particularly like doing it but we did it. If you were on an exercise you just went and you didn't pay any attention to anything else. I think we were supposed to keep to the roads but often we didn't, we just took the short cut. Those exercises were very interesting. They went on for perhaps five or six days and you slept outside, or inside the tank.

We went into Hamburg when we could. I remember the Reeperbahn of course, because we were always looking for sex. The object was to try and find a girlfriend. Sometimes you went to a brothel and sometimes you found a girlfriend in the wives of the officers, but that was a lot more dangerous. A major or someone could be sent back to England on a course but the wife had to stay in Germany because the kids were out there with them in the barracks. A lot of not very good stuff went on, because some of those women were very attractive. We were very young, we were eighteen or nineteen, and they might not necessarily have been our first girlfriends, but in many cases that was where we had our first fuck. Maybe the marriage had been going for ten years and the wives were lonely and bored and a young subaltern comes along . . . it's just human behaviour.

I went sailing a lot up in the Baltic. Five or six of us would get a weekend leave and we'd go up to Kiel, rent a boat and set sail across the Baltic Sea towards Denmark.

When Suez broke out we were told that we were being held in reserve but we could expect to be sent down there shortly. Of course we'd been in northern Germany and we'd had no desert training at all, so God knows what sort of a fist we'd have made of it if we had gone. We were supposed to go as peace-keepers. We weren't first forces in but we'd have gone in like they've done in Iraq to mop up after the first wave. I've had a soft spot for the Egyptians ever since Mohamed al-Fayed put up half the money for *Chariots of Fire*.

I started putting on concerts, sketch shows for Christmas and special occasions like that, written and performed by the guys in the regiment. Some of them would dress up as women, classic stuff like they did in prison camps. Remember that scene in *The Great Escape* when the escape is happening whilst the Germans are watching the concert party? It was a bit like that. I ran that and of course everyone thought I was gay. I was not, though I was a bit different – I didn't like riding for a start – but the key thing for me was that I was already directing.

I know I struggled to win that commission in the Royal Armoured Corps but when I was commissioned as a second lieutenant I really enjoyed the experience of command. I loved working with the troopers. It was like a film set in that everyone had some sort of expertise. You have an expert cinematographer like you have an expert driver who is brilliant at driving a tank. You have a navigator like you have a first assistant director. Everyone has a job to do – like an air crew. Everyone depends on everyone else, so it's perfect training for being a film director.

From the age of fourteen all I wanted to do was to be in the film business, so as far as National Service was concerned my only thought – at least at the beginning – was to get it over with as soon as I could and come home. Before the end, though, I was thinking I might stay in for a bit longer on a short-term commission. There was a bit more money involved and I enjoyed my time in Germany. We were sent down to Salisbury Plain to do some training for tanks, gunnery – all that stuff was great fun. Moving across the countryside at high pace and having that machine under one was really quite attractive. I ended up having six Conqueror tanks under my command. It was a pretty good life. Officers didn't have to do much. They were reasonably well paid, all their food was paid for, they had good accommodation and if they were married they had married accommodation. What a wonderful carefree life. There was no major war. I enjoyed my creature comforts as an officer. I had my own room, a batman, the officers' mess and so on. The drink was flowing and it was cheap.

I got on very well with most of the guys on National Service. I did not go into a clique with guys of my own class. National Service mixing people up from all the classes was a great idea. They should do it now but I suppose it's not much of a vote-winner. I was twenty when I left National Service and I had no doubts that what I wanted to do was somehow to get into the film industry. If I'd not done National Service, if I'd gone from school say into the City or even straight to Sandhurst, I wouldn't have got to know other people outside my own class and I would have been a less interesting person.

JOHN SNOAD

1955–1957

RAF Photographer

The day I arrived at Cardington happened to be the same day that Colin Cowdrey was called up. He was met by twelve group captains, so my first impression of the service quite frankly was bloody awful. We were treated like animals and he had twelve senior officers greeting him. I never saw him again.

I was born on 9 January 1934. My parents were both brought up in orphanages, my father in a most Dickensian one, and I know almost nothing about it. My mother came from a very unusual place (it would probably be called today being 'in care'). She was brought up by an upper-middle-class gentlewoman who had inherited a large home but very little money. My mother therefore had no money but she was very well read, very well educated, and had very middle-class values. I sense there was a slight conflict between my parents on that score.

My father managed a jeweller's shop and was surprisingly well educated considering his background. I learned to play the piano when I was young and it was years before I realised he could read music. My mother then explained that he used to play the banjo in a cinema orchestra for his beer money. That was a surprise. I started life in a flat in Tooting in south-west London and just as I started National Service they bought a house out in Raynes Park. I have to say I had rather an unhappy childhood and I went off family life a bit.

I didn't like primary school but after the eleven plus I got into a technical school. It was a small unusual school in Westminster, only twelve or thirteen to a class. From there I went to Dorman Long, who had a huge steel works and drawing office next to Battersea Power Station. It was very strict, no talking, very harsh discipline, but it probably set me up quite well for National Service, which was a holiday in comparison – an unwelcome holiday but easier than the drawing office. I was an apprentice at Dorman Long for five years before I was called up for National Service. My exemption ran out the day my apprenticeship finished and I got my call-up papers a week or two later, so I went into the RAF on 22 June 1955. I was asked which service I wanted to go into and I chose the RAF. Very few people got into the Royal Navy and I didn't fancy the army, so I thought the RAF was a realistic choice. I started out at Cardington and then got sent to Hednesford.

The day I arrived at Cardington happened to be the same day that Colin Cowdrey was called up. He was met by twelve group captains, so my first impression of the service quite frankly was bloody awful. We were treated like animals and he had twelve senior officers greeting him. I never saw him again.

I think he had flat feet and was invalided out so he could play cricket. He certainly never went into an airman's mess.

I had always been very interested in photography and though I had no money I saved my pennies and made my own camera and slide projector. I made some 10×8 prints from the best work I'd done and some little 5×4 prints that would go in my wallet. When they asked me in the RAF which trade training I wanted, I said that I knew it was difficult for National Servicemen but I wanted to be a photographer. I thought if I was going to be in the cookhouse peeling spuds I wouldn't have access to the 10×8s but I'd always have the 5×4s, and that's exactly what happened. Some chap looked at the prints and much to my surprise he picked up the phone and called RAF Wellesbourne Mountford near Stratford, where the School of Photography was based, and I was booked in for an examination.

Eventually I got a call to go off to Hednesford for basic training, and when I got there ... I don't want to sound conceited, but there were only three of us. The other two were professionals and they both failed – I was the only one who passed. It was an absolute pantomime. Despite the fact that I owned a Weston Master exposure meter at home, when I got there they wouldn't give me one. They said I was an amateur and I wouldn't know how to use one. They were very annoyed that they were given an amateur photographer and two professionals. They were furious with the selection officers and they were quite rude to me. It was a long test, four or five days, but I passed it easily. Mind you, I had a friend in the barracks at Hednesford and he got two stripes because they made him a dispatch rider. I thought when I'd passed that test they'd make me a marshal in the air force but all I got was AC1.

I'd always been interested in industrial photography, technical things. If they sent me off somewhere to take photographs I always came back with the goods and the others didn't always do that. The sergeant who ran the place couldn't afford that because very often there was only one chance.

There were two schools at Wellesbourne Mountford. One was airfield construction, teaching people how to mix concrete and build runways that they would dig up a week later, and the other was this school of photography. I did the eight weeks of basic training at Hednesford and I got taken away to do the week's trade test, and when I came back I had to do the small arms test, which I managed to get through otherwise they would have back-flighted me. I had to go up in front of someone and present arms and all that silly sort of thing. They didn't like back-flighting so if they could get you through they would, and I stayed with the same group for the rest of basic training so I only did seven weeks in the end. I was quite fit, I used to cycle to work; I wasn't athletically fit but actually I found basic training as far as the fitness was concerned to be a bit of a doddle – though I did find it stressful, I must admit.

The shouting didn't bother me but it seemed to me that some of the training corporals were very aggressive and that did worry me. I found that the NCO who shouted the loudest was actually quite lenient, he was really all right, but the quiet-voiced one ... he was the one you had to watch because he was really nasty. I thought he needed a psychiatrist, he was a baby-faced nasty box of tricks. I kept my nose clean and my head down, although I nearly got into trouble once for smiling on parade. This corporal put his nose almost against mine and yelled.

They did try to persuade me at one point to go into the RAF Regiment – that's an infantry regiment within the air force for protecting airfields. It was a tough place to go and I wasn't having any of it, though they tried their hardest to make me sign on for it. By that time I had my trade and the last thing I wanted was to do soldiering, which I'd tried to avoid in the first place. I hated all those inspections, if you got things half an inch out of line they threw it out of the window, but to be honest it wasn't that difficult. The people who got things wrong were stupid. One lad did his shoelaces up crossed even though we'd all been told to do them up straight.

It was a real mixed bag in the barracks. Some were very well educated, obviously officer material, and some were quite badly educated. What shocked me was the poor living standards. Some things annoyed me intensely. There was a washhouse but we never had any hot water and even the cold water ran out sometimes. The sanitation was awful although the food at the training camps was much better than the food I had afterwards. Somebody must have made the decision that men under training needed to be fed properly. I was quite surprised at how good the food was but the washing and the toilets were an absolute disgrace. When I got to the main station it was different but during basic training you had no time for anything apart from running round the countryside, polishing boots or your brasses. Or you were asleep. My National Service coincided with rock and roll and Elvis Presley but one of the things I hated about the services were those loudspeakers with all that horrible piped music. I missed classical music and I didn't respond to rock and roll at all.

At one point I got German measles so I missed another few

days. Reporting sick on basic training was a serious matter but in the end I had to go. I found out afterwards that they fumigated the station after they'd diagnosed what I had. Again I had to prove myself so that I wasn't back-flighted. I got a bit of a bad name for bringing German measles into the camp. How I got it I don't know, but as I said the sanitation was very poor. We had only cold water for eight weeks and that couldn't have helped. It was a good job it was summertime.

I could have – should have – applied to become an officer and, looking back on it, it seems silly that I didn't. But the truth is that I resented being there. I thought it would be joining the Establishment. One day I and about four hundred others were marched off to a building I'd never seen before with a lot of men from other flights I'd never seen before, and we had a lecture from an officer on what a good life we would have if we had a career in the services as officers. Apparently Hednesford had a reputation as a training camp for officers, so you were sent there originally if they thought you had potential. He said at the end that anyone who didn't wish to become an officer could leave, at which point everyone in the room got up and started to file out. He then lost his temper completely and screamed at us to sit down again. He thought 390 out of the 400 would apply and when he found no one did it undermined the whole philosophy of the camp.

I remember thinking at the time how crass the whole event was. Not one thing had been said or done during the previous few weeks that would have made a service career the least bit attractive to anyone who was not already interested. In fact they could not have done a better job of putting us off. One idiot had ordered us to cut a lawn with scissors – and blunt ones at that! This made me realise that men in the ranks were looked upon as low-class labourers, were of no importance, and that the services were really divided into two – the real service consisting of the officers, who seemed to live in a different world. I thought this ridiculous, particularly on a highly technical station where all the aircraft servicing was carried out by men in the ranks. In fact, the lives of the flying officers depended on them.

I did my technical photography at RAF Odiham, near Basingstoke in Hampshire. When I was at trade school they asked me where I wanted to go and I suggested the Far East so of course they sent me to RAF Odiham. It was a 1930s station with conventional brick buildings. People were divided according to trades, so all the airframe fitters were in one building and I was in the odds and ends collection. There was a flight sergeant there who couldn't count past twenty and I spotted this, so I took a huge gamble and avoided parades because he hadn't realised that I was there in the first place. I spent the next eighteen months on that station never going on parade, apart from the big annual one where you had to wear your best blues. When that came up for the first time I got a bit worried because he'd see me, so I marched across the ground looking like I knew what I was doing and crawled through a hedge towards a large tree. I started to climb up the tree when I heard a voice saying, 'Give us your hand, mate,' and there were thirty blokes sitting in the tree camouflaged from the parade ground. We all hid in the tree and watched the parade with the band marching up and down. When it finished we got down and nothing happened.

I was friendly with the people I worked with in the photographic unit but they were all time-servers; I was the only

National Serviceman. Most of them had signed on for years and me getting that very good job didn't go down too well. On two occasions it all turned very nasty. They tested new aircraft by running them for a thousand hours with the engines on and refuelling without turning them off. When the aircraft came in it was the duty of my colleagues to go out to them and take the cassette of 16 mm film out of the camera. Whenever the pilot pressed the firing gun it photographed the record they wanted to make. One of the guys who didn't like me asked me to take over for a while. I couldn't see any aircraft on the field at all, but he knew there was one that had been there out of sight all the time and he tried to get me court-martialled. The officer came into the room and blew his top at me, so I had to explain that I'd only just come on duty. I didn't want to get other people into trouble, so my policy was to try and get out of trouble without causing problems for others. I didn't tell him the whole truth. Anyway, he wasn't a bad bloke and I got away with it.

The other occasion was much more serious. I went to a crash site, as I often did, to take photographs, and there was this other man there, a civilian from the Air Ministry. He asked me if I would take his photographs back for processing, which I did, and they turned out to be blank. That had never happened to me before. I never made mistakes. I checked everything very carefully. Looking for an explanation I found that one of the glass bottles in the lab had some acid crystals at the bottom. It had been sabotaged by someone. My background in photo-graphic chemistry was good, so I knew exactly what had happened, but I had to go back to this chap and apologise and say there had been a terrible accident and the film had been lost. I could see the shock and disappointment in his face but he didn't say anything. We parted and he obviously thought that I was some kind of idiot.

I never found out who had done it. There were two men who were very anti-National Servicemen and I assume one of them had done it, but I never found out which. They must have seen me as a pain in the neck, but my behaviour was not bombastic. If anything I was too quiet, so this was just another streak of nastiness. It struck me that some of the men who had signed on full time were a bit odd, as if they didn't belong in the world outside, almost like they were in a monastery. I had very few social graces but these blokes were really just misfits and they saw the services as a hiding place from society.

The time I spent in National Service really dragged and when I'd done a year I groaned because I had to do the same amount all over again. On Wednesday afternoons I used to play golf whenever we had time off because we had free access to the local golf club, and I also did long-distance running which got me away from the place. I had a serious approach and I thought it was all a disgraceful waste of time and national resources. We had a fuel tanker every fifteen minutes, twenty-four hours a day, 365 days a year into that station. That was the consumption level there.

We had lots of crashes. There was a hooter in the office and when it sounded I knew someone had gone off the end of the runway. I had my equipment in a suitcase and a bicycle, and when the hooter went off I grabbed the bike and the suitcase and set off following the fire engine. Very often the planes taking off or landing went through the hedge at the side of the runway, over the country road that ran alongside,

and into the adjacent farmer's field. He never planted anything there, he just ploughed it up and collected the
compensation. They put traffic lights on the road, so anyone
driving along it must have wondered what was going on,
because there were no side roads. When the lights went red
it was because an aircraft was coming through the hedge. We
had an overrun and a serious crash about once a week. On
one day we lost seven aircraft.

My instructions were to proceed to the crash site as quickly
as possible and photograph the altimeter in the cockpit, if it had
survived – amazingly, even with the technology then available,
these were based on the barometer, so if the weather changed
the pilots would fly into a hillside. Sometimes there were bits
of the pilot lying around. I then recorded everything possible
of the remains of the aircraft and of the general damage to the
site. The resulting prints were then used by courts of inquiry,
which I never attended.

A lot of aircraft were fitted with huge wing tanks before they
were flown to Cyprus. Now this must have been around the
time of Suez, and I distinctly remember being home on weekend leave and hearing on the wireless someone saying that the
RAF was not involved, so I knew they were lying. I was very
shocked by Suez. The idea of going to war in a foreign country when we hadn't been attacked appalled me, though I don't
think I ever discussed it with other National Servicemen at the
time. I felt ashamed about it and I thought it was a disaster, but
I wasn't politically sophisticated. None of us were.

When I came out I went back to Dorman Longs and lived
with my parents until I was thirty-two, when they both died.
I then moved to the BBC and spent twenty-five years as an

engineer with them. I built all the high television masts when they extended the broadcasting system.

I appreciated home when I came back after having been deprived of so many things for two years. National Service food was a disgrace. Fancy cooking peas so they tasted like ball bearings! Complaining was a waste of time. There was always a duty officer who never took a blind bit of notice, so nothing happened if you did complain. You only got junk food at the NAAFI.

I think that National Service can only be understood by appreciating British society as it was at the time. It was a very mixed bag of people I met there and if I got anything out of National Service at all it was learning about humanity in general. When I worked in the drawing office there was a terrific feeling of co-operation. We all worked together and when I came out of the RAF and went to work for an American consulting engineering firm, I found exactly the opposite. High pay was there as an incentive but instead of people co-operating in the office they were competitive with each other.

I had been an apprentice for five years in a drawing office where we had to work hard. I had one day a week at college where I took two Higher National Certificates, and I attended night school as well, so that I had experienced no social life whatever and had earned almost no money. Consequently, although I resented being forced to serve, at twenty-one years of age, I found many aspects of the change welcome and the low pay, often the source of complaints from others, was actually more than I had ever had.

I found the lifestyle much easier than my civilian life, with its long hours and hard work. A friend who had been a scientist at

Aldermaston told me that he too had had no social life, and had no intention of returning to his career and his one visit to the local cinema each week. This resentment at having a career interrupted but then having doubts about wishing to return to it and to a lifestyle of routine was also fairly common in the 1950s. It could only have had an adverse effect on the country as a whole.

More seriously, many of my National Service colleagues said that if they had never done it they would have willingly served if there had been a third world war, but, having experienced their treatment and conditions, there was no way they would ever serve again, regardless of the consequences. I was surprised at how common this feeling was and at the strength with which it was expressed. It was entirely believable and I left the service feeling that whilst a few may have benefited, those who had already acquired a worthwhile trade or profession felt it a complete waste of time.

I also felt strongly that the government used National Service to keep the unemployment figures down. I hear people saying, 'Bring back National Service and give the young lads some proper discipline,' but I could have spent two years with dirty underpants as long as there was a crease in my trousers. What sort of discipline is that? Why should the services be saddled with a bunch of hooligans? I think the services were actually relieved when National Service finished.

HAROLD RHODES

1955–1957

Royal Army Medical Corps, Derbyshire & England (RF)

I could give one command to produce maybe a dozen movements, 'By the left, quick march,' and they wouldn't get another command till they finished. That took a lot of practice. I got commended by the drill sergeants for that bit of imagination. You can compare the rhythm and the timing and the balance of a good drill to a fast bowler's run-up to produce a great delivery.

I was born on 22 July 1936 in Hadfield, near Glossop in north Derbyshire, which is where my grandparents lived and where I was evacuated to. My father was a professional cricketer who played for Derbyshire. When the war finished and cricket started again our family came back to live in Derby. We'd lived there before the war but we were evacuated from it during the war because we lived near the Rolls-Royce factory, which was a big target for the German bombers. My father played for Derbyshire until 1953 when he retired. Then he went on the umpires' list and became a Test umpire. I had a trial for the county round about the time my father retired – I was an off-spin bowler then and I batted at no. 5. Walter Robins offered me a contract to go on the ground staff at Middlesex but I preferred to stay in Derby. It had been good enough for my father.

My father was in the Artillery and served in Italy. I can't remember him coming back on leave but I remember when he came back for good. I hadn't seen him for five or six years. I was nine when Labour got in and I think that was the soldiers who thought Churchill was a bit of a warmonger – I don't know. Everyone was fed up with war. My parents were both Conservatives so they were quite surprised.

I joined the ground staff at Derby after I left school when I was fifteen. I was paid about four pounds a week during the summer but I wore a dark blue boiler suit as often as I wore cricket whites. I had to help the groundsman put up the nets and prepare the wicket, I had to move portable stands and screw them together – frightening when you think of how vital your hands are as a bowler! I had an interview at Rolls-Royce but they wanted people who were more mechanically minded to put aeroplanes together. Then I got a job as a clerk with the Electricity Board in the welfare office. I did that for a couple of winters before I did National Service.

I wasn't looking forward to National Service. I didn't know what those two years would do to my cricket career or what it would be like to be away from home for that long. I was apprehensive, but I had a better time than most, I suppose, because I played a lot of cricket. I probably had more leave than most people because I played for Derbyshire during my National Service. In fact in the middle of my second year I took five for 52 against Yorkshire at Chesterfield and we won by six runs.

I had my medical in Derby and a few weeks later I was told to report to Aldershot. The doctor decided I had something called hammer toes, which meant he marked me down so I wouldn't go into the infantry. I went into the police and after I'd done my training, which I started in January and finished in April, I was asked to play cricket for the Army and the Combined Services. I was then transferred to the Royal Army Medical Corps at Crookham near Aldershot. Roger Bannister was there when I was there. He was a second lieutenant, a commissioned officer, because he was a doctor of course.

Basic training was a shock to the system – the discipline and the bulling. You were up till 2 a.m. because you didn't have the expertise to do these things. It takes time. To get rid of the pimples on your boots was a work of art. It wasn't spit and polish because spit made it come out grey. You became quite keen on your smartness. I got bicycle chains that fitted round the bottom of the trousers so you had a nice round fold next to your gaiters and your boots. The regular soldier wouldn't do things like that. He'd just tuck them into his socks or his gaiters. They didn't look smart at all. We had to box the blankets up every morning and make the beds all in line so everything looked smart. You went to a lot of trouble with the ironing. I'd never done any ironing before – and to be honest, I've never done any since – but you learned from other people.

It was a lot like being back at school. The slightest thing would make someone shout at you. To be shouted at for tiny things you'd got wrong was part of the life. You expected to get a bollocking from the corporal. At first I was upset but you got used to it. I did ten weeks' basic training altogether. The physical stuff was no problem for me. There was plenty of homesickness at first but when everyone had settled there was a lot of laughter too. There was a heavy sleeper in our barracks and five or six of us took hold of his bed and moved it whilst he was asleep, so when he woke up he found himself in a different room.

The first fortnight was all about square bashing and getting your jabs and a lot of bull. Then you were transferred to a company, C, D, E, F and so on, for shooting and the rest of it. There was a major in charge of each one. I was in B for the first two weeks, then I went to D. The first fortnight was spent getting kitted out, looking smart and getting used to sleeping away from home. I wrote home to my mum and said I wasn't enjoying it. My dad thought it would do me good so he was all for it. Once I did it I didn't regret it. It felt like a waste of two years at the time, but looking back I understand that it did do me some good.

As the basic training went on you got used to your rifle on the shooting range and to throwing a hand grenade. When I first started firing a .303 I had a bit of trouble with the recoil – I wasn't gripping it hard enough. It was a bit frightening firing that .303 till I got used to it. When I finished basic training I went to F Company, still at Crookham, under Major Ball who was nuts about cricket. I was in the police at the start and we were a bit lenient with the cooks on their haircuts provided we got food in the guardhouse. We used to get extra eggs and toast and things like that. For a period I ate very well. In fact we had a competition in the guardhouse as to who could eat the most eggs on toast. One chap ate fifteen – nobody beat that. It reminded me of Paul Newman in *Cool Hand Luke*.

When I was in the police I had to go to Leeds to pick up a guy called Lynch, who had gone AWOL and committed a burglary. The police had got him but he had to answer the army charge first, so me and a private went up by train and we collected him and signed for him. We had an easy time getting him as far as Waterloo and we had about half an hour before the train was due to depart. He'd been handcuffed to the private and he'd given us no trouble at all, so when he asked if he could use the gents' before the train left I didn't see why not. I told the private to check there were no windows he could get out of, then said he could take the cuffs off and give him a bit of dignity. The private stood outside the gents' and I was leaning on a W. H. Smith's stall so I could keep an eye on the entrance as well. Suddenly this lad came out hiding behind a great big man so that the private couldn't see him. But I did and I yelled out immediately, 'Shoot him!' It was just instinctive. Lynch stopped immediately as soon as the private took his gun out, but of course there were people on Waterloo station hurling themselves to the ground. I got a reprimand for that. I had to report what had happened because some civilian might if I didn't. The reprimand was fair enough. I knew I'd made a mistake.

The police didn't think much of me because I was never there. I was always playing cricket. So they transferred me out of the police and I went into the Royal Army Medical Corps. I was there during the Suez crisis, which blew up after the 1956 cricket season was over. People did go from our place to Suez but because of the cricket I had an idea I wouldn't be sent overseas. Some guys were looking forward to the possibility of action. I think we all felt the canal was an international water-way and Nasser had no right to close it. That meant we had a right to go in there and sort him out. After all, he was a bit of a Hitler, wasn't he?

At the end of forty-eight hours' leave I would return to Aldershot as late as possible. I'd catch the milk train from Derby, which got into St Pancras about 3.30 a.m., and there'd be seven or eight of us piling into one taxi to save money to get to Waterloo and the train to Aldershot. Going over Waterloo Bridge and seeing London all lit up was a magnificent sight.

Ken Higgs from Staffordshire, who went on to play for Lancashire, was just up the road in H&D Company – that was the holding company, which kitted you out when you were about to be posted abroad – and the two of us opened the bowling for the RAMC in Crookham. We won a few cups locally playing sides like Fleet and Aldershot. Ken and I both got picked to play for the Army and then I played for the Combined Services with Roy Swetman. I opened the bowling with Bob Platt, who played for Yorkshire. Roy was the wick-etkeeper when I first played for England. There was a lad in our barracks who played for Chelsea, Frank Blunstone, the outside left, and he was doing his National Service in the 1954–5 season when Chelsea won the Championship. They used to joke in the barracks that he had a pass to get in because he never needed one to get out. He played for the barracks. So did Ken Higgs, because he was on the staff at Port Vale.

I became an instructor and I was responsible for twenty-odd guys in a barrack room. I must have overseen about eight sets of lads, but at the same time I was always likely to be off for a few days playing cricket somewhere. I knew how to drill people and I could do a demonstration with weaponry, and I could do part of the medical side. Some of it needed a doctor but I could do the basic nursing, putting on a Thomas splint for a broken leg or arm. I was taught how to carry a stretcher in a hostile situation with people firing at you. They threw stuff that went bang and gave off smoke, and you had to carry a stretcher in those conditions. I learned how to do a tracheotomy, which I can probably still do.

I kept in touch with Derbyshire CCC all the time. If I got a 48-hour weekend pass I used to go down to the indoor school on a Sunday morning and bowl. I played a lot of cricket for the base and when Higgs and myself opened the bowling we were very successful. Higgsy never went abroad either. We were never close friends. He didn't have much to say. We were rivals in a way, competing to see who could take the most wickets, and he was in a different company. He finished his career like me, playing in the Lancashire Leagues – he played for Rishton and I played for Burnley, starting in the same season.

I was discharged in January 1957. I never thought it had been a waste of time. I did something worthwhile – not just playing cricket. I put maybe 160 to 200 lads through training in a way that they'll remember for the rest of their lives. I always thought I got the best out of people by encouraging them. There was a competition with the other groups at the end of basic training and we won it three or four times out of eight. I could give one command to produce maybe a dozen movements, 'By the left, quick march,' and they wouldn't get another command till they finished. That took a lot of practice.

I got commended by the drill sergeants for that bit of imagination.

You can compare the rhythm and the timing and the balance
of a good drill to a fast bowler's run-up to produce a great
delivery. I enjoyed a lot of what I did in the army – drilling and
weapons training. Many years later I was talking to Stuart
Surridge, who had captained Surrey to County Championships
in the 1950s, and I asked him how he dealt with someone like
Tony Lock or Jim Laker, who could be a bit awkward. He said
he couldn't bollock Jim because he'd go away and sulk. He had
to tell him he was the best off-spinner in the world. He told
Locky he couldn't bowl a hoop down a hill and that he was
lucky to be in the bloody side. Locky would swear and show
the bastard. That kind of man management was something I
used in National Service, perhaps without thinking about it in
quite the same way. It gave people discipline doing National
Service and I think the country was better off when we had it.
I always feel it did me a lot of good. I've often thought that
with all the crime we've got today we should bring back
National Service for a year, but apparently the forces don't want
them.

NICOLAS HAWKES

1955–1957

Royal Hampshire Regiment, 3rd Battalion Ghana Regiment

One evening when my friend James was duty officer one of the drivers came to see him and said in pure Cockney, 'Permission to go to the station and get the pipers, sir.' James said, rather bewildered, 'Pipers? What pipers?' 'You know, sir, the pipers what we get regular like.' 'My dear man,' said James, 'the regimental band isn't expected, is it?' That is not invented. That is a true story because I heard that exchange. So after eighteen months James had no idea how his own men spoke or that he was referring to the newspapers.

I was born in London. My father was an archaeologist at the British Museum. My mother was also an archaeologist and I think they were more in love with archaeology than they were with each other. They produced me in August 1937, and then

I was shunted away first into the country and then to Cambridge. It was a private family evacuation rather than an official one. My parents divorced in the early 1950s and my mother married J. B. Priestley when I was fifteen. It was upsetting because it was so public and in the newspapers. There was of course a great stigma attached to divorce then. Many archaeologists held it against my mother and my father was emotionally wounded for years. At boarding school there was one boy who was nasty about it, but everyone else just got on with their lives.

I went to boarding school at Bryanston in the beautiful Dorset countryside. I missed the eleven plus because I was at a fee-paying school, though the fees then didn't decimate your post-tax earnings the way they do today. I had a background that was very secluded from the mainstream of British society, but it certainly wasn't one of thoughtless privilege. There was plenty of left-of-centre thinking in there. At my public school our image of grammar-school boys was that they were very hard workers. We had an ethos that we worked hard but we couldn't be seen to be too serious about it, whereas the grammar-school boys were going to be seriously hard workers and get the scholarships. We were nervous about them and certainly didn't look down on them – but then we weren't Eton or Harrow. It was more of a literary, artistic and cultural school – we had Robert Donat's sons there and Mark Elder and John Eliot Gardiner. Having said that, outside of my family and friends I don't think I really came into contact with children who had not gone to a fee-paying school. My interests were natural history, sailing and my stamp collection.

My view of Britain's place in the world was formed at first by my time at prep school in London. It was the late 1940s, the immediate aftermath of the war, and we did a lot of history emphasising the success Britain had had over three centuries, but I also understood that there were a lot of economic differences. People were very hard up. I was certainly patriotic and I learned through Jack Priestley that patriotism could be of a socialist kind. I can't date when it first occurred to me, but I did become aware that you could have a vision of your country that was not necessarily based on militarism or nationalism.

From the age of about ten or eleven I read large quantities of boys' adventure stories written by men like G. A. Henty. Many of them were about the Empire and I got very interested in that. When I went to Oxford I maintained my interest, having been posted to West Africa during my time in the army, but because I was now swinging to the left as a general response to the Conservative government of the late 1950s, I turned it on its head and became someone who wanted to go to those countries in order to help them move forwards.

I left school in July 1955 and knew I would go up to my father's old college in Oxford in October 1957 after I'd completed National Service. I was very immature when I was called up. I looked very young and although I had these interests in politics and the world I went about it in a very immature way. My social experiences were very specialised.

I was pretty fit when I was called up. I spent as much time outdoors as I could – sailing, archaeology and natural history were my principal interests. I suppose I was nervous when I was called up, but everyone I knew had done it or was doing it and on one level it was quite exciting, because it was going to be like nothing I had ever done before. Priestley had been in the First World War and he told me stories about the army, which helped. His home out of London was on the Isle of Wight so that was why I was told I was being sent to join the Royal Hampshires. I had to report to Winchester Barracks on 29 September 1955. It seems to my recollection that I had only been there a few days when they started talking about potential officer selection, so the whole question of class reared its head immediately. There were two distinct groups. There were about fifteen of us who had been to public schools and a great mass of men from Portsmouth and Southampton, most of whom had never lived away from home before. A few of them were utterly miserable.

I think the public schoolboys were very anxious not to be prejudiced in any way whatsoever towards the working-class lads, but that wasn't always reciprocated. There was a man called Sid who said to me in his strong local accent, 'I can't stand a bloke what talks with a plum in his mouth.' Instead of always calling each other 'mate', these lads often called each other 'mush'. Being eager to join in I remember calling out to one chap in my public-school accent, 'I say, mush . . .' and they all roared with derisive laughter.

To be an officer you had to have five O levels, so that automatically restricted the choice and cut out most of the working-class men. The September intake of course would obviously include a lot of well-educated boys who had just had their exam results. We did tend to sit together in the NAAFI, as you might expect, so quickly there was a clear social divide. I suppose you could argue that if they said that no National Serviceman could become an officer that would have been much better socially, but of course they needed the officers so they perpetuated the class divisions.

There was a strict process of selection for officers which operated very efficiently. It started with USB, the Unit Selection Board, where extremely gauche young men were weeded out. Later in the training you went to Wosbe, the War Office Selection Board. A tall young captain at Winchester with a weak moustache and spectacles was the personnel officer and we had go along and be interviewed by him. I told him I didn't want to be an officer because I wanted to fit in with the other lads, but he said that he thought all my other friends would go away for officer training and that I would be very lonely.

National Service was a shock because I thought that my personal goodwill would be reciprocated. You could say that this was in parallel to the way I thought Britain's goodwill would be reciprocated by the former colonies.

The last meal on Sunday was at 5.30 or 5.45 and we were doing very energetic things all day so that by 8 p.m. you were ravenous again. I started smoking a pipe just to put something in my mouth.

Those of us who were better educated could internalise things like the number of paces you had to march forward in a certain drill procedure, so we learned quickly. Then we would get bored and our attention wandered and we would get successively worse at it and more ragged, whereas the other men who were less well educated took longer to learn the routine but when they did get it they kept it up till the passing-out parade.

Most of my friends found the NCOs and the army generally just a great big joke. We would do imitations of them and laugh at them all the time. It was quite class conscious because it was the corporals and the sergeants screaming their abuse that attracted our contempt, not so much the officers. They used 'nig nog' a lot – which didn't mean a black person – and they used 'fairy' to mean weak and feeble.

Anyway I did consent to go to Usbe. I passed that and after two or three weeks we were all sent off to Wessex Brigade head-quarters at Topsham Barracks in Exeter. That was effectively the end of the social engineering, because I was on the conveyor belt to becoming an officer already. Some of the people selected were not toffs by any means, although the majority were certainly from public schools. There was a man called Pete whose father was a tobacconist. He smoked like a chimney and at six o'clock every morning he'd get up, he'd suck in his breath and exhale, 'Bastard arseholes!' That's how he began every day. It was best if you just took people as they were.

We did a lot of square bashing, exercises on Dartmoor, and we learned about Bren guns. Because we had passed Usbe we were trained as a separate squad. We took Wosbe during that time and that was when we learned whether we'd be going off to the officer cadet school. There was a nice man called Jim, a slightly owlish youth, as I remember, who didn't pass. Later on in Germany, I was telling a young professional officer about chatting to this man when he was duty clerk and I was duty officer. The lieutenant just looked at me scornfully and said, 'But you're an officer!' So much for social engineering!

I think I looked about fifteen and was very unimpressive when I did Wosbe, but they still gave me a commission. I was OK in discussion groups but there was a practical task where I had to lead a group of men across a 'ravine', represented by a pair of parallel bars, and with cross-pieces that weren't long enough. I'd got my group halfway along when I discovered the bars weren't parallel at all but divergent and we all fell down into the ravine – and yet they gave me a commission! I couldn't work it out and thought they must have mixed me up with a man called Hawker.

We had a hard time at Exeter because the NCOs had complete power over you. I went without weekend leave for a long time. The company sergeant major was sympathetic and one day promised me I would have leave the next weekend to go home to the Isle of Wight. I was on my way to the gate when I bumped into a well-known and ferocious sergeant who seemed to me like a galvanised turtle. But he had many war medals on his chest, and shouted, 'Get over to the cookhouse and report for fatigues!' I said, 'But Sergeant, I've got a forty-eight hour pass.' He didn't care and the officers were too remote to help. You couldn't appeal to them. I did in fact get the pass from the CSM, but this man wanted to cancel my leave just like that.

In that winter of 1955–6, in those bitterly cold conditions at Topsham, I became very ill with pleurisy and was transferred to the Royal Naval Hospital in Plymouth. I also injured my knee very badly on an assault course. Anyway, I was in quite a bad way, but I survived and I got to Eaton Hall for officer training in March/April 1956 just as the weather was improving. I passed out on 7 July 1956 as a second lieutenant. Eaton Hall belonged to the Duke of Westminster; it was an enormous Victorian country pile on a huge estate which was later demolished. We had a very nice man, Captain Ashby, as our immediate commander. The men were interesting there and the food improved slightly.

After I got my commission I was sent back to Winchester with a lot of other second lieutenants, where there was nothing to do. They passed too many people. The officers' mess had been designed by Christopher Wren and it was opposite another parade ground that was used by the Rifle Brigade and the King's Royal Rifle Corps. The Rifles regiments are socially superior to the basic footsloggers. They had to sign our visitors' book in the officers' mess and we had to sign theirs, and we were instructed we were not to be seen while doing so. We had to go out of the building and round the corner and slip in unobserved. There was this great divide between us even though we were the Royal Hampshires. Above the Rifles were the Guards. I don't remember ever speaking to a Rifles officer. We were in the lower barracks, literally and figuratively, even though we were also allegedly officers and gentlemen.

At the end of that boring summer of 1956, maybe in September, about a year after I had been called up, we were posted to the BAOR in Münster in Westphalia. The very first night we arrived, a friend and I wanted to go into town and look at the shops and the people and so on. Most of the officers and nearly all the men rarely went out. It was a foreign country, which by definition I found interesting, so I was interested in what Germany was like, although few of my colleagues were.

As duty officer I knew that from time to time the code word was 'Caribou'. If the phone had rung and I had heard that word I would know the army was mobilising to fight the Russians. As the tension in Hungary worsened in October 1956 we grew increasingly alarmed that we might have to fight. We were young officers and we knew we'd be on the front line pretty quickly. The Russians were a genuine ever-present threat. What was happening in the Middle East at the same time didn't concern us quite so much – a friend of mine thought the whole Suez crisis was a joke – but I had a friend in the Service Corps who was murdered out there. He was lured into a back-street carpet shop in Suez itself and killed.

Now in the 1955 school election, which coincided with the General Election, I had stood as the Conservative Party candidate, and that was only just over a year previously, so even though when I got to Oxford I became relatively radical, I must beware of seeming too anti-government during Suez and Hungary in 1956. I thought the Egyptians might have been perfectly capable of running the canal, but just grabbing it the way Nasser did was wrong.

One evening when my friend James was duty officer one of the drivers came to see him and said in pure Cockney, 'Permission to go to the station and get the pipers, sir.'

James said, rather bewildered, 'Pipers? What pipers?'

'You know, sir, the pipers what we get regular like.'

'My dear man,' said James, 'the regimental band isn't expected, is it?'

That is not invented. That is a true story because I heard that exchange. So after eighteen months James had no idea how his own men spoke or that he was referring to the newspapers.

It was a great blessing, a life-changing blessing, when the signal came through that Second Lieutenant Hawkes was to be transferred to the Gold Coast on New Year's Day 1957. This was because when I'd been at Eaton Hall I'd applied for a colonial regiment, inspired by those G. A. Henty adventure stories. I later heard that the Nkrumah government, which was self-governing and approaching full independence, had asked for military reinforcements because Nkrumah was afraid that the eastern part of what is now Ghana, beyond the River Volta, was going to break away and join Togo. There was a breakaway movement because, geographically and ethnically, the eastern side had formerly been part of German Togo and the western part was given to Britain as mandated territory to add on to the Gold Coast but the people there didn't feel part of the new Ghana. They asked for professional soldiers, not amateur National Servicemen, but what the British army did – which was contemptible – was they pretended we were regular officers when we weren't, although they paid us as regular officers. I drank nothing but orange squash for eight months, saved money and bought a car, which gave me an advantage with girls at university even though we were poor value as army officers. It was just like Winchester that previous summer. There were too many of us, there was little to do and we were falling over each other.

I did exercises in the Togoland area and that was quite exciting, far better than Germany. It was an adventure. I was on secondment from the Royal Hampshires to the Royal West African Frontier Corps, which stretched all the way from Nigeria to the Gambia. Within that was the Gold Coast Regiment, which became the Ghana Regiment, and I was in the 3rd Battalion. The HQ was in Accra where there was a lieutenant general and a major general. There were three battalions in the regiment and they each had a commander.

I certainly didn't think I was there to keep the natives down. I was far too idealistic for that. Our numbers, compared to the population of Ghana as a whole, were quite small. It was only after independence that the numbers of security personnel went shooting up. The colonialists managed the country with very few people. The first Sandhurst-trained Ghanaian officer came to our battalion whilst I was out there. A couple of Ghanaians had been sergeant majors and they were given commissions, but there were only a few black officers and the rest of us were white British.

When we arrived we went to see the brigadier. We soon discovered that if you liked horse riding you went up to the north of the country, but if you were a social person who liked parties you stayed in Accra. I was keen on sailing, so I went off to Takoradi in the west and loved it. Takoradi Harbour had been one of the first big colonial development projects in the 1930s and there was a sailing club there. I couldn't believe my luck. The brigadier, Pat Heywood, was a nice old-fashioned man who took snuff and wore a monocle. He had a young wife and three children scampering about in short trousers, and he took a fancy to me because I understood his Latin jokes. I got the impression that he liked the company of this fresh-faced young Classics scholar. I drank orange squash in the mess and sometimes played High Cockalorum on Saturday night. That was supposed to be a team game but really it was just upper-class roughhousing. It would be banned by Health & Safety now but it was great fun in the mess.

I was in Accra for independence on 6 March to help manage the independence parade. There was a big camp where all the Commonwealth troops were based – British, Canadian, Nigerian, Indian and so on – and they needed latrines, which I had to check. There was a dreadful man in charge who smoked cigars with the label on, which was considered very low – he was a major but he was not a gentleman. Anyway I had to go off and check the latrines. I came back and reported and then I asked what I was to do next, and he would sniff and say, 'Just go off and check the latrines, Mr Hawkes.'

I would say, 'But sir, I've just checked them.'

'Check them again please, Mr Hawkes.'

The other thing I had to do was to collect twelve gross of French letters to give to the men for their visits to black prostitutes, who didn't interest me at all. I was very virginal. And of course we didn't understand the damage the sun could do. I remember seeing men with dreadful blisters on their shoulders from sunburn.

Princess Alexandra represented the Queen and I thought it was a good thing that Britain was conferring independence on Ghana. I went back to Takoradi at the end of March 1957 and stayed there until August. It was only about fifty miles to the Ivory Coast from there. I shook Nkrumah's hand in June that year when he came through Takoradi on the way to boarding a ship that was taking him to the Commonwealth Prime Ministers' Conference. I was in charge of his meal in the officers' mess. I was very keen on Nkrumah though my mother, despite her very liberal opinions, was a bit racist about West Africans. The old-style African politicians, who were well educated but who had worked in collaboration with the British, were firmly rejected at the polls in favour of the less well educated and much more self-interested Nkrumah people and the net result of that was bad. I think Ghana would have had a far better first few decades if those older men had been left in charge. But it was democratic and it was much like the people of Gaza electing Hamas.

We had to wait until there were enough trained officers to take over. The emergence of Lawrence Okai from Sandhurst showed this was starting. In the meantime we continued to enjoy ourselves. Recruits from neighbouring territories like Niger and Burkina Faso poured into Ghana because they were far better treated by the British – pay and conditions were much better than where they came from. Like most British soldiers I loved the men from the north and the local villages, but we had no time for the clerical lower middle class, savvy boys who were neither 'properly' native nor 'properly' British. Of course that was very condescending.

On my way home I made what I considered to be a semi-corrupt deal. My parents had a lot of connections all around the Mediterranean. With two friends I arranged that the first-class tickets which, being officers, the army had provided for us should be converted into second-class tickets for a longer, more interesting journey. We went to Tripoli, Malta, Rome and Nice and we had a whale of a time. The other two had had enough leave to have got as far as Timbuktu; I had wanted to go there but the best I could do was a trip on a motorcycle to the Ivory Coast along the beach road. We had a lot of time because there was so little to do, and there was little to do because they had passed too many officers. If I had spent my two years mucking in with the rest of the chaps I would have become a much more rounded person socially. There would have been more social mixing, more social engineering if you like, if far fewer people – especially from privileged backgrounds – had been commissioned.

My life, my career followed this pattern. G. A. Henty, the colonial regiment in Ghana, the left-wing shift at Oxford, and finally going to work overseas as a teacher, so you can see how vital National Service was in shaping the rest of my life. In the short term National Service meant that I was less immature when I got to university, but in the long term it was part of that process that dictated the course of my life.

BRIAN SAYER

1955–1957

RAF Driver/Mechanic

We found our camp at Mafraq surrounded by Iraqi troops who arrived overnight, covered the entire perimeter and dug in, so there were 25-pounder guns pointing inwards at our camp. It was total panic in the morning, because if they had wanted to wipe out the whole camp it would have taken them no more than ten minutes to do it. We were told to dig slit trenches, and we were all wondering what bloody use was a slit trench when you were facing a 25-pounder artillery cannon.

I was born in December 1937 in Carlisle and my connections with Carlisle have stayed pretty strong. I still have a lot of friends and relatives there. My father was very badly wounded in the First World War. He ended up working in a bakery on the delivery side, looking after the wagons and the horses. My mother was born in Sunderland, though she moved to Carlisle when she was five, and she had a very difficult background too – her father died when she was very young. She worked at various jobs including Liptons, the grocery store in Carlisle. In 1937, with the aid of his war pension and a loan – I think from his own father – my father bought a new house on London Road, which was quite a nice part of town. It was a comfortable three-bedroom semi-detached house which had cost eight hundred pounds to build. My parents had received only the most basic education but they were entirely supportive of whatever I chose to do.

The smallest class I was in had forty-two kids and the largest was fifty-one. You had tests at the end of each week and the result determined where you would sit for the following week. I was about sixth or seventh in the class as a general rule. When I sat the eleven plus I didn't pass for the grammar school, though I was expected to, so I went to the Creighton School for Boys. I don't think my parents were particularly upset. It was an odd school because it wasn't a secondary modern. I thought about being a cartographer but eventually I decided I wanted to be a teacher.

There wasn't a sixth form at the Creighton but you could transfer to the grammar school if you wanted to do A levels. That's what Hunter Davies did before he went to Durham University, and if I'd had the right kind of advice that's what I would have done because it would have meant that I missed doing my National Service. You could defer if you went to university but if you were going to a college you had to do your National Service first. If you decided to go to college it was only a two-year course, whereas for a university it was three years, and of course there were financial implications in that. When you go into the armed forces you get paid peanuts – not even your national insurance. There were no continuing benefits.

The careers advice at school was very poor and my parents were just pleased that I wanted to become a teacher. Nobody in the family had done any higher education before. I was planning to go to a Church of England teachers' training college in Chester which was well regarded at the time. I was pleased to get in there and they held the place open for me whilst I did my National Service.

My father had been a sporty young man, but he'd had most of his legs shot away in the First World War when he was eighteen and he told me that if I went into the army I'd be cannon fodder. I knew I got seasick easily so I applied for the RAF. I had my medical in Carlisle Castle, which I passed A1. My call-up date was 1 September 1955. My parents were going away on holiday at the end of August and my mother didn't want me to go off to RAF Cardington from an empty house, so I went with them to Cornwall for a few days' holiday and then I got the train from Cornwall to Cardington.

I got kitted out and then I went to lectures on what the RAF was about and what being in it entailed. I was apprehensive and anxious. This was the first major move for me from being a schoolboy to doing something that men did. I knew I was going into another world, but I didn't know what it would be like even though I'd heard all sorts of tales about square bashing. My father could enhance those dark tales quite graphically, so I wasn't exactly filled with joy when I went in through the gates. Everyone felt the same way, but I felt very young on the bus going from Bedford station. There were people there who were twenty-two or twenty-three and they seemed very old.

The shouting at Cardington wasn't too bad and for a couple of weeks it was quite gentle. At the end of the second week we were on the parade ground and this guy read out 'Sayer – Hednesford.' There were a lot of places I could have gone to, like Padgate up near Warrington, but I'd never heard of Hednesford. It was near Cannock Chase and very much off the beaten track. When you went in you didn't know what to expect. They had a parade ground the size of four football pitches. You also had tests to decide which trade you were going to follow.

I can still remember Corporal Beacham, the most foul-mouthed man I had ever met in my life. I'd never come across anyone like that. The language was a shock at first, but when I was in a billet with twenty other men and I was eighteen and they were older you soon got used to hearing it and swearing became the norm. The humour I sometimes found difficult to take because it was directed against someone personally. It could be very cruel.

I could march in step with a rifle, but one guy called Cox who was very bright – he'd been accepted at Oxford or Cambridge – he simply could not march and keep his arms and legs in the right order. I can still hear the cockney drill sergeant shouting at him: 'Fackin' 'ell, Cox, 'ow many fackin' O levels you got?'

'Twelve, sir.'

'And how many fackin' A levels you got?'

'Four, sir.'

'You got twelve fackin' O levels and four fackin' A levels and you can't put your right fackin' foot in front of your left fackin' foot.'

Now if you're not the one being picked on that's quite funny – until later, when you realise that poor guy must have gone through agony. This drill sergeant would have the poor lad marching by himself up and down the parade ground from one end to the other. Then he would get to the end and the drill sergeant would shout 'About turn!' and he would have to march all the way to the other end. And he had to do this for an hour. He was a very withdrawn guy and for all his academic skills he had few social skills, so no one asked him to go down to the NAAFI and have a drink, however much we sympathised internally.

We had the inspections of course, and you got used to getting up in the morning and folding your blankets in a neat arrangement and making sure that there wasn't a speck of dust anywhere in the billets. The corporal, who had a little room at the end of the hut, and the officer would come round and inspect and I kept thinking what a waste of time it all was. The officer would put his stick in the middle and drag it off the bed onto the floor and say, 'Do it properly.' You couldn't see anything wrong with it but there'd been one tiny crease somewhere. I thought that was stupid and there was a lot of bitterness about what these people were doing to you. However, we were powerless and the best thing you could do was to keep your nose clean. Otherwise you'd get the same sort of treatment that had been meted out to poor old Cox.

The discipline affected different people in different ways. The way I grew up I questioned things – though that was due to my naivety. Corporal Beacham would have said it was the way to instil discipline. As he used to put it, 'When I tell you to jump you jump, and you ask why on the way down.' The discipline was probably less severe in the RAF than it was in the army, but it was still there and that was what the square bashing was for.

We also went on exercises on Cannock Chase when we had to camp for the night and make our own food, which was better than square bashing, and we also had rifle practice and handling machine guns, which I found quite interesting. I learned a lot about how to fire a rifle – which I never did – but I knew how to strip it down.

The guys in my billet came from all over the country. The one in the next bed to me came from Wigan, so we had a northern connection, but there were men from London and Scotland, all over the country. There was one Scottish guy and when I asked where he came from, he said something I couldn't understand at all so I said 'Sorry' and he repeated it four times, but I was no wiser. Eventually it transpired it was a town near Glasgow, but I simply couldn't understand what he was saying. People came from diverse backgrounds – from school, from jobs, from university. I didn't have any friends who had jobs and those who were earning decent money suddenly found themselves on twenty-eight shillings a week minus deductions. Regulars got five pounds a week but if you signed on it had to be for three or five years. Some people took the money, but I had no interest.

You could volunteer for officer training, but I remembered my dad talking about life in the trenches and how the officers were the first to be killed, so I wasn't that keen. However, you had mess bills to pay and you could end up with a debt when you left, which I didn't want either – though I think that was more the army than the RAF. I was too young and immature to have been chosen anyway – I just didn't think I was mature enough. Most people didn't want to go down that path. Maybe I should have had the experience of applying.

It was suggested to me that I follow a technical trade like an electrician, but I refused. I said I was going to be a teacher, so I'd quite like to train as a driver, but I was told I'd have to sign on for five years. Eventually I was allowed to put down 'driver/mechanic' because I really didn't want a clerical job. I was told they never gave driver/mechanic postings to National Servicemen, so I was astonished when eventually they read out who was going where and the man said, 'AC Sayer 2768290, you will be sent to RAF Weeton near Blackpool to be a driver/mechanic.' I thought I'd won the battle, but as it turned out it was a false dawn.

I knew Blackpool pretty well because I'd been there quite a bit on my holidays. We used to go the first week in September so my dad could go to a couple of football matches – we were also quite near Bolton, Blackburn, Burnley and Preston North End, as well as Blackpool. I found the trade training to be OK in that at the end of the week, when we had tests on what we'd learned, I did pretty well. But although I acquired some technical knowledge which I could reproduce, I'm not sure I was any the wiser as to how to repair a truck if it broke down. I came out after eighteen weeks not knowing much more than I went in. That was the nature of the course and the way it was taught – all I really got was the very basics. There wasn't much driving, I have to say. The emphasis was always on the mechanical aspects, which was disappointing. And if I'd been on the front line during the war and had to mend all these wagons I'd have had a lot of difficulty. What I did learn came mostly from other people who were much more competent than I was, rather than from the course itself.

I met up with a friend who was on the permanent staff at Weeton and he asked me if I wanted to go abroad. I said that I didn't particularly, so he advised me to ask for an educational posting, because he knew I was going into teaching and that would mean I wouldn't be sent abroad. You can imagine my surprise when the postings came out and it said 'Sayer, Middle East Air Force.' I thought he'd led me up the garden path, because he told me it was an absolute certainty that I wouldn't be posted overseas. I found out later that they needed large numbers of National Servicemen who had done my kind of trade training to service the vehicles in the camp at Mafraq in Jordan. They had a large number of vehicles which had come from the Canal Zone and from Aden and we were the people who would be looking after these hundreds and hundreds of vehicles. Nobody told us that at the time, even when we got to the Middle East Air Force HQ in Cyprus. From Cyprus you could be sent anywhere, even back to Gibraltar. We could have gone to Libya or Aden, which is a hell of a long way from Cyprus.

We were kitted out at RAF Hendon and I'm pretty sure we flew out from Stansted, which wasn't a commercial airport then. It was too far for the Hastings plane to get to Cyrprus in one hop so we landed in Malta, which I thought was a really nice place. It had been the winter of 1955–6 when we left England and here it was warm and sunny and beautiful. I was delighted the Hastings had engine trouble because it meant we could stay in Malta for a couple of days.

When we got to Cyprus we were given lectures from

officers on the political situation out there – EOKA and all that, the Greek Cypriots wanting union with Greece. The lectures were of course from a British point of view. Then we realised how difficult the situation was, how many soldiers had been killed in Cyprus at that time. You couldn't go out on your own, you had to go in a party, and you couldn't go into the old city of Nicosia. There was a notorious street there called Ledra Street. We stood at the top of it looking down, while someone who had been there for a while pointed out that was where someone had been killed by a sniper, that was where someone had been blown up. That was quite frightening because it was the first time I felt as though I was in real danger.

Because we were in transit I had to do quite a lot of guard duties, especially at night – two hours on and four hours off. There were six of us, plus the corporal, and we had to go into remote areas where there were ammunition dumps. Two of us had to march in opposite directions round the dump, and that was hairy, because we knew there had been numerous occasions when a guard had been shot and the ammunition dump robbed. It never happened to me but I was aware that it could have, and I was still pretty young at the time. We were supposed to be stopping terrorist activities but really we were there to defend British interests. There was a large RAF base at Akrotiri and that was the base from which they flew to Suez.

I was in Cyprus for six weeks until I was told I was going to Jordan. To me Jordan was just the name of a country in the atlas, but I soon found out there was an RAF base in northern Jordan at Mafraq – the main base was in Amman but I was sent to Mafraq, which was part of a ring of bases built at huge cost by NATO to counter the threat posed by the Soviets. There was a massive runway at Mafraq, which meant that any plane in production in 1956 could land there. King Hussein, who had just dismissed Glubb Pasha from his post with the Arab Legion, came to visit the camp once and his motorcade passed along the main road outside of the camp with very high security.

There were quite a few civilians on the base. Some were skilled tradesmen who worked on the wagons, some worked in the office and others did the menial jobs. Cumbria, where I come from, is a pretty cut-off part of the world – there were no Indian restaurants or anything like that – and so meeting these Arabs was the entry to a different world for me. People spoke to the local Arab civilians in what I thought was a very unpleasant way. Terms like 'wogs' were commonplace, though I didn't like using them. Even at that stage some people held attitudes that were quite offensive towards others who were not of their colour. There was a local Arab who worked in our section – he was a lovely guy and he invited me to his house for a meal on two or three occasions. He lived by the railway station in Mafraq village itself. I was slowly starting to learn about different cultures and how this chap cared for his kids like my parents cared for me. A lot of the guys on the camp didn't want to do that. That's why I was less inclined to call them 'wogs'.

However, the reason everyone thought I was really weird was because I didn't smoke. I'd always played a lot of sport and the idea of smoking never appealed to me. I was taunted for not joining when the tin of tobacco was being handed round, but I got used to the abuse after a while. I could banter back with them and I suppose that meant my confidence was growing, because I wouldn't let them get the better of me. I also played a lot of football and that made me more friends and won me a bit more respect. The no smoking made them think I was weak, but the football told them I wasn't. I was happy to go for a drink in the NAAFI, but it all ended in a fight so often. I really couldn't see the point of that.

There was one guy I was friendly with – Denny King from Torquay – and he was desperate to go into Amman and get a tattoo. Everyone said to him, 'Don't be so bloody daft,' but after three months he still wanted it. He went into Amman one afternoon and came back with a bloody mess on his arm. He was so proud of it. You met all sorts of people on National Service. There was one chap who came from Staithes near Scarborough. He was from farming stock so he was a naturalist and he was fascinated by all animals and insects. Whereas some of the crasser lads used to catch scorpions and put them in a bucket and watch them kill each other, he was a collector. I remember he had a room of his own, which he shared with the insects that people didn't much care for. When he left the camp he left behind a long snake in a box – we had to get one of the local Arabs who cleaned our shoes to put it in a bag and take it out to the desert.

I remember listening to Elvis singing 'Hound Dog' for the first time. We were out in Jordan, so it was some time in 1956, and someone had got hold of the record. Opinion was very widely split between those who loved it immediately and those who didn't. I think I was somewhere in the middle. I was keen on Frank Sinatra and this was so different. Sinatra was such a huge contrast with Elvis and Little Richard.

The reputation of Nasser was growing all the time. We went into Amman, which we liked – we would go and have a meal there and then on to the cinema. One night we did that and when the news came on, there was a newsreel of Nasser addressing a large crowd in Cairo. That was frightening because it was just like a reincarnation of Hitler. This was before Suez of course. At least three-quarters of the audience, who were all Jordanians, were standing up and shouting and cheering him on. 'Nasser is good!' We got out of there as fast we could.

We took a trip to Jerusalem, which was a divided city in those days. We were in the Arab part, of course, and I'll always remember looking across into the Israeli half and seeing neat new roads and houses and factories while on the Arab side it was rambling chaos. The contrast was radical. We had a drink in the Shepherd's Inn in Jerusalem and then got back into the wagon for the return trip to Mafraq, but went back past the refugee camps on the West Bank. I have never seen such unpleasant squalor in my life. I couldn't believe it. I'd never seen anything like it and I was horrified. I suppose that's given me an interest in what's happened in the Middle East ever since.

Mafraq was only a few miles from the Syrian border and the Syrians were a very intransigent bunch. We had quite a few vehicles stolen from the base at Mafraq, because they knew that if they got them started and drove them across the border into Syria the British couldn't pursue them. I suppose we lost maybe ten vehicles like that. The military police would race after them, shooting at the tyres trying to blow them out.

I realised about a month before Suez started that I was going to be in a war zone. The planes that started to arrive had yellow strips on the wings to facilitate identification. As soon as the crisis erupted and our planes started bombing Egypt, we found our camp at Mafraq surrounded by Iraqi troops who arrived overnight, covered the entire perimeter and dug in, so there were 25-pounder guns pointing inwards at our camp. It was total panic in the morning, because if they had wanted to wipe out the whole camp it would have taken them no more than ten minutes to do it. We were told to dig slit trenches, and we were all wondering what bloody use was a slit trench when you were facing a 25-pounder artillery cannon.

That was a horrendous time. Faisal was still on the throne of Iraq and the Arabs were talking about being united. Freeing themselves from the British was all part of this movement. I think there were some Saudi troops in Jordan as well, and they were all stationed outside our base to stop any of our planes taking off and being used in missions in Suez. At that time you didn't know what was going on and the threat of being wiped out by those guns was very real. Certainly if the Suez fighting had gone on and escalated that was a very real possibility. There were negotiations with the general in charge of the Iraqi army and the deal was done that if there were no flights out of the base they wouldn't open fire. We were in no position to fire back. We couldn't do a thing. The main road from Baghdad came right past our camp. There was nothing in the press over here about it.

We heard the details of the attack on Suez on the wireless, either from the BBC World Service or the local English language stations. There was no real television input – we didn't have a TV in the camp, so it was radio and newsreels in the cinema. I suspect that the way it was sold to us was that we had a perfect right to seize back the canal because Nasser had illegally nationalised it. If you listened to the BBC you'd hear that so many missions had been carried out, no planes were lost, troops were advancing on Alexandria and huge damage was inflicted on the enemy. If you listened to the Egyptian radio they said, 'We were attacked today by fifty planes but we shot down thirty-two of them.' You wondered who was telling the truth. It was lies on both sides, I suppose. The Egyptians thought that Suez was a huge victory. We were thankful that we were pulling out, because that meant a lot less trouble for us. The Iraqi army went away after about two or three weeks, when the invasion was called off. They left as quickly and silently as they had arrived.

Back home my parents knew nothing, because all the news was about Egypt – there was nothing about Jordan. I knew nothing of how unpopular the war was back here until I got home and then I read the newspaper articles that my mother had saved for me. Out there when the war was going on, the overwhelming feeling was that we were right, no question about it. We were right and it was the bloody Gypos who were causing all the trouble. They'd always caused trouble, that lot, etc. To take any other line would have been almost impossible. Besides, I had no knowledge beyond what I was told. I learned it all when I went home and started reading and talking to people in Carlisle who had fought – one had been a para-trooper and he said he'd never been so scared in his life. He was a National Serviceman too. There was a big reluctance to believe that we might have been wrong to invade Egypt.

Just before the invasion started I'd arranged to take some local leave in Cairo and Beirut and Lake Habbaniyah in Iraq. Everything was scrapped and that was a great regret, though I did get to Petra, the 'rose-red city half as old as time'. In those days there was nobody there – no tourists like now. It was absolutely fascinating. Aqaba was like heaven. The rest of Jordan was so inhospitable, just desert, but Aqaba had a wonderful sandy beach. A stone's throw away was Eilat, which was in Israel, and down the coast was Egypt and Saudi Arabia. Being in Jordan you got a very negative view of Israel. We weren't allowed to go there, so it was forbidden territory.

I came home at the end of the summer of 1957. It was officially supposed to be the end of August but I found out you could be officially demobbed four or six weeks before your time. I went back to Cyprus and I was in transit for quite a long time – the RAF flights back to the UK had other priorities and were constantly full, so I couldn't get a seat. One day though the flight sergeant (he was Scottish, it seemed they always were) said, 'I've got good news for you lot. You're all going home. On the *Empire Clyde*.' And of course I hadn't applied to join the navy because I get seasick so easily. I told the flight sergeant and he said, 'If you take my fucking advice, laddie, you'll get on that fucking boat tomorrow because otherwise you might never get home.' I didn't argue. I was sick the whole way from Cyprus to Malta.

When we docked at Liverpool at 7 p.m. there was a brass band waiting to greet us, but they wouldn't let us off the boat till 7 a.m. the next morning. Before that time we got our final pay and they asked how much leave I'd taken. I said I hadn't taken any leave when I was out of the country, so they paid me in lieu and I went back to Carlisle feeling very rich. Well, a day or two after I got back, a telegram arrived telling me to report to Gloucester. I just told my mother to tell them I'd gone away on holiday. A few days later I came back home to discover that apparently I shouldn't have declared I'd taken no leave – or at least I shouldn't have been financially compensated for it – so I had to return to the government all the money I'd been given. They made me feel like a fraudulent deserter! I feel I got a particularly bad deal because I was trapped in Jordan during Suez. There were all kinds of places I'd have liked to have gone whilst I was out there but I couldn't because of Suez, and that was very frustrating. However, it did leave me with an abiding interest in Middle East affairs.

National Service wasn't all beneficial for me by any means, and I have quite a few criticisms of what army discipline does for you. I certainly had a natural antipathy to being told what to do all the time. I didn't like that part of it at all. I felt like a tiny pawn in a huge game and I felt absolutely powerless. I didn't like those humiliations. People say their time in National Service matured them, but between eighteen and twenty most young men grow up anyway. I am not one of those advocates of National Service being the saviour of the country and disaffected youth. It's so much more complicated than that.

PART 3

THE END
1958–1962

In the aftermath of the humiliation at Suez, Anthony Eden resigned as Prime Minister and was succeeded by Harold Macmillan. In April 1957 Duncan Sandys, the new Minister of Defence, announced a radical series of defence cuts. Britain was going to place its faith in long-range missiles rather than aircraft and troops. As a consequence the need for constant reserves of manpower diminished, and the rationale that had justified peacetime National Service was rendered superfluous. However, the process was to be phased out slowly, and for more than three years after the announcement, men who increasingly didn't want to be there had to give up two years of their young lives to serve Queen and Country. They were not pleased.

Of course, they had rarely been thrilled at the prospect. In 1955 a government committee reported: 'Our overwhelming impression is that, with few exceptions, the National Service man regards his ... period of service as an infliction to be undergone rather than a duty to the nation.'

As the men whose reminiscences make up the final part of this book attest, there were great frustrations with National Service as it began to wind down. We should beware of imposing history with hindsight, but whilst the men who had been sent to Korea, Egypt, Kenya, Malaya and Cyprus in the early 1950s were never too far away from real fighting, the National Servicemen who were called up after Suez and the cuts proposed by the Defence White Paper were mostly bored. There simply wasn't enough for them to do and what they were given, those dull pointless boring jobs, could not by the wildest stretch of the imagination be described as important or in the national interest.

The failure at Suez affected the men who were yet to be called up, because in its wake the Empire continued to contract at a rapid rate as the former colonies sought and received their independence. The conflict areas of the 1940s and early to mid 1950s dwindled as Nasser held on to control in Egypt and Cyprus was partitioned between the Greek and Turkish Cypriots. Jomo Kenyatta in Kenya, like Dr Hastings Banda in Nyasaland, Kenneth Kaunda in Northern Rhodesia and other African nationalist leaders who had once been considered a serious threat to the peace and stability of British rule in Africa, were transformed into responsible leaders of the emerging Commonwealth states. There was consequently less need for an army of National Service conscripts to police these territories. There were still uprisings in Muscat and Oman in 1957, civil unrest in Gan in 1959, riots in the Cameroons in 1960 and assistance to be given to the Emir of Kuwait in 1961, but some-how this all lacked the glamour of serving Queen and Country in India and other former jewels in the crown of the British Empire. The troubles in Aden that both Stuart Atkinson and Mike Clark recall were typical of this frustrating obscurity. Very few people knew and even fewer cared where the Crown

Colony was or what was going on there, or what the British armed forces were supposed to do about it. Stuart Atkinson's rather worrying story of the 'goolie chit', however, lets readers know that honest, uncomplicated British soldiers were still subject to frightful foreign practices as late as the last year of National Service.

There was simply too much happening back home in these years for any young man to be happy at the enforced incarceration of an army or RAF camp. The experience of Stan Richards, who appears to have done his National Service from his own bedroom, is astonishing and comic; at the same time it is a very clear illustration that by the end of the 1950s National Service had outlived its usefulness and the armed forces simply didn't know what to do with the young men who were still appearing in their thousands at the barracks gate every month.

A small element in Stan's story indicates that the residual problem of class had not been significantly eased by the growth in social mobility and the percolation of rising affluence. He mentions the fact that he and his wife-to-be Penny came from different classes as well as different parts of the country. Penny was a middle-class girl from London and Stan was the son of a small grocer from a fishing village in Cornwall. When I talked to the charming Penny, she was very open about the problems that emerged when she and Stan started courting and they were entirely based on her middle-class parents' unwillingness to approve of Stan. Penny saw that Stan was an ambitious young man who was determined to start his own electrical business, which in due course he did. For Penny's parents, however, the son of a village grocer was not the prize they had in mind for her. This attitude, combined with the fact that the marriage has lasted for fifty years, suggests both that class suspicions remained entrenched in Britain for many years after the end of the war and that they were slowly easing. The barriers might have come crashing down in the 1960s but they were significantly weakened in the 1950s.

Nearly all the National Servicemen did 'better' than their parents. Stan's father was an employed grocer, but Stan started his own firm and employed six electricians. Mick Meredith, who grew up on a diet of bread and jam and bread and dripping as one of nine children in a tied cottage without electricity, ended his days as a union official. Dave Blackman's father was a painter and decorator when he came out of the navy at the end of the war, but Dave went on to succeed as the manager of Burton's shops all over the country. It would be difficult to quantify what part National Service played in the success of men such as these. Certainly the frustration of having nothing to do and watching their peers get ahead in life seems much more pronounced the later a man began his National Service. A certain amount of bitterness is evident in the stories of the men whose memories of National Service are shortly to follow.

Although they could hardly have been expected to articulate the reasons at the time, it becomes possible with the benefit of hindsight to look back at the Britain of the late 1950s and early 1960s and see that it was undergoing enormous social and cultural changes. The battle for control of the national culture was won during these years by the new ITV companies and their advertisers. They were the years in which the BBC's captive audiences of the 1930s and 1940s on the wireless, and the rapidly growing numbers of its television viewers in the first five years of the new Conservative government, were deserting the Corporation in their droves, seduced by the sophistication of commercials for washing powder and cigarettes, enchanted by 77 *Sunset Strip* and *Wagon Train*. It needed the Pilkington Report of 1962 to criticise ITV, praise the BBC and recommend the award of a second channel to the Corporation. BBC2 started transmission in 1964.

Richard Hoggart's well-received book *The Uses of Literacy*, published in 1957, denounced the imposition of a mass culture by an unholy alliance of the tabloid press, unscrupulous advertising agencies and Hollywood glamour. The British desire to ape American tendencies became very obvious as Diana Dors and Sabrina were styled entirely along the lines created by Marilyn Monroe and Jayne Mansfield. The British version of Elvis Presley was Tommy Steele; Shirley Bassey's rise to fame was the result of her talent, but her marketing owed something to the success of Eartha Kitt in the United States.

The social and cultural influences on Britain were not exclusively American in origin. The late 1950s saw the rising popularity of Italian suits as well as blue jeans, espresso coffee as well as Coca Cola, Scandinavian furniture, pasta and cheap Italian or French wine. They had only managed to infiltrate a minority of British homes, but in hindsight the small advances they made were to become increasingly significant. A classic fusion of traditional British fare and Continental sophistication was spotted in the window of a North London café advertising 'Try Pizza and Chips – the Italian Welsh Rarebit'. It was in the 1950s that Elizabeth David wrote her recipe books in praise of Mediterranean cooking and advocated the use of olive oil, although it transpired that the item was only available in Boots and other chemists. Most people in Britain used it for softening ear wax, although I do remember that my grandfather bought it as a cheap alternative to Brylcreem.

Insofar as it was possible for our National Servicemen to be aware of these cultural innovations behind the wire of their army and RAF camps, the belief that Britain was entering a new era of affluence and consumption would only have increased their already corrosive frustration. The final years of National Service were also the years of the Macmillan affluence, which concerned the Prime Minister so much that he wondered aloud in a speech he made in Bedford if it could last. Immediately after he declaimed that 'most of our people have never had it so good', he went on to wonder if it would be possible to keep a lid on inflation and prices if economic growth and employment continued to expand at the current rate. That, he said, was 'the $64,000 question', instantly rooting his speech in the new, exciting, American-originated game show vocabulary of the time. The classic phrase was not meant to be emblematic of the smug triumphalism with which it was thereafter forever associated but was intended as a warning, equally familiar in recent times, about the philosophy of boom and bust economics.

Nevertheless the British public were too busy acquiring cars, kitchen gadgets and white goods for the first time to worry too much about the nuances of economic philosophy. One thing that struck me when I was interviewing the men, and still strikes me consistently as remarkable, is the easy acceptance of employment. Their fathers, who had gone to war in 1939 and 1940, mostly did so with some relief that the unemployment problem was being solved, or at least that they would not have to worry for the duration about the soul-destroying fear of unemployment and poverty. None of the interviewees seemed to have the slightest anxiety that after their National Service they might not return to their jobs or might be unable to find another one. Most of them were cross that they were expected to sacrifice a decent wage of ten pounds a week for the Queen's shilling – or, to be precise, the Queen's twenty-eight shillings (minus deductions for barrack-room damages).

Some, like Dave Blackman, were worried that their careers would take a long time to recover from their enforced absence, and Shaun O'Connor thought it was extremely unfair that his contemporaries who managed to avoid National Service had gained a two-year advantage and he was left lagging in the attempt to get married and buy a place to live. Mike Clark makes the point that there was so much work around in engineering companies you could never work enough hours. He worked every Saturday from 8 a.m. to 2 p.m. and every other Sunday as well, earning over seventeen pounds ten shillings a week, a relative fortune for a young working-class lad of twenty-two. Dave Blackman earned more from working the occasional Saturday at Burton's than he did for a week in the service of the RAF. Any sense of patriotism – if it ever existed, and it probably didn't the moment the Japanese surrendered in August 1945 – was long gone by the late 1950s. At the same time the booming economy simply made them desperate to get back home and join in the fun.

Here they are then, the last of the many. Most of them didn't want to be there and the country didn't quite know what to do with them. It was a somewhat inglorious way to bring the experiment of National Service to its conclusion.

ROLL CALL

STAN RICHARDS	1956–1958	RAF
MICK MEREDITH	1958–1960	1ST BATTALION, GLOUCESTERSHIRE REGIMENT
STUART ATKINSON	1960–1962	ROYAL ARMY SERVICE CORPS
DAVID BLACKMAN	1960–1962	RAF, QUEEN'S COLOUR SQUADRON
SHAUN O'CONNOR	1960–1962	GRENADIER GUARDS
MIKE CLARK	1960–1962	ROYAL EAST KENT REGIMENT, 1ST BATTALION, QUEEN'S ROYAL SURREYS

STAN RICHARDS

1956–1958

RAF

I suppose I could have been sent off to Suez to be killed but in fact I was living at home, playing rugby and driving to camp in a Standard Eight. Some weeks it was a three-day week, some weeks two days, and some weeks they didn't want us to turn up at all. I'd go down to the telephone kiosk on Newlyn Bridge and phone up the guardhouse. If there was a parade we'd get in the car and drive down there, but if not we wouldn't bother.

I was born in Newlyn, near Penzance in Cornwall. My dad was an employed grocer and his parents before him were fishermen. On my mother's side, her father was also in fishing and she was the oldest of ten children, eight girls and two boys. I lived in Newlyn till I did my National Service. It was a very friendly place but everyone knew what was going on. On Sunday evenings after chapel we would all go walking on the promenade. The girls would go in one direction in waves and the boys would go in the opposite direction in waves. That was how you met girls. By half past eight, curfew time, everyone had linked up and that was the end of the evening.

My father worked for quite a large grocer called R. Chirgwin's & Sons, who had shops in the Isles of Scilly, Penzance and St Ives as well as Newlyn. He worked there till he was sixty, but then they ran out of sons and daughters in the family and the likes of Tesco came along, and that was the end of it. My dad then opened a small shop himself in Upper Newlyn Town and he traded there till he retired. On Friday evenings I used to deliver groceries in a small van. My dad was a Methodist lay preacher and I was also brought up in that faith, which was very strong.

During the war aircraft would bomb Plymouth and on the way back, if they had any left over, they would bomb Newlyn. They made a mess of one or two of the streets. Rationing wasn't a problem. People in Newlyn were so used to scrimping that rationing seemed a very fair way of doing things. I think people were in favour of the 1945 Labour government, because it was a very working-class area.

The NHS saved my life. I was cycling with two other lads and we were coming out of a minor road onto a major road when my front wheel touched one of their back wheels, and I wobbled and went over. Luckily I hit the back of a double-decker bus rather than being Flat Stanley. I was lucky again because there was a surgeon down from London whose wife was having a nervous breakdown, and he was in Cornwall chaperoning her. He was on duty after five o'clock and he performed a miracle on my pelvis when I was brought in.

There was a very good local grammar school, but I had no ambitions other than to go into a trade. At secondary modern school I enjoyed rugby football and I played centre for the Pirates – the Cornwall Pirates, they are now. By the time I was fifteen I was thinking about becoming a funeral director because that was all I could get, but my father got me into South Western Electricity. I was two weeks into my first job laying bricks when I came back in the morning and the wall I was building had fallen over. I would have been hopeless as a carpenter because you have to be very precise, but when I got into the Electricity Board I did my six-year apprenticeship and deferred my National Service for three years.

I was called up in April 1956 and went off to RAF Cardington. That was my very first time out of Cornwall apart from a day playing rugby in Plymouth. I was very worried that I might not get there and I'd be accused of desertion. I had no idea where Cardington was and I just trusted the guy on the train who told me where I was supposed to go. I'd never been anywhere. Anyway, I did get there in the end and I was kitted out – that took about four days – then I was off to Bridgnorth in Shropshire.

I didn't do the regular eight weeks of basic training – I only did five. You see the Royal Tournament was on at Earls Court and we were used as cheap labour to show people to their seats. There were two shows a day, six days a week. It was wonderful in a way, but of course I couldn't go out of sight of Earls Court because I'd never have found my way back. If I'm being honest I was frightened – frightened to do anything, talk to anyone. I was very reticent, didn't like to talk to people I didn't know. I was fine at home and in a social environment I was comfortable with. When I was taken out of it I had to mind my Ps and Qs. I didn't swear, and people respected that – even in rugby circles.

There were twenty-two of us in my hut during basic training and I was made the senior man – I have no idea why, maybe it was because I was the oldest. I was AC1. Those first few nights at Cardington and Bridgnorth I don't remember a lot of talking going on because we were all basically scared and we knew we couldn't run away. I met some lovely people though – one in particular, a lovely chap from Swindon. There was a bloke from Wolverhampton and he could get home in an hour or so. He had a Black Country accent and I couldn't understand it very well. We decided to turn his wardrobe round so when he came back in the dark late on Sunday . . . There was only one public schoolboy I can remember on basic training. He was from London but he was actually quite a nice guy and we got quite fond of him, because we were pretty much all working-class lads. You had to get on with everyone because we were all in it together. The sergeant and the corporal were both working class as well.

After the Royal Tournament, which lasted about a week, instead of being sent back to finish basic training I was posted off to RAF Helston, which I was thrilled about. Instead of a large RAF camp with three thousand men miles from home, I was at a small camp with perhaps two hundred airmen on it, two planes, and about twenty miles from home. It meant I could live at home and continue to play rugby, so I was delighted. One of my mates was also posted there and he could drive a car – his dad was Jack Reynolds, who had taxis and lorries in Newlyn – so we bought a Standard Eight to get from Newlyn to the camp. I had some money put aside from my apprenticeship and I think his dad helped him out.

We found that as long as you got there in the morning in time for parade and you left when they told you to leave, it was fine. It was like a normal job, and to be honest I can't actually remember doing anything. I was an electrician but they didn't give me any electrical work. I wasn't allowed to touch anything to do with the planes because I was ground crew and they had civilian electricians to do the regular electrical work. We couldn't do much square bashing because there was no real parade ground to march on. I suppose I could have been sent off to Suez to be killed but in fact I was living at home, playing rugby and driving to camp in a Standard Eight.

Some weeks it was a three-day week, some weeks two days, and some weeks they didn't want us to turn up at all. I'd go down to the telephone kiosk on Newlyn Bridge and phone up the guardhouse. If there was a parade we'd get in the car and drive down there, but if not we wouldn't bother. It was all right as long as they kept to the same times, because we could plan for that. It was unbelievable really. We couldn't believe our luck. I still can't. Before I'd finished there were about four or five of my mates posted to Helston, so we all piled into that Standard Eight.

I met my wife Penny when I was on National Service. We met at a garden fete and we danced together that night at St John's Hall. We had a lovely week together because she was in Cornwall on holiday. I took her to the Royal cinema in St Ives and to the Savoy in Penzance. I somehow fitted that into my National Service. She went home and I wasn't a big letter writer, but three or four years later I'd started my electrical business and she came back on holiday, and the rest is history. Penny was a middle-class girl and I was a working-class lad but we didn't see that as a problem, although her parents did. They wouldn't have much to do with my family but we didn't let that bother us. I think Penny was much more conscious of that class difference than I was.

Even the limited amount of National Service I did made me grow up, because you had to adapt to the direct discipline. I couldn't be happy-go-lucky Stanley all the time. There are situations in life where you cannot do what you want to do. You have to knuckle under and National Service taught me that.

My National Service was purely the luck of the draw. I never left Helston during my whole National Service and I was a senior aircraftman by the time I left. I decided that I didn't want to leave Penzance because I was still playing rugby for the Pirates, so the best thing to do was to start my own business. Besides, I am very much a Cornishman.

MICK MEREDITH

1958–1960

1st Battalion Gloucestershire Regiment

I didn't have much interaction with the local population but the Germans who worked on the base were very nice people. We knew about Belsen and all that, but you've got to forget about things like that, haven't you? Mind you, there were certainly some Germans who were nasty to the British, or they were rude and they ignored you. You had to be careful if you left the base to have a drink and you were on your own. You could easily be set upon and given a beating. That German beer was very strong.

I was born on 22 April 1936 in Hereford, one of nine children, but we were living at the time in Staunton-on-Arrow just outside Pembridge. I went to school in Kington and when I left school at the age of fourteen I went to work for a farmer called

David Edwards. In those days it was all tied cottages on farms, so you all moved wherever your father worked. I shared a bed with a couple of brothers. We mainly ate bread and dripping and bread and jam but I never felt deprived. I did little jobs from an early age – carrying the wood for the fire and so on. I think my dad worked a forty-eight-hour week for three pounds. He was a cripple. He was born with a twisted thigh so he was never called up during the First World War. There was no electricity in the house so we had oil lamps, but they didn't leave them upstairs in case we knocked them over and caused a fire.

We were a happy family. We didn't have much money but in those days you could get eggs, potatoes and milk even when there was rationing on. Milk was a penny a pint and eggs a couple of coppers for a dozen.

I left school in 1950 and went to work full time for David Edwards on the farm. I worked a forty-eight-hour week for one pound. I was a stockman, so when I was eighteen I wasn't called up – I should have gone in 1954 but I didn't because they didn't take people who worked on a farm. Eventually I got to earning fifty-five shillings a week but after a few years, when I was eighteen, I left David Edwards and went to work for a chicken farmer for more money. When I became twenty-one they called me up and suddenly I was back down to twenty-eight shillings a week.

I went for my medical in Worcester and I had to go for chest X-rays in Corporation Street in Birmingham, because when I was younger I suffered from asthma and they wanted to make sure I was OK for the forces. It was a challenge to do something different, so I was looking forward to it. I have to be honest, I enjoyed it – I was seriously thinking about staying in the army. I hadn't lived away from home before but I was looking forward to it, even with all the shouting and the horrible haircut. You had to accept it. It was like going to work for somebody else. You have to adapt.

I was called up on 8 May 1958 but before that I had a letter from the Ministry of Defence telling me to report to Devizes to join the Wiltshire Regiment. A few weeks later I had another letter telling me not to go there but to report on the same day to the Gloucestershire Regiment. When I got off the train in Gloucester there were trucks there to meet us, and they shouted out names and said, 'You on this one, you get on that one.' Then you'd get into the barracks and line up in your civilian clothes, and you'd go to the quartermaster's stores and you'd line up again and they'd throw this kit at you. You checked it and you went to the barrack room and you were off.

I did eight weeks' basic training at the Robinswood Barracks in Gloucester and shooting practice at Seven Springs ranges just outside Coney Hill. That was the first time I really talked to people from London. I could understand them all right, but they must have thought I was Welsh because they called me 'Taffy', even though I was born in Hereford in England. My father was born in north Wales though. I was also called 'Farmer'. Everyone on basic training got on with one another. The only one I didn't get on with was called Corporal Green. He was arrogant and he obviously hated us. I didn't like him at all.

I remember the inspecting officer would wipe his handkerchief across the top of the lockers and if there was a dirty mark on it we all had extra duties. It was good because it instilled discipline and that's what young people lack today. You had to warm up the spoons in the oven and remove all the marks from the boots. Several people struggled and they asked me to help because I'd always been good with my hands. So I did and they paid me by buying me an extra glass of milk in the NAAFI. I never resented the discipline and the food was all right. We got all the vitamins we needed for that kind of work.

After basic training I was told I was going to join the battalion at Quebec Barracks in Osnabrück in Germany. Nearly everyone in basic training went there. I was there from August 1958 to January 1960. We went by boat from Harwich to the Hook of Holland. I was thrilled because it was different being out of England and on the Continent for the first time. I noticed those endless flat lands in Holland and Germany.

I didn't have much interaction with the local population but the Germans who worked on the base were very nice people. We knew about Belsen and all that, but you've got to forget about things like that, haven't you? Mind you, there were certainly some Germans who were nasty to the British, or they were rude and they ignored you. You had to be careful if you left the base to have a drink and you were on your own. You could easily be set upon and given a beating. That German beer was very strong.

As soon as I got to Germany and the 1st Battalion of the Gloucestershire Regiment, I was appointed to Signals branch and I went off to do signals training. The dispatch rider, a bloke by the name of Hazell from Cheltenham, got demobbed and they asked me to take on the job. I was the DR for the rest of my time in the service, based in the signals dispatch office where all the mail comes in. I couldn't go for a meal unless another DR came to relieve me. We used to take it in turns to go to meals – me first one week, him the next. What was great was I could be called on to deliver a message by bike at any time, night or day, so I was excused from all parades. So DR was a really good job. I had a BSM20. I'd ridden a bike in England before call-up and they knew my history.

We didn't have much entertainment within the barracks, apart from the NAAFI where you could have a drink – though only in the evenings. You couldn't have alcohol during the day or if you were going on duty. There was also a wireless set in the NAAFI.

When I was doing my training I was on coal duty, shovelling coal into bags with German civilians. I used to take the coal from one barracks to another and fill up their bunkers every week. I was driving a wagon with the bags of coal on it when a lorry with a trailer of sand behind went straight through the traffic lights and smashed into us. My arm was broken and I was unconscious for four days. I had to go to the military hospital in Münster. I didn't become conscious again until 5 November 1958. I was then transferred to the military hospital in Hostert where they did the operation. I was off duty for about three months. Then I went back to Münster but I had to go back to the hospital every few weeks. The arm is OK but it's been significantly weaker than the other one ever since.

We always thought that the officers were no better than us, that they only got to be officers because they'd gone to university and got a degree, and they'd only been able to go to university because they'd gone to a good school and had got the O levels you needed. We didn't find it unfair. We just accepted it. Anyway, we didn't get bad treatment from the officers – or indeed from anyone. That's why I can recommend National Service today – it would give those kids some sense of discipline. That's what it gave me and it gave me a different outlook on life. I think I was typical of most.

Coming to the end of National Service I had the usual interview where they try to persuade you to sign on. I was asked if I wanted to be considered for promotion to lance corporal, but I didn't because I'd lose my job. If you got promoted they could take you off it and put you somewhere you didn't want to be. I just wanted to do those two years and get out – like everyone else. I didn't resent the time I spent in National Service. In some ways they were the best two years of my life. I was doing something interesting and it was so different from life on the farm. That was the way most of the boys looked at it.

When I got back from Osnabrück I was sent to Connaught Barracks in Dover; then I was asked by an officer in the Signals if I would go and look after the beagles down in Deal. I went to Deal twice a day until I was demobbed. I didn't count the days to my release like some others. In fact, I came out three days early because it was Princess Margaret's wedding and they said I could go to avoid the crowds in London. My release papers said: 'Mick Meredith is a very cheerful Welshman who works hard and has proved extremely reliable. He is of above average intelligence and learns easily and is honest.'

When I came back after all those months in Germany I found it really hard to settle down. I liked the fact that in Germany I was alert in case something would happen quickly, but in England life was much more relaxed. You were away from the dangers. We were always prepared to see action in Osnabrück and when I came out I didn't have a job. The place I was working in when I got called up in 1958 had closed down, so I had to go back in the end to David Edwards's farm where I started. I worked there as a stockman. I earned more than I did in the army but it wasn't much. I had to come back to live with my parents and it was a job to settle, so after twelve months I left and went off to work as a lorry driver for a firm in Kington. Eventually I joined the Royal Mail where I stayed for thirty-four years until I retired.

I missed army life, I must confess, even though I was a Z reservist, so after a few months back on Civvy Street I wrote to Hereford TA and joined them. I stayed with the Herefordshire Light Infantry, which kept changing its name when it was amalgamated with the Mercian Volunteers. I got to be a sergeant and I wore six different cap badges. I was called up again in 1968 to serve in Aden during the emergency out there because I was part of the Ever Readies – volunteer reservists who were supposed to bolster the main army in an emergency. Eventually I reached the rank of colour sergeant and I was in charge of the motor transport pool, then I went on to become a staff sergeant in the Royal Army Pay Corps in Ross on Wye. I finally retired from active service at the age of fifty-nine in 1996.

I can say quite honestly that National Service did change my life, because I had no real prospects beyond a job on a farm when I went in and when I came out I had a career in a way. It gave me the confidence to become a union official and I did all sorts of jobs – treasurer and secretary and so on –

and I went off to conferences. From nothing I was learning and progressing and I've had a good life, I think. National Service was a positive experience for me and I'm glad I went through it.

STUART ATKINSON

1960–1962

Royal Army Service Corps

*We had one guy who Blancoed everything he had –
trousers, coat, raincoat, the lot. He tried to make
out he was doolally so he could get out of it. At
night he was writing letters home by candlelight,
just trying to get out of it. In the end they sent him
off for psychiatric observation. There were other
chaps who instead of marching normally along the
road, they marched like penguins. They used to do
all sorts of things to get out of the army.*

I am Stuart Frederick Atkinson and I was in the Royal Army
Service Corps Air Dispatch. My army number was 23813646
and I joined in 1960 as one of the last National Servicemen to
be called up. A chap I was in with was the very last National
Serviceman to be demobbed. Not everyone who was called up
together got demobbed on the same day. Some men had to do
another six months because they were called up to go to
Germany.

I was born just round the corner here in Barnet in 1939. We were bombed out in 1940 when a land mine exploded and we were buried in the cellar. I was only one at the time so I don't remember much about it, but I know my uncle got me out, though he couldn't get to my mother and my sister. They were pulled out later on. My sister was only two. My mother said later they were trapped there in the cellar for a day. It was very frightening.

My uncle was only sixteen at the time and after that he went missing. When he came back he was in uniform, he'd joined the infantry. When the officer in charge found out he was only sixteen he wrote to my grandmother and asked if she wanted him back, but she said, 'No, you can keep him.' There were eight of us living in the same house – it's still there, a little white house, two up and two down, so it was a bit crowded. When my uncles came home from leave they stayed there as well.

I never passed the eleven plus so I went to a secondary modern school. I had no problems with that. I was in the Boys' Brigade and then I joined the TA, so there was a service nature to the family and I was really looking forward to National Service. One of my uncles was a regimental sergeant major in the Artillery. When I left school at fifteen I knew I only had three years before I went into the army. I started work in a place called Watsons, which was a factory near here which made microscopes and gun sights and things like that.

I was eighteen in 1957 but I got a deferment for three years, because by then I was an apprentice at Watsons. I was on about four pounds a week but I was living at home so I gave my mum half. If we worked a bit longer at night or on a

Saturday morning we got overtime. We were paid in cash in sticky brown envelopes. At that particular time we were working on a special gun sight they were using for ack-ack guns and a special kind of ventilator for breathing. The film star Liz Taylor was the first one to use it, I believe, but it was for army use as well as medical and we could get deferment on that – it came through automatically. I had the medical at Acton at the age of eighteen but they asked me what I was doing, so I told them and they said they would defer me for three years. Obviously I nearly missed it altogether.

In 1957 they seemed quite keen to defer me because they were trying to cut back on intakes anyway. In 1960 I got the letter and I went in during October. By then most of the people who were going in had had deferments. I had an IQ test, a written test, a complete medical. If you're A1 after that you go before a board and they ask you which service you'd like to join. I put down the army and they asked if I wanted a particular regiment, so I said I was in the TA and I was serving at the time in the Royal Army Service Corps Tank Transport, which was in Barnet. They wrote down Royal Army Service Corps and when the papers came through it said Royal Army Service Corps, report to Aldershot.

I was looking forward to it because I knew what the army life was about, whereas the majority of conscripts I joined up with had no idea what was going on. I went to Aldershot for two weeks. We were issued with our kit and shown how to clean it and lay it out. I'd already slept with twenty other blokes in a hut when I was on manoeuvres with the TA, but the majority of people couldn't take it.

The NCO who was in charge of us at Aldershot showed us

how to Blanco our belts. We had one guy who Blancoed everything he had – trousers, coat, raincoat, the lot. He tried to make out he was doolally so he could get out of it. At night he was writing letters home by candlelight, just trying to get out of it. In the end they sent him off for psychiatric observation. There were other chaps who instead of marching normally along the road, they marched like penguins. They used to do all sorts of things to get out of the army. There were tough guys, I mean real tough guys, from tough working-class districts, and they'd be crying. They just couldn't take the discipline, because you were shouted at from the minute you got up in the morning to the minute you went to bed. It wasn't so bad in the first two weeks, but when you went on to the next part of basic training it got really bad.

You had to Blanco your stuff, lay it out on the bed, clean the floor with razor blades, clean the windows and clean those dustbins till they shone. The rifle had to be cleaned and ready for inspection and so did your locker. The inspecting officer would come and he'd walk around very slowly inspecting someone, and when he found the tiniest spot of something he'd open the window and throw that man's kit straight out. It didn't matter if it was raining or snowing – the whole lot went out of the window. It was very disheartening. I never got it. I knew how to do it. You helped one another out, but it just took the slightest thing and it would go out of the window. Sometimes the officer said he'd come back and inspect at ten o'clock at night, and after you'd done all your duties and had your evening meal, from 6 p.m. to 10 p.m. you'd be cleaning everything till it was spotless. It was to get you to work together. I can remember being on the parade ground in the snow marching up and down for five hours. It was sadistic.

If you were any good at sport though, you were OK. Boxing was the main thing, they used to make us knock hell out of one another, but if you were any good at boxing you never did any duties, you just did boxing, and you got the best life. There was one guy who played football for Barnsley, and in those days Barnsley were a decent team. He never did any duties. He was spotted when we were at Watchfield near Swindon and all he did after that was play football, like Bobby Charlton. I had two weeks in Watchfield, followed by ten weeks in Yeovil – that's where I learned to drive one-tonners and three-tonners. So I became a driver, I was Driver Atkinson. But also we had to learn how to load an aircraft, where the loading points were, how much weight to put on, plus basic aircraft drill and parachute jumping. We jumped from eight hundred feet, though after basic training there was no more compulsory jumping.

I was asked by the commanding officer where I wanted to go and I said I wanted to go into Air Dispatch. He asked me where I'd heard about Air Dispatch because it was such a specialised unit, and I said one of my school friends was in it. Air Dispatch was loading aircraft and supplying troops on the ground. Our regiment had been at Arnhem in 1944 and lost 90 per cent of its troops. There's a memorial in Arnhem to Air Dispatch. We went first to Aldershot, then to Hendon. Then we flew out of Stansted on an RAF Britannia.

I did four weeks' training on how to load the aircraft and drop supplies to the troops on the ground. We used to fly out of Abingdon on Dakotas, Vallettas and Hastings aircraft to drop supplies. You get a badge to put on your arm after so many drops. You got extra money for flying – that's also why I wanted it. In this country I was earning four pounds ten shillings a week. I was told within a week that I was going into 47 Company.

When I got into Air Dispatch I could have been sent to Malaya or Cyprus or Aden if I was going to be sent overseas. Everyone knew there was trouble in Cyprus and Malaya, which was Singapore, but no one here knew anything about Aden. In fact, I can say that no one in this country in 1960 even knew we were on active service out there, or anything about the fighting in Yemen.

I could have opted for a UK posting, because there was always a company at home in case of emergencies – like there had been with the Berlin Airlift. I actually said I wanted to go to Malaya – I didn't mind the danger – but I was told Malaya was full, no vacancies, so I took Aden. You could also go to Bahrain or to Muscat in the Gulf. In the end I spent more time in Bahrain than I did in Aden.

I didn't know anything about the political situation in the Middle East but when we got out there we were told that we would all be expected to take part in special missions on active service. We'd had rifle training but all we had were .38 pistols and twelve rounds of ammunition. I knew a bit about the Middle East because my father had been at Tobruk with the Australians, and then he'd gone missing but showed up in the Eighth Army at El Alamein. He'd been to Palestine as well, but we never really found out much about what happened to him. He would never talk about it.

Out in Aden we didn't have much time off. We got up about 6 a.m., worked till lunch at 1 p.m., then we were back to work till 9 p.m. In our time off we just slept. Our billets were three storeys high with no windows. The doors were always open. The only time they were closed was during a sandstorm. You just slept on your bed naked, apart from a pair of trunks or a towel draped over your middle. I mean it was hot. During the day it went up to 120° F. Even at night you couldn't walk on the pavement in bare feet, it was still so hot.

Compared to the officers at Yeovil and Aldershot you couldn't ask for better. There was a Lieutenant Weir, a Scotsman, who I thought was very fair – so were all the officers out there. In the company we had a Geordie called Dennis Potter, who's now a multi-millionaire, and when we were out there he always said to our corporal, 'I'm going to be a millionaire.' Everybody took the mickey out of him because he was just an apprentice pattern maker in one of the shipbuilding yards on the Tyne. Now he's a friend of the Sultan of Brunei. I could understand his Geordie accent but I had a big problem with a couple of Glaswegians. Not Lieutenant Weir, he was Scottish but he spoke what I would say is normal. But those Glaswegians . . .!

We did air/sea rescue with Shackletons and patrols with helicopters. In 1961 we were on attachment from Bahrain to Kuwait. We were unloading rockets that went onto Hunter aircraft and we dropped one. It took two of you to hold one of these things. They were very heavy, and one chap lost his balance and it slipped. You never saw anyone jump out of an aircraft so quick in your life. We had a few scares like that. We were in planes that might come back full of shell holes in the fuselage. If one of those shells had hit the fuel tank and not the fuselage we were gone.

Much of the shooting was between the royalists and the communists – they were shooting at each other and we were caught in the middle, though we were supporting the royalists against the communists. It was sort of part of the Cold War, though we didn't see it like that. When we flew up there we had an escort, two Hunters and a bomber. The bomber would go in first and drop leaflets telling the insurgents that in a few hours' time there would be a supply plane coming up. If anyone fires on this plane, we said, we shall retaliate. Then they'd send the two Hunters in.

We all carried what was called a goolie chit, because when the insurgents got hold of a British soldier they used to cut his goolies off and stick his cock in his mouth. The goolie chit said that if our dead bodies were not mutilated in this way and were returned to the British authorities they would give them five hundred quid. We were fighting savages – that's why we didn't really see it as part of the Cold War.

By the time of the Cuban missile crisis I was back home. I was out in Aden and Bahrain for about eighteen months and by the end of it I'd had enough. It was pretty rough out there. The ones who were going out there to replace us were all regular soldiers because National Service was over. I have to say, though, there had been no division between the National Servicemen and the regulars when we were out there.

I'd changed my mind about becoming a regular soldier myself. Some of my mates had to stay in another six months after the two years were up, I think something had happened in Germany and they needed the manpower. I know the Berlin Wall had gone up while we were out there and there was trouble brewing, but by then I'd had enough and I just wanted to get back to Barnet. We'd never had any time to come home on leave when we were out there, though the RASC had a company in Kenya and some guys used their leave to get to Mombasa and go on safari.

After I got home and was demobbed I went back to work at Watsons, but I could never settle there again. I got into a few arguments, had a few punch-ups and got the sack. Civilian life didn't seem to agree with me. The RAF were recruiting and money was short. I was tempted to go back into the RAF. I wouldn't have had to do the basic training and I had all the papers ready for signing. I can't remember quite why, but in the end I didn't sign them. Something must have come up.

Looking back on my days in National Service, I'm glad I did it and I think in many ways it was a shame they abandoned it.

DAVID BLACKMAN

1960–1962

RAF Queen's Colour Squadron

We didn't know the guy was coming in on a helicopter, so we were all lined up in three rows, and the rotor blade blew all our hats off, and our CO went bananas as if it was all our fault. The NCOs must have known, but their hats blew off as well and of course we had to stand there, we couldn't go and get them back. So the Duke of Norfolk inspects us and nobody has a hat on and there's a pile of 120 hats at the back of the field.

I was born in July 1939 and christened on the day war was declared. I was born and brought up in Gosport. My very first memory was of living in a reasonably sized flat with my mother and my younger sister whilst my father was in the Royal Navy during the war. One day I came back from school and one of the neighbours stopped me and said, 'Your dad's come home.'

284

I went in and there was a sailor sat on a chair, a man I didn't know, and he was my father. It was not a happy homecoming. I grew to hate him because he was a sadistic bully. He made our lives hell until eventually my mother kicked him out. I remember that as a kid I was given massive punishments for the most trivial things. He completely wrecked any confidence I might have had for quite a long time.

We moved into a council house on a huge estate just outside Gosport. A lot of people from the Portsmouth area went to a naval boarding school in a village called Holbrook, near Ipswich, called the Royal Hospital School. It was started by William of Orange in Greenwich and it moved to East Anglia about eighty years ago. It's a beautiful school in a gorgeous place. I convinced my parents to send me there when I was twelve. It was free – no fees – and all my school clothing was provided for me. I had three incredible years there. I cried my eyes out when I left.

My father, however, was annoyed that I didn't want to leave school at fifteen and get a job so I could contribute to the household. He was a painter and decorator and he had a chip on his shoulder that his parents didn't pay for him to further his education, because he thought he was more intelligent than was recognised. They had six or seven children though and they couldn't afford it. He was very bitter about that. When he left the navy he got a job as an office worker, but he resented that too because he constantly complained that his superiors were not as intelligent as he was. He stuck it out for a few years, then he became a telephone operator and progressed to being a postal and telegraph officer and that's what he did for the rest of his life until he retired. He did some part-time janitor work, but he died at sixty-nine of lung cancer.

At Easter 1955 I came home from school and got a job on a building site as a tea boy during the holiday. I earned three or four pounds a week, which was taken off me by my parents. I had very little non-school clothing and I desperately needed something formal – I was sixteen years old and this was the mid 1950s. We went to the outfitters in Gosport looking for a sports jacket, but Mother didn't like any of them and we ended up in Burton's. I looked around this beautiful emporium and compared it to the tatty little shops we'd been in and I wondered what it must be like to work there. My mother asked the manager, 'Do you take apprentices?'

Well, about three weeks later I started work there. My plan had always been to get my O levels and then an apprenticeship as an aeronautical engineer at a place called Fleetlands, which was the Royal Naval aircraft yard, about a mile from where I lived. However, when I went back to school after Easter I was called into the headmaster's office and told that I was leaving to go home because I had a job – which I knew nothing about. When I got back to Gosport my mother told me I had a job at Burton's. They agreed that I should go to night school and take the O levels, and if I passed I could leave and become an aeronautical engineer. After three weeks I told them I didn't want to leave and I stayed working at Burton's for thirty-six years, moving all round the country, and finally becoming an area manager.

At the end of the 1950s the government decided to stop National Service, but they didn't say exactly when. I think they thought they'd get enough men into the regular forces, but it didn't quite happen and it started to stretch, so I was nearly twenty-one when I went in, though I hadn't been officially deferred. They just weren't calling everyone up at eighteen any more. They didn't get the recruitment of regulars they expected, so they had to keep National Service going to make up the shortfall.

It all started when I got a letter telling me to go down to the town hall in Portsmouth on 10 January 1960 and register. I then received a brown envelope telling me to go to the recruitment office in Southampton for my medical and service selection. That would be around March 1960. Burton's, like every other employer, had to keep my job open as long as I stayed in the RAF for the length of my National Service. Of course, I'd been earning decent wages and the pay in the services was absolutely abysmal. I went from eight pounds a week to one pound ten shillings, but if you signed on for an extra year as a regular your pay shot up to three pounds a week and a lot of them succumbed. A lot of them also signed on to get out of going into the army and get into the RAF instead.

I really didn't want to go in at all. It was 1960. I just couldn't see the point of it. I would be almost twenty-three when I got out. I was determined to have a career in Burton's and missing two years would set me back in my progress. I used to drive friends mad talking about Burton's. Burton's ran through me like a stick of rock.

When asked my choice I said first the navy, then the RAF, then the army. I thought I might swing it with the navy because of the naval school I'd gone to. About five of us went to see a chief petty officer and he asked us if anyone was in the RNVR. Nobody was, so we were told there was no question of us getting into the navy. At one point I had thought about joining the navy at sixteen and becoming an engine room artificer because I thought that might be the way to get a commission, but my father and mother wouldn't let me do it. Anyway, I joined the queue outside the selection office. Everyone who went in and asked to go into the RAF was told, 'No. You're going into the army,' but when it was my turn the officer looked at my name on the list and said yes, they were going to take me. To this day I don't know why. I think they drew my name out of a hat. It was typical of the services. Nobody ever gave you a reason for anything.

I wanted to be in the RAF partly because the uniform was more comfortable and nicer. We had to wear a stiff collar with collar studs, but I was used to doing that for Burton's. It had, to my mind, more allure for the opposite sex. That was a major factor.

When I was called up on 16 May 1960 I went for four days to RAF Cardington, which was a reception camp where we were given our uniforms and our number, which you never forget as long as you live – 5077734. I was 734 Blackman for other purposes, they always use the last three numbers. On the 17th, 18th and 19th we were given our equipment, eating irons and mugs, which kept getting smashed; we parcelled up our civilian clothes and sent them home and we were checked for diseases.

On 20 May we were sent down to RAF Bridgnorth, where we were put into huts with about thirty other people and called a flight – I was in Blue Flight. In the hut you wore bits of blanket under your boots so you wouldn't scratch the floor and there was a table with a shiny surface that nobody touched. Nobody dared to put anything on it. If an NCO came into the hut you jumped to attention, no matter what you were doing, and he would march up and down in his hobnailed boots and wreck the floor. There was one chap who thought it was a joke when someone shouted 'Corporal present,' so when the corporal came into the hut he didn't get up. Immediately the NCO made him put his full kit on and then stand on this table for an hour, and when he got down he yelled at him for messing up the table and made him spend the rest of the evening polishing it. It was nothing but bullying really. We all made sure that didn't happen to us. Of course they wouldn't call it bullying, they would call it discipline, and the purpose was so that you would react to an order instinctively without questioning it. In combat that is what is needed.

We had to make up our bed in a manner which displayed all our personal equipment – blanket, sheets, socks, underwear, vests and so on. The presentation was easy. There was a diagram on the wall and you just followed it. You had two sheets and three blankets, which had to be presented in a perfect cube. In front of that were two pairs of socks, because you were issued with three but you were wearing one, and in front of that were two pairs of underpants. And then razors and boot polish and so on. That was checked every week, not just in basic training. My friend Jim, who was with me at Bridgnorth, had never made a bed in his life, but I'd been to boarding school and I knew about hospital corners, so I made his bed for him. The corporal or the flight sergeant would come in and if your blankets weren't perfect he'd throw them all on the floor. I thought it was all so unnecessary.

I am very rarely sick, but I remember one time when I was in training at RAF Bridgnorth and I was really ill. I was told by the corporal that I had to change out of my denims and into my best uniform and report to the other drill inspector corporal. I said, 'I don't feel very well.'

'Don't feel very well what?' he shouted back.

'I don't feel very well, corporal.' That was the attitude.

I never came across anyone who crumbled. I saw people cry – that was a mixture of homesickness and the bullying and the stress. They got over it, because the one thing you get in the services which you never get in Civvy Street is an incredible *esprit de corps*. If someone is faltering, someone else will help them.

You passed out after seven or eight weeks a fully rounded airman. You knew what was going on, you knew what was expected of you and you did it. I couldn't ever quite get to grips with never being allowed to show any initiative. You were never allowed to voice an opinion that we could do something better by doing it a different way. You simply did what you were told.

There were some accents I found difficult to understand and you had to ask them three times what they'd just said, but they found you hard to understand as well. The Scotsmen were always a class on their own. There was never an Englishman or a Welshman in their group. They didn't ignore you but they gravitated towards each other. Most of the people I came across were normal people. Most of the upper classes became officers because they had the education. That was all it came down to. You couldn't become a commissioned officer unless you had four or five O levels. I suppose in that hut of thirty men in basic training I'd be about halfway if you ranked us in terms of social class. There was a very well-to-do accountant, and also an architect from London, so we had all sorts of classes, but in the ranks of the National Servicemen, you're all the same.

I thought the whole selection thing was a bit of a farce.

You'd go through basic training and you'd take a sort of eleven plus exam and then you were graded. There were four grades in two sections – Engineering and Non-engineering. On either side of each grade were the jobs that that grade qualified you to do. I got a Grade 1, so that qualified me to make maps from aerial photographs, which I wanted to do. Another one was signals, which I didn't mind, but down at Grade 3 was 'typist'. I thought I'd put that down as well because I thought it would be useful to learn to type.

One afternoon every single recruit, regular and National Service, was called out onto the massive parade ground they had at RAF Bridgnorth. We fell into flights and were marched up and down. I could see the NCOs were tapping a few people on the shoulder and telling them to go and stand in the corner, and I was one of them. That was how they selected the Queen's Colour Squadron, which is the RAF drill team. No reason, no logic as far as I could see.

We were sent off to RAF Catterick for basic trade training. I was trained as a gunner and then sent down to Uxbridge as part of the first lot to go down there. There were some jobs I didn't want to do – working in the cookhouse or as a medical orderly emptying bedpans. I was a little miffed I couldn't get the cartographer's job – I would have enjoyed becoming a cartographer or a signaller – but I didn't get upset when they told me I was going into the Colour Squadron. Because I was going to Catterick I didn't pass out at Bridgnorth in July 1960. We were taken out early, which delighted me because I managed to get home for my twenty-first birthday.

Catterick was enormous. You walked in and a cloud of depression would descend on you. There was a guy there from

Kent. He was a little dumpy short boy and they wouldn't pass him out till he had lost weight, and when the rest of his barracks passed out they kept him back for a further two weeks because he wasn't making the grade. They could be very harsh. On exercises they'd dump you in the middle of the countryside with a map and wearing full pack; you were on a route march to a point on the map. It was torture. Then, when you got to the meeting point, all the NCOs were having a great time in the pub.

Eight of us went down from Catterick to Uxbridge to form the first batch of the Colour Squadron. It gradually built up and at its peak there were 160 airmen there. We were three flights: 2 Flight, 3 Flight, 4 Flight. The ceremonial drill unit, which was the original RAF drill squad, was being disbanded and the Queen's Colour Squadron was being formed, and 1 Flight was being filled by personnel from the Queen's Colour Guard. They were the cream, everyone stood in awe of them, but some of them got demobbed very quickly. They picked four people from 2 Flight to go into 1 Flight and I was one of those four.

I did it for a year, from September 1960 to October 1961. The Colour Squadron went where the job went. Every service has a flag that's used at all the ceremonies. Usually a flight lieutenant carries the flag and three NCOs – a flight sergeant and two sergeants – form the escort party, and the Queen's Colour Squadron goes with it. Our job was to do all the ceremonial occasions in the RAF. We went to France for a day once. If I'd signed on for a third year I'd have had a bit of choice, but I didn't want to do that.

We went to all parts of the country. We might form a guard

of honour for General de Gaulle when he landed at Heathrow, say, or at a funeral for an officer who had died. We would do the tattoos and other shows, like the Bath and West and the Monmouth Show in Abergavenny. It was quite an easy life, which suited me because all I wanted to do was get my two years out of the way and get out. That was always my attitude and fitting in, doing what I was told, seemed the best way to do it.

There were some silly things we had to do. We were once doing a guard of honour for the Duke of Norfolk. National Servicemen were issued with two T63s, which was the official title of the RAF dress uniform. Because National Servicemen weren't normally issued with them, we were also given two greatcoats and two service drill hats as well. We didn't know the guy was coming in on a helicopter, so we were all lined up in three rows, and the rotor blade blew all our hats off, and our CO went bananas as if it was all our fault. The NCOs must have known, but their hats blew off as well and of course we had to stand there, we couldn't go and get them back. So the Duke of Norfolk inspects us and nobody has a hat on and there's a pile of 120 hats at the back of the field.

The CO decided that everybody would be punished because he had been embarrassed by the spectacle. We always wore a white webbing belt and white gloves, which had to be spotless even though you were doing drill with a rifle that was covered in oil. The webbing belt had two brass slides that pushed up to hold the buckle in place and as you pushed it took all the white Blanco off it. I sandpapered the hob nails on my boots because I knew that if the CO saw they were slightly rusty I'd be sent back, and I had a short back and sides haircut. I got away with it on the first inspection but some men had to repeat it over and over for two days. They wouldn't tell them what was wrong. They just said, 'Go away and do it again.' It was nobody's fault that those hats blew off – I just didn't understand the punishment.

In May 1960 I had take-home pay of one pound two shillings a week after deductions. After my twenty-first birthday I got a rise of two bob. Then after six months I was made a leading aircraftman and I went up to two pounds two shillings. After a year I passed my exams, became an SAC – senior aircraftman – and I was then up to two pounds fourteen shillings. And after eighteen months I was on three pounds three shillings, but I also earned thirty bob a week working for Burton's on Saturdays when I got weekend leave. I had a girlfriend at home and that thirty bob enabled me to take her out on Friday and Saturday nights.

In the last few months I got myself a job in the squadron office, which was lovely because I didn't have to go out on the parade ground. One of my jobs was to do the kit inspection for the new recruits who were coming in to replace the last of the National Servicemen. I was astonished that they kept losing stuff – a sock, a pair of underpants. They would then have to buy their own replacements and bring them to me to prove they'd done it, and I'd sign them off. Then as people left they'd leave me their spare kit, and when the new recruits lost theirs I'd flog 'em the stores I'd built up. When I left I had a sale because I had so much of it.

Towards the end we did an annual Air Officer Commanding's Inspection. He was an air vice marshal, scrambled egg all over his hat. He stopped at me and told me that I was the smartest man in the Royal Air Force. Can you imagine the pride I felt? To be honest I didn't think I looked any different from my colleagues – we all looked immaculate – but for some reason he said it to me. Afterwards I was taken to one side and congratulated by my flight commander, who said, 'You do realise you'll be on every job from now on.' I might not have wanted to be there but that made me feel really good. I was still elated when I got back to Burton's though.

In the office I dealt with queries and made arrangements for anything going on, because not every job needed all 120 of us. And I made tea and coffee for the officers. I was the office wallah. Sometimes we only needed thirty-six men – six by six made a perfect square – and when the Central Band of the RAF stopped we would do fifty or sixty drill movements without any beat at all and we'd do them immaculately in perfect unison. If you had a funeral for a high-up wing commander, there could be all 120 there – the escort party, the firing party and the burial party, which I did with five others.

I was aware of things happening in the outside world, but only dimly – I knew there was a trial going on about *Lady Chatterley's Lover*. We talked about it but I never met anyone who'd read it. We knew the Berlin Wall had gone up but we never really talked about the implications. I saw television once in my whole two years – I watched a bit of Wimbledon. I was on fire picket. We went to the fire department and had to stay there for three days in case there was a fire. We were given some training the first morning as to what would happen if there was a fire and for the next two and a half days we sat on a bed and watched TV, and Wimbledon was on. We didn't have a wireless; what we had was a Tannoy system broadcasting in every room. You could switch it on and off. It wasn't the news or any-thing, it was just popular records. It was a bit like hospital broadcasting on a closed system.

I made a sort of Advent calendar to count off the last hun-dred days. I came out on 14 May 1962, so I got out a day or two early. Two days before you left you were given a card, and you had to go to every department on the camp and get them to sign that you were clear from them. There was cash accounts and pay accounts – that was the money side of it – and the third one was stores, where you'd hand in your bed and the rest of your equipment. The fourth and last was the Colour Squadron office, which I ran.

About a week before I got out, Corporal Roberts was made up to a sergeant and he decided he wanted to flex his muscles. He came into the office, had a go at me about my hair and told me to go and have it cut. I thought to myself, if this bloke thinks I'm going to have my hair cut a week before I get out he's got another think coming. I said to him that I was going home at the weekend and I would get it cut on the Saturday. 'Right,' he says, 'I'll inspect it next week.' I thought, you've got no chance.

At the weekend I went home and I did have a trim, the hair-dresser really just waved the clippers at my head. When I got back to camp I had three days to serve. Roberts took one look at my hair and put me on a charge, Form 252 – the only one whilst I was in the RAF. I was marched into the CO's office, Squadron Leader Babbage. He dismissed the whole thing but told me to get it cut like his, which wasn't a short back and sides! Roberts said he would check it out on the Wednesday, but I got demobbed on the Tuesday, a day early. I would love to have seen his face when he realised that I had gone – without a haircut!

Looking back at it now I know I resented doing National Service, and I can honestly say I never met anyone who wanted to be there – except perhaps the regulars, and even some of them wished they hadn't signed on.

SHAUN O'CONNOR

1960–1962

Grenadier Guards

We did so much exercise we were always starving, which was the only reason we managed to keep down the food they served us. The beef could have been used to repair a fell walker's boots, but we chewed it up and forced it down, followed by tasteless veg and lumpy gravy and then inedible sponge pudding and lumpy custard. It was all washed down by the undrinkable tea. The odd thing was I did feel better having eaten it.

I was born in Kingston-upon-Thames in 1938. We were evacuated from there when I was about two years old, down to Wheddon Cross near Minehead on the top of Exmoor. We stayed there for the duration of the war and then moved back to London. My father ended up as an RSM in the Irish Guards and at the end of the war, though he wanted to be a career officer in the army, they had more personnel than they needed and he was one of the many thousands they made redundant.

He got a job at the Gamages department store in Holborn Circus as a floorwalker but he didn't like it very much. He went off to work each day in his pin-striped trousers with his bowler hat on, but it wasn't him. Having been an RSM he expected things to be done when he snapped his fingers, but he was now in charge of a bunch of civilians, spotty faced youths, and he couldn't get anything done the way he wanted it. He was forever being hauled up in front of management for talking to the staff like they were in the army. He was Irish – that's why he was in the Irish Guards – and he was a Catholic, so eventually he got a job as the RSM of the Combined Cadet Force at Downside School at Stratton-on-the-Fosse, between Radstock and Shepton Mallet. That's when we all moved back to this part of the world again.

I'd been at a little primary school on Wimbledon Common after the war, near the camp for Italian prisoners of war. I remember talking to them through the wire. That's what I mostly remember about those early years – and of course the very cold winter of 1946–7. In my memory the winters were freezing and the summers were glorious. I'm not quite sure which year we moved, but I know I was down in Somerset when I took the eleven plus exam. I failed mine because we'd only just moved and I was still getting used to a new way of life.

Wimbledon and Raynes Park, where we lived, was very different from this part of the world. When we came back here the local children all thought I spoke very posh; now I speak like an old wurzel, but back in Raynes Park we had been allocated a requisitioned house in a very nice street. One next door neighbour drove a Rolls-Royce and the guy on the other side had two open-topped Morris Minor tourers with consecutive registration numbers – one for him and one for his wife. I played with the kids of a dentist and a doctor, so it was rather nice, and I began to speak rather nice but that changed when I came back down to Somerset.

My parents wanted me to do well but there was no pressure from them at all. Life was obviously going to be better than it had been during the war and we were all very optimistic about the future. I just wanted to make a reasonable living with a few bob to spare for a holiday somewhere – nothing spectacular, flying in an aeroplane was just for rich people. There were only two people in the village with a car – the local doctor and the abbot. The nearest train station was Chilcompton, which was a two-mile walk away across the fields on the slow and dirty line between Bath and Weymouth, and there was another line at Radstock, four miles down the road, which would take you to Bristol.

If I'd passed the eleven plus I'd have gone to Midsomer Norton Grammar, but I won a place at the art school in Bath when I was thirteen and I had a wonderful three years there. We studied architecture and pottery and painting and draught-manship as well as the traditional subjects, but I'd always been out of doors and the idea of sitting at a desk doing technical drawings for the rest of my life didn't appeal to me at all. Nobody told me that if you're an architect you don't spend much time in an office once your apprenticeship is over, but that was what I thought back then.

I stayed on at art school till I was sixteen but at weekends I used to work on the Downside School farm, mucking out the cowsheds and helping with the milking. I didn't worry that I didn't know what I was going to do when I left school because there were so many options about in those days. Eventually I was offered a five-year apprenticeship as an agricultural engineer in Frome and I thought that would be OK because it would be outside in the country. I learned how to do everything from building milking parlours to repairing combine harvesters, shoeing horses and putting handles on shovels. We got paid almost nothing. My first week's wages were one pound seventeen and six. The bus fare was ten bob and I gave my mother a pound, I think. If I had enough pocket money left to go to the pictures on Saturday night I had to find some way of getting there that didn't cost anything. So in the summer I would cycle to work, which was a good hour's run from where we lived. It's eleven miles and it's all up hill and down dale.

They'd been talking about packing in National Service, so I thought with my apprenticeship I might get away with it altogether – they'd already announced that National Service was stopping in 1960. I finished my apprenticeship and went up to ten quid a week basic and they still hadn't clocked me. I stayed on the farm another year, so I was twenty-two when I finally got my call-up papers. I went off to Bristol for my medical but I knew I'd pass because I was so fit. The papers said I had to report to Caterham Barracks on 6 February 1960. My first choice was the navy, my second choice was the RAF and my third choice was REME, because with my apprenticeship I thought I might be some use. But they sent me to the Grenadier Guards – that's why I went to Caterham, because that's where the Guards do all their training. Anyway, they sent me a rail warrant to get there and I set off on the train on my own for the first time in my life. Because I'd been posted to the

Grenadier Guards, my dad knew what I was going to. He said it would make a man of me, because he even knew the barrack buildings had been condemned as unfit for habitation before he went there in 1919.

There was only one more intake into the Grenadiers after ours; they came in a fortnight later on the 20th. The Grenadiers, the Coldstream, the Welsh, the Scots and the Irish all do their own basic training, which is six months rather than the six weeks that most other regiments have. You have to be not only a first-rate fighting soldier at the end of it, you have to know how to do all that nonsense outside Buckingham Palace, Windsor Castle and the Tower of London.

I was apprehensive about it, but after the first six weeks it's not so bad because they give you your civilian clothes back then – assuming you've passed of course. If you don't pass you get back-squadded and you start again back at the point they think you've reached. So there are two passing-out parades, one after six weeks and one after six months.

There were no three-tonners waiting for us when we got to Caterham railway station. We had to walk from the station to the barracks. As soon as I got there I got shouted at – some spotty youth with a bad haircut called me 'a dozy turnip'. Lance Sergeant Smith – the Guards don't have the rank of lance corporal because they feel that one stripe doesn't look very elegant on the dress uniform. So the first promotion is to corporal, which is the same as a lance corporal, then to lance sergeant which is the same as a corporal. But then all the other ranks are the same as the rest of the army – came into the barrack room where we all rather nervously assembled and took us down to the quartermaster's stores where we were issued with our kit. It was the usual stuff: 'socks grey, boots leather two pair, shirts khaki, ties khaki, greatcoat khaki, knapsack, mess tins, eating irons' and finally 'blankets wool and mattress'. These were piled onto our open arms until we were invisible except for our feet. Then we were supposed to sign for it all and most of the kit fell onto the floor as we struggled to write. We got called 'prat' and 'imbecile' and so on, and then we knew we were really in the army.

I was in Block C third floor, so we had to go up six flights of stone steps carrying this stuff. The room was about seventy-five feet long and two-thirds of the way down it was an iron stove. There were fifteen iron bed frames on each side of the room and beside each bed was a locker. The walls were painted cream but the bottom three feet were brown and at the top were painted the names of the Grenadier battle honours. We put all our stuff away in the bedspace, and then we went down to the cookhouse for unlimited quantities of undrinkable tea and food which I couldn't eat. The stove warmed you up if you were within three feet of it, but it was the beginning of February and everyone froze. Lights out was at ten but I woke up several times because I was so cold, so I used my greatcoat as an eiderdown.

There was a lad called John Stowe. His dad had recently died and he was now the head of the family business, a shop in Ipswich. He should never have been in there and we could all hear him crying at night. He stayed with us for about three or four weeks and then he got a compassionate discharge from the army because his family was in such a state and the shop was falling apart. We never saw him again.

On our first Sunday I was hoping we might get a bit of lie-in, but we were up at six and Training Sergeant Ellis showed us how to fold our blankets and lay everything out for inspection. Breakfast was porridge, fried eggs, tomatoes and fried bread and more undrinkable tea. Apart from the porridge everything was black and hard to identify. Ellis told us we had to buy Blanco and Brasso and boot polish from the NAAFI which we had to pay for ourselves, which made us all very annoyed. Then we were sent back to C3, where Ellis showed us how to sew a tag with the last four digits of our army number onto every bit of kit we possessed. We soon learned to get up quickly, because there was only a limited amount of hot water to wash and shave in and if you weren't there till after it ran out you had to do it all with cold water. I was too far away from the door to get into the first ten to arrive, so I got used to an invigorating wash and shave in cold water at half past six. The same problem with hot water applied to the small shower block, which was used by eleven other squads besides us.

We soon learned from Lance Sergeant Smith that the Guards wasn't going to be all poncing about Buckingham Palace in a furry hat and a red coat. We were going to be an efficient fighting force. We were told we weren't to answer 'yes' to a question or order but 'sir' or 'sergeant' or 'corporal'. One lad called Dungate when asked if he understood these instructions replied 'yes'. Twit.

That first morning we had a haircut. I say a haircut but it was more of a scalping by an Irish barber called Paddy. The whole point was to be shorn of your individuality. We all looked the same, we all dressed the same. We were doubled back to C3 and told to change into our PE kit. When we came out our legs were soon blue with cold because it was a freezing cold February morning. Then it was into the gym and the vaulting horse and ropes suspended from the ceiling and beams suspended from the wall. We went up and over and round every bit of equipment. When we got back to our beds, all we could talk about was how to escape this hell and join something easier, like the Foreign Legion.

We did so much exercise we were always starving, which was the only reason we managed to keep down the food they served us. The beef could have been used to repair a fell walker's boots, but we chewed it up and forced it down, followed by tasteless veg and lumpy gravy and then inedible sponge pudding and lumpy custard. It was all washed down by the undrinkable tea. The odd thing was I did feel better having eaten it.

For the first days it was really bad news. You didn't know if you were coming or going. You were being shouted at and hurried along all the time. If you didn't get your boots done up quick enough you were in trouble. At least everyone got the same treatment. It was really cold and these draughty old barracks just had this miserable little stove in the middle that didn't warm anyone. You were allowed two buckets of coke per day and that went in an hour. We were told that it was easing off a bit by the time we were called up. We heard stories of people sleeping on the floor in the early days of National Service so they would have their kit laid out on the bed properly, but that didn't happen in our barracks. Eventually we got our weekend passes and I came back to Somerset for a few days.

After the passing-out parade we had our leave and we came back to Caterham for a few days before being transported over to Pirbright, where we did all our field training for the Grenadier Guards. We didn't know if we'd see action. I mean

Suez had come up a few years before with little warning. We had a battalion in Germany and we could have gone there. The second lot of training was not as horrible but still, I remember one time I had a bit of Blanco on the inside edge of my belt buckle that I hadn't seen and I was put on punishment parade for that. That meant you had to turn out in full battle order and march round the square for an hour. This must have been the end of March or beginning of April 1960, so the weather was getting a bit warmer. Anyway I learned not to leave any Blanco inside my belt, even though I'd been wearing it at the time when they found it. They knew where to look, I suppose because lots of others had been caught that way before.

Coming to the end of the second lot of basic training they asked what we wanted to do when we got to the battalion. I'd already got a civilian driving licence so I thought I'd put down for the motor transport platoon. I'd be off barracks a lot of the time, driving officers around or driving three-tonners and picking up supplies, or taking troops to the firing range. I went straight into that but then we were posted off to the Cameroons. This would have been about March/April 1961, because we were scheduled to be out there during their independence celebrations in October 1961.

Anyway, before we went out to West Africa I was posted to the motor transport platoon at Tidworth on the eastern edge of Salisbury Plain in Wiltshire. That was a real home posting for me because I could hitch-hike home from there in an hour. We did a work parade in the morning and then went back and polished the wheels on the truck, had a tea break around half past ten or eleven o'clock, then went back and polished another wheel until lunchtime. Then perhaps you might get a detail to go somewhere to pick up something. That took up the afternoon and we would knock off around four o'clock. It wasn't difficult.

I never wore the red tunic and busby until right at the end of my National Service, though we had to practise putting them on and cleaning them and all that sort of stuff during training. We didn't actually get to wear them until we were asked to perform public duties after we came back from the Cameroons.

That was the first time I'd ever been abroad and it was a big adventure for a 22-year-old who'd hardly ever been outside of Somerset. The MT platoon was part of the advance party and we were flown out on a Bristol Britannia from Heathrow. That was an amazing experience in itself. Everyone else came out on a cruise – well, a troopship that took four weeks. We landed in Libya to refuel. We couldn't get off the plane at Tripoli airport but I could see the only building on the whole airfield was a little shed about half a mile away. All you could see in any direction was desert.

The Cameroons was quite a pleasant posting. The only trouble came from the Chinese, who were out there stirring up the local population to become Communist and fight the old British imperialist regime. The communists were planning on taking over Africa, as they are still today, for all the natural resources. Anyway, between us and the French on the other side of the border we dealt well enough with the insurgents who wanted to make trouble. During that operation one of our men did get shot and killed, but that was way up on the high ground, about two hundred miles away from where our camp was. We lost twice as many on swimming parties when two guys got washed out to sea. The sharks'll have you pretty quick out there.

I'm not sure I gave much thought to the idea of giving away the Empire. We knew we were at the top end, we were the ones who had put all that red on the map of the world, but it was taking time to sink in that the Empire was going – India and so on. I suppose I thought it was a pity that we were giving away these places, because we'd had them under our control for the best part of a hundred years and more. I never gave a thought to the implication of us owning those countries – I mean immigration and so on. In those days England was still full of white people and you hardly ever saw a black face or a brown face – certainly not in this part of the world.

We had a native from the local village, a dhobi wallah as we called them, who came into our section of the aluminium hut and did the washing and ironing for the three of us for ten bob a week each. He was a rich man. You've got to remember we were only on two pounds a week or so ourselves, though we did get some extra money for being abroad – nine shillings or something, so that paid for the dhobi wallah.

One night I heard English music coming out of one of the huts. All the radio music was African music. I listened and I couldn't hear a bass, so I stuck my head in the door and said, 'You need a bass in there, Sarn't.' He said he did but there wasn't one on the camp. I said I could help him out because I played a tea chest. He told me to go and get myself fixed up, which I did, and that's how I became part of the battalion band. It was like an instrument in a skiffle band but a bit more sophisticated. We did the camp dances and then maybe during the week we'd go to one of the local plantation manager's houses and play for his birthday party. We had a whale of a time.

They wanted me to stay on – they wanted everyone to stay on – and they offered me more money and promotion, but I never wanted promotion. I just wanted to be out of the army at the end of my two years, whatever happened. I'd been court-ing Marie for two or three years before my call-up and I just wanted to get back to her. She worked at Clark's the shoe-makers in Shepton Mallet. I'd met her at the local dance at Colford and the plan was that as soon as I was free I'd come back here and get married. None of the guys out in the Cameroons got a Dear John letter, though whether that was unusual I can't say. We'd been in a steady relationship for two or three years and things were pretty much cut and dried for us.

I was out in the Cameroons for about nine months. I came back in November 1961, about a month after their independ-ence. We had a couple of weeks' leave, and after we reported back to Tidworth we were told that we were going to do public duties through till the end of January. I didn't do Windsor Castle but I did do all the others – Buckingham Palace, St James's Palace, the Bank of England and the Tower of London. You get trained not to react to the staring. You're trained to stare straight ahead and never to react to anything people do or say.

In those days when we were on Buckingham Palace duty we were outside the building and the population was fifty yards away, but at St James's Palace you're standing in a little box and you get people coming up and wanting to take your photo-graph. You do two hours on and four hours off and in the middle of winter that takes care of your daylight, so you might hardly be on in daylight at all. The rest of the time is in darkness, so there's no tourists. By that time we knew we only had a few weeks left to do and it was better than loitering about at Tidworth. Everybody had a chart to tick off the days – many of them did their demob chart from the first day they went in.

I think they should have gone on with National Service because I was one of the last ones to go in and I had two years of my life taken away from me by the Queen for two pounds a week. Most of my younger friends didn't go in and by the time I came out they were skilled men and they'd had a year or so of earning twelve or fifteen quid a week – in two cases twenty quid a week. I, on the other hand, was coming out of the army with no savings because all my money was spent on Blanco and boot polish and getting back home at weekends. These guys were buying houses and settling down. In my opinion it would have been fairer if everyone had started off in life on the same footing, that's why I thought it should continue. It gave those who didn't do National Service a big financial advantage which I would never catch up with.

After National Service I was on what they called the Z reserve for ten years, meaning you could be called up at any time. I wasn't. I went back to being an agricultural engineer for a couple of months, which is a very badly paid job – you get paid farm labourer's wages – but I hadn't any other real skills that I could use, so I went into the motor trade because the two cross over. I was in the motor trade on and off for the rest of my life.

I found I could get on with most people in National Service, though I'd never come across Geordies before and we had two of them in our squad. I found them very difficult to understand.

For a long time I thought they were speaking Welsh and I just couldn't understand a word they said. Mind you, they couldn't understand much I was saying either. On the second part of basic training we had one guy who was back-squadded and sent to join us. He had a bad reputation and he was a dirty uncouth bugger, but that was really the only one I didn't take to. Most people have something good about them and that's what I found in National Service.

One thing National Service taught me was that nothing in life is ever as bad as you think it's going to be. You can put up with a lot after you've done two years in the army. People who come out of the army today and need all this support . . . I don't know, I mean there was none of that in my day. You came out of the army and got on with things – that's what the army taught you to do. You were a self-sufficient operation. Just think of those men who came out of the First World War – seeing their mates blown to bits next to them in the trenches and they got nothing when they came out. A lot of them suffered very badly, but they were just sent out into the wide world to fend for themselves, weren't they?

MIKE CLARK

1960–1962

Royal East Kent Regiment, 1st Battalion Queen's Royal Surreys

I can never understand how they got treated so well in the RAF ... The food they had on that RAF base ... I'm telling you it was out of this world. In the infantry we'd never seen food like it, and that was for the ordinary men, it wasn't for the officers or anything. It was like Mum's cooking. The food in our regiment was so awful.

I am 23800968 Corporal Clark on parade. You never forget that number. I was born in 1938, so my first memories are of the war. We lived in Teddington, Middlesex and my dad worked at the local gasworks. When there was an air raid warning we had to go over to Bushy Park where there was an air raid shelter which was owned by the gasworks. We'd be in there overnight and stay till the morning. As the war progressed, in 1944 I was evacuated with my two sisters and a brother to Newport in south Wales. I hated it because I was only six years old, and the people who took me in were not very good, I'm afraid. Fortunately we were only there for three or four months and then we came back, though I don't know why. We'd been sent away from the flying bombs, the doodlebugs, but I was so happy to come back to Teddington, even though we only lived in a two up, two down, no bathroom or anything like that.

I got a decent education and I left school at fifteen. I was fortunate at St Mark's because we had a very good maths teacher called Mr Edwards who said I should do well as a bank clerk but my background made me feel like I couldn't go into a bank. My mother worked when she could because she was raising a family, but between them my parents never had much. That was how it was for a great many families in those days. I come from quite a poor background and my parents couldn't afford to pay for an education. I did feel I was left out a bit. Big poor families didn't have the opportunities.

At fourteen, I went out with a man who used to go round engineering companies and I helped him delivering tools to them. So before I left school I was thinking I'd like to become a toolmaker and I became an apprentice engineer toolmaker with a company called Kingston Instrument Company in Surbiton. I was on a six-year apprenticeship and I was still going to college till I was twenty-two. That's why I never got called up till right at the end.

Anyway, like a load of others I ended up having my medical at Croydon where I was passed A1. You were allowed to put down where you'd like to go to but I ended up in an infantry battalion – which was not where I wanted to go. I didn't enjoy it, not to start with anyway, but if you went in there with a bad attitude it was going to make it worse than if you went in determined to make the best of it.

On 7 July 1960 I left home to report to Howe Barracks, Canterbury to go with the 1st Battalion Buffs Regiment, which was the Royal East Kent Regiment. In the First World War there was the cry 'Steady, the Buffs!' and we heard that cry a lot. We were trained by the Buffs, but that didn't mean we would automatically go into the Buffs at the end of basic training. Anyway, a week before we passed out as infantrymen they told us we were all going into the Queen's Royal Surreys because they were short of men to be posted to Aden. Most of the men who joined with me on 7 July 1960 were also ex-apprentices and most of them were in engineering.

I was over a year past my time so I was earning top money by then – I remember four shillings and elevenpence an hour was the rate for skilled workers, which made two quid a day. The pound went a lot a further in them days than it does now. If you had a pound you could really enjoy yourself, and in them days there was so much work around in engineering companies you could never work enough hours. I was working every Saturday from 8 a.m. to 2 p.m. and every other Sunday as well. I was earning over seventeen pounds ten bob a week and I was only twenty-two. I could go up to Berwick Street in Soho to have a suit made, buy the material, have it made by a tailor – that would cost twelve pound ten bob. Now that was most of your week's wages. Then you went into the army and right away you were brought down to less than thirty bob a week and made to salute for it as well.

I didn't even have a suitcase on that train to Canterbury. I was in civvies and because I left early there wasn't even a lorry waiting at Canterbury station, which there was for the later train with the others on it, so I had to make my own way to Howe Barracks. Once you cross the line and you're in the army you don't have time to think about anything else. Everything starts moving – shouting – getting your gear at the quarter-master's stores in the afternoon – you just hold your arms out and they load you up. Those first three days it's all work, work, work till the lights go out. It's all Blancoing and doing your boots. The lance corporal starts you off for those first few days, then the sergeant gets involved and then it's your first parade.

The first night there was a lot of banter. No crying – I heard about it, but there was none of that with us. Everything about Howe Barracks was wonderful because it was a very modern block. They said we'd have good food and we did. I've got nothing negative to say about that training. We were the last lot to go in and they did look after us. The training sergeant would shout at us, but I was twenty-two years of age by then and most training sergeants were only twenty-three. The first Monday morning he came in for inspection at seven o'clock in the morning. There were forty men in four rooms in our block and we were in the last room, so we could hear what was going on in the other rooms – the shouting, the bawling. The windows had to be lowered to eighteen inches and they all had to be in line. He'd take his stick and hit the top of the lockers, and all the gaiters and anything on top would go out of the window. We'd have to go outside afterwards and sort it all out. This was how they started you off in the infantry.

I can never understand how they got treated so well in the RAF. We heard they were treated like humans. There was none of that in the army. When we were out in Aden we sometimes had to go over to Khormaksar airport and look after the children, accompany them to the Isthmus School on their coaches. We were their guards and when we'd done it we had to go back to Khormaksar – we had lunch there while we waited for the kids to finish at school, because we had to act as guards again on the way back from school. The food they had on that RAF base ... I'm telling you it was out of this world. In the infantry we'd never seen food like it, and that was for the ordinary men, it wasn't for the officers or anything. It was like Mum's cooking. The food in our regiment was so awful.

At the end of basic training they frightened the whole intake by telling us, 'You're all going in the Queen's Royal Surreys and you're going to Aden. We were there two years ago and a few men never came back because they got killed there. Now you can sign up for the extra year and get more money and you won't go to Aden.' I thought, there's no way I'm signing on. I'm twenty-two years of age and a skilled man. I never wanted to come into the army in the first place but I've got to do what I've got to do. I'll take whatever's ahead of us. Because it was all coming to an end they were losing so many National Servicemen at that time, and they weren't being replaced by a new intake.

I was physically fit for most things but when we came to the last week we had to go through the swamp with full kit. If you drop your rifle you go down in that mud and pick it out. A week before I got piles, haemorrhoids, but I didn't know it was that, I thought I had an abscess. I'd had to do a mile run just after dinner and I couldn't do it, I was in so much pain, so I saw the sergeant who was in charge of PT and he told me to report sick. Now the worst thing you could do was to report sick, because you had to take all your gear with you in case you went to hospital. So anyway I went down and saw the MO and he diagnosed I had piles and it was bad. I took medication and was told to rest for two days, then I was put on light duties for the next three or four days. When it came to that swamp and I saw what I had to do I said to the PT sergeant that I didn't think I could do it, and that got all the boys having a go at me. Anyway I sort of enjoyed watching all the blokes do it and seeing their rifles falling in the mud, but I had to clean all the rifles afterwards. I was lucky I wasn't back-squadded. I was afraid of that because I thought I couldn't go through all that again, but luckily they pushed me through.

When you start off and you see them in front of you doing their passing-out parades, you think you could never be as good as that. But in the end you are like that, and to give the army its due I didn't think personally it was that bad. There were some who were weaker than others and they were bawled out, I'm afraid. There was a bloke there whose name was Girl, so you can see he got bawled out many a time. You only saw the RSM of a training battalion seven weeks into training. We got him on the square after seven weeks. You could see he must have had a good night with the Scotch the night before because his face was all red. He got us all tangled up because he had us all out on the square and he was shouting out things and it was a windy day. So you had two platoons of forty men marching with their studs clicking all the time and you couldn't hear what he was saying. I think he did it deliberately, as a ploy, because he disintegrated two whole platoons. Then they could keep us out there all afternoon working harder. It made us better, I suppose, and at the very end I suppose we felt a sense of pride when we passed out. However, there were some blokes who couldn't do, say, press-ups, things like that – just couldn't do them. I was strong in the neck and shoulders so I could do lots of them. I was like a monkey.

After eleven weeks' training we had a week off, so we went home. We had to report back to Canterbury and then we were bussed to Colchester, and that's when we went from the Buffs to the Queen's Royal Surreys. Within two days they told us that there was an advance party going out to Aden within four to six weeks. They wanted volunteers. Because we'd just come out of training we saw all the bullshit at Colchester – that was the word we used as soldiers – we said right, let's get on with it, and nearly all our lot went out with the advance party, so we only had about a week at Colchester. Fifty per cent of our basic training unit had volunteered to join the Buffs and took the extra year to avoid going out to Aden and getting shot. So that left the other forty out of the eighty to join the 1st Battalion Queen's Royal Surreys.

We left Southampton in October 1960 in a force-eight gale on board HMT *Dunera*. We went through the Bay of Biscay in gale force twelve. Everybody was ill. We had jobs to do on the boat but after a while we couldn't do even that. When we got to Gib, we couldn't believe it, it was like a millpond and they wouldn't allow us off the ship. They put the flags up, which was a signal to say we had something wrong on the ship and they wouldn't allow us to land. We saw the rock and filled up with water and things but we went on to Malta where we could get off. Then we went on to Famagusta in Cyprus.

When I was called up I had a girlfriend. It was quite a strong relationship. We might have got engaged and married, but it never worked out because I was in Aden for so many months. Eventually I got a Dear John letter from her. She didn't say it in so many words, but I realised she'd met somebody else and she was asking me if I would marry her when I came out of the army. I didn't feel I could give her that answer, so the relationship finished. I wasn't devastated – maybe I was a little bit upset for a while – but I was so fortunate, because the year after I came out of the army I met the love of my life. Which changed me again in many ways, because I'd been a bit of a tearaway. Once I'd met my future wife, though, I was committed and we had forty-one happily married years together.

On the way to Aden we went through the Red Sea and we acclimatised to the hot weather, which was the reason for going by boat. We arrived at the end of October, which was the end of the hot season – September is the hottest month, and maybe April and May – it was midnight and dark and we all off-loaded onto lorries. My first reaction was amazement at seeing Arabs living in fifty-gallon oil drums at the side of the road. We were wondering what we were coming into. We arrived at the camp and they gave us a sheet – you wouldn't want a blanket. Mind you, the sheets could have been a lot cleaner. I don't know where they'd come from – maybe the medical side.

We were at this camp for about three or four days and then we set off north in a big convoy. We left Aden and went into the desert, heading for Mukeiras near the Yemen border. For a couple of nights we slept out in the desert under the stars. Eventually we got to our camp, which was on the edge of the desert, and there were forty or fifty big tents with a sandbag perimeter around it. We were taking over from the Royal

Highland Fusiliers, which they told us about though they didn't tell us much else. We were there to make sure the Yemenis didn't attack the local Nayib. He was the local leader. I don't suppose it's much different now, because it's all tribal round there. We were there as a peacekeeper in case of any problems, but luckily in the four and a half months I was upcountry there was no real problem.

There was a local village, though, where there were all these young girls aged about eleven or twelve. They were being educated by the Arab women to know everything about marriage and then they would be married off at thirteen or fourteen. We were told to keep away from that village when we went out on patrol with loaded rifles. I think it was called Er, or maybe that was how we pronounced it, but if you got too near Er you would hear a rifle shot. They had guards there, and that was just to let you know you were getting near. Still, it wasn't too bad up there. You'd be much more in fear of your life down in Aden itself.

We all went down there in March 1961 when another lot went upcountry to relieve us. We flew in RAF Beverleys, which was my very first flight. I got something very akin to malaria, although I'd taken anti-malaria tablets. I went down with something that caused me to sweat non-stop. It was coming off me like a hosepipe and I heard some corporal saying about me, 'Oh, he'll be all right. Just give him an aspirin.' We didn't even have paracetamol. It knocked the life out of me for a few weeks. I couldn't run in that heat with my full gear on, so when a job came up elsewhere for a ration corporal they decided to get rid of me. I was offered the job in the camp commander's office and I accepted immediately. They made me up to a lance corporal and within three or four days I left the regiment and went off to Headquarters Middle East Command at Fort Morbut, which sounded grand but it was only a ramshackle collection of huts. Mind you, Fort Morbut was like a holiday camp compared to being in the Surreys. I was still wearing the Surreys insignia and I still had to be smart because I was representing the regiment and all that.

Of my twenty-four months in National Service I spent nineteen months in Aden. I had no leave whatsoever. To be honest I had no idea what leave I was entitled to and neither did anyone else. My quartermaster from the East Anglian regiment, who was a lovely man, said, 'Right, corporal, you haven't had any leave so I'm going to send you back a few weeks early before you finish your time. Go on leave for a week when you get home, then report to your barracks and see what they say.'

I'm not saying this was true in every case, but once you've done service you get this terrific camaraderie. Also I suppose the army taught me how to save, because I'd saved a bit when I came out of the army and I'd never saved before. I think I was on five pounds ten shillings a week, because you got another quid a week when you got two stripes and a further quid when you got three. National Service certainly showed me how other people live in foreign countries and it told me how lucky we are in this country. I think it's the best country in the world. I would still like to see one year of National Service for all men who are fit because it would give them discipline, which would then become self-discipline. I think we wouldn't have all the drug problems we have today. Discipline and morals have certainly deteriorated in this country.

I didn't think I needed the discipline the army gives you.

Don't forget I'd gone through a six-year apprenticeship and I was twenty-two years of age when I was called up. I was right at the end of my apprenticeship when it was announced that anyone who was deferred until after 31 May 1960 wouldn't have to do National Service. I was deferred until 31 May 1960, so I missed getting out of it by a single day!

POSTSCRIPT

The history of the 1950s is never written now without some reference to the cultural upheaval of that decade, frequently dating from the first night of John Osborne's play *Look Back in Anger* at the Royal Court Theatre in May 1956. To a nation of theatregoers who had grown up with Noël Coward and Terence Rattigan (the latter of whom is now undergoing a timely renaissance), the appearance of Mary Ure as Alison standing downstage left in her slip and ironing when the curtain went up came as a surprise. Soon it would be the presence of the French window on the stage and of Rattigan's Aunt Edna in the audience that would be the surprise. The revolution in the theatre that took place with the emergence of Osborne, Wesker, Pinter, Rudkin, Kops, Simpson, Whiting and others pretty much passed most National Servicemen by, as did the new novels of Alan Sillitoe, John Braine and Stan Barstow. The men in uniform led such circumscribed lives that this sort of change would only have appeared to them if they went to see a film like *Room at the Top*, *Lucky Jim* or *Saturday Night and Sunday Morning* on their weekend leave from camp.

One of the few cultural phenomena that must have struck a

chord with these men would have been the first Carry On film. *Carry On Sergeant* (a parade ground order which has nothing to do with *Carry On Regardless* or *Carry On Camping*) was made in 1958, very loosely adapted from a play called *The Bull Boys* by R. F. Delderfield. It starred Bob Monkhouse, called up on his wedding day, and William Hartnell as the gruff sergeant who wants to win for the only time in his army career the honour of training the champion platoon at the passing-out parade. Unfortunately, as he is due to retire it is his last chance and he is saddled with, among others, Kenneth Williams, Charles Hawtrey and Kenneth Connor.

Carry On Sergeant was conceived as a single film making fun of National Service and only by virtue of its success did it become the first in the celebrated series of British comedies. It is a long way from the glories to come of *Carry On Cleo* and *Carry On Up the Khyber*, but it succeeds very well in capturing some of the absurdities of army life and it is no coincidence that Joe Trotter referred to it when he remembered his medical. The holding out of one's arms in the quartermaster's stores as a variety of clothing and other equipment was placed on them until it became impossible to see over the top is captured faithfully. The film was budgeted at less than £100,000 and grossed more than five times its negative cost, principally because it would have appealed enormously to those who had experienced National Service. It was men like that and their partners who formed the bulk of regular cinemagoers.

Carry On Sergeant, a curious and interesting historical document to those of us who escaped National Service, worked as a comedy on its release in 1958 largely because it tapped into the divided feelings most British men had about the army.

During the 1950s *The Goon Show*, the wildly successful BBC radio comedy, was used by the former soldiers Spike Milligan, Harry Secombe, Peter Sellers and, in its early years, Michael Bentine as a vehicle for venting their spleen about army life. Apart from the character of the cowardly and venal Major Bloodnok ('Let me lift this heavy wallet off your chest'), the jokes about idiotic officers were constant. 'Silence when you speak to an officer!' was one command that received huge cheers from the studio audience. When the description of Colditz as 'a camp full of British officers who had sworn to die rather than be captured' was greeted with similar roars, Milligan quickly ad-libbed, 'Thank you, fellow cowards!'

It is perhaps then not surprising that there remains in nearly all the men in this book a deep ambivalence about National Service. On the one hand, although a few enjoyed the experience, most of them hated it, were bored by it or resented its unnatural and unwelcome intrusion into their lives. On the other hand, most of them, frequently the same people, recognised that it gave them some sense of discipline and other qualities which they used in their lives and for which they have remained grateful. They manage to reconcile their memories of how unpleasant National Service had been in its early days with a recognition that it had helped to shape their characters for the better.

Many of them advocate some sort of reintroduction, if not in the same shape as they knew it but in some form of community service that would give the disaffected youth of modern Britain some urgently needed discipline. I have never been entirely convinced by this argument. I can hear in it an echo of the classic jail scene in *Monty Python's Life of Brian* as Michael Palin's Judean prisoner calls for the wider application of crucifixion to solve the problem of juvenile delinquency in Roman-occupied Jerusalem. 'Listen, if we didn't have crucifixion, this country would be in a right mess. Nail 'em up! Nail some sense into them!' The Monty Python team were born just too late to be called up for National Service.

You can, of course, argue that National Service changed lives. Certainly those who saw action, those who saw their friends killed by local insurgents in foreign countries far from home, would have been changed, as millions of men have been changed throughout history by similarly traumatic experiences. As Stanley Price said so succinctly, 'You don't die for your country; you die for your mates.' However, as Brian Sayer pointed out, the years between eighteen and twenty are always years in which young men change and to his way of thinking he was sufficiently self-disciplined that he had no need of the extra sadistic and destructive discipline imposed on him by the armed forces. Certainly one of the benefits of three years or so at university or college is that it allows young people to 'find themselves', in the phrase so popular in the sixties. Going up to university straight from school, as so many of these inter-viewees went into National Service shortly after leaving school, young men and women inevitably graduate as more mature and more thoughtful people after what might be the first lengthy experience of living away from home and having to fend for themselves. The abolition of National Service in no way altered this common process.

There were clearly far too many sadistic NCOs; living and working conditions were frequently primitive, verging on the barbaric, particularly during basic training. There were how-ever plenty of officers whom the men liked and conditions invariably improved after basic training was over. To a great extent the quality of a conscript's National Service experience depended on the luck of the draw. How bad or good it was related entirely to the individual barracks, platoon and officers he was assigned to. In that regard it was much like life has always been for the rest of us.

There is no point in calling for the reintroduction of National Service. The British armed forces do not need pure manpower in the way they did in the early postwar years, because though Britain has NATO obligations they are nothing like as demanding as the old imperial ones. The current call is for tactical missiles and small, elite, highly trained professional forces. I wonder whether any of the men who went through National Service would recognise the British armed forces of today compared to the traditional outfits they first encountered.

National Service was of its time. I have tried to paint a picture of that post-1945 world, one in which the preservation of democracy and peace that had been fought for over six long brutal years was paramount. David Niven, ostensibly plunging into the sea in his burning plane at the start of Powell and Pressburger's 1945 film *A Matter of Life and Death*, calls himself 'Conservative by instinct, Labour by experience'. It was symptomatic of that wartime consensus and the widespread desire to rebuild a world that would not be plunged back into the economic and political disasters of the 1930s. National Service persuaded young men of the late 1940s that they had an obligation to serve their king and country as their fathers and possibly their grandfathers had done in two world wars. They didn't resist. They weren't necessarily thrilled but they recognised the validity of such an obligation. National Service was part of a British way of life that celebrated Empire Day and stood solemnly as the national anthem was played before the start of a play or a concert and at the end of a film in the local cinema. It was a country that would take seriously the classic newspaper headline, FOG IN CHANNEL: CONTINENT CUT OFF. It was a country that was overwhelmingly white and insular in outlook, a country that took pride in its imperial glories and its island history, 'This earth, this realm, this England'. 'The past,' writes L. P. Hartley in the opening page of *The Go-Between*, 'is a foreign country. They do things differently there.' That is where National Service belongs.